Human Rights and U.S. Foreign Policy

Human Rights and U.S. Foreign Policy provides a comprehensive historical overview and analysis of the complex and often vexing problem of understanding the formation of U.S. human rights policy.

The proper place of human rights and fundamental freedoms in U.S. foreign policy has long been debated among scholars, politicians, and the American public. Clair Apodaca argues that the history of U.S. human rights policy unfolds as a series of prevarications that are the result of presidential preferences, along with the conflict and cooperation among bureaucratic actors.

Through a series of chapters devoted to U.S. presidential administrations from Richard Nixon to the present, she delivers a comprehensive historical, social, and cultural context to understand the development and implementation of U.S. human rights policy. For each administration, she pays close attention to how ideology, bureaucratic politics, lobbying, and competition affect the inclusion or exclusion of human rights in the economic and military aid allocation decisions of the United States. She further demonstrates that from the inception of U.S. human rights policy, presidents have attempted to tell only part of the truth or to reformulate the truth by redefining the meaning of the terms "human rights," "democracy," or "torture," for example. In this way, human rights policy has been about prevarication.

Human Rights and U.S. Foreign Policy is a key text for students, which will appeal to all readers who will find a historically informed, argument driven account of the erratic evolution of U.S. human rights policy since the Nixon Administration.

Clair Apodaca (Ph.D., Purdue University, 1996) is an associate professor in the Department of Political Science at Virginia Tech University.

Routledge Studies in Human Rights
Series Editors: *Mark Gibney, UNC Asheville, USA,
Thomas Gammeltoft-Hansen, Raoul Wallenberg Institute, Sweden, and
Bonny Ibhawoh, McMaster University, Canada*

The Routledge Human Rights series publishes high quality and cross-disciplinary scholarship on topics of key importance in human rights today. In a world where human rights are both celebrated and contested, this series is committed to create stronger links between disciplines and explore new methodological and theoretical approaches in human rights research. Aimed towards both scholars and human rights professionals, the series strives to provide both critical analysis and policy-oriented research in an accessible form. The series welcomes work on specific human rights issues as well as on cross-cutting themes and institutional perspectives.

Sovereignty, State Failure and Human Rights
Petty Despots and Exemplary Villains
Neil Englehart

Understanding Statelessness
Edited by Tendayi Bloom, Katherine Tonkiss and Phillip Cole

Human Rights in Democracies
Peter Haschke

Extraordinary Rendition
Addressing the Challenges of Accountability
Edited by Elspeth Guild, Didier Bigo and Mark Gibney

Truth, Silence and Violence in Emerging States
Histories of the Unspoken
Edited by Aidan Russell

Human Rights and U.S. Foreign Policy
Prevarications and Evasions
Clair Apodaca

For more information about this series, please visit: https://www.routledge.com/Routledge-Studies-in-Human-Rights/book-series/RSIHR

Human Rights and U.S. Foreign Policy
Prevarications and Evasions

Clair Apodaca

NEW YORK AND LONDON

First published 2019
by Routledge
52 Vanderbilt Avenue, New York, NY 10017

and by Routledge
2 Park Square, Milton Park, Abingdon, Oxon, OX14 4RN

Routledge is an imprint of the Taylor & Francis Group, an informa business

© 2019 Taylor & Francis

The right of Clair Apodaca to be identified as author of this work has been asserted by her in accordance with sections 77 and 78 of the Copyright, Designs and Patents Act 1988.

All rights reserved. No part of this book may be reprinted or reproduced or utilised in any form or by any electronic, mechanical, or other means, now known or hereafter invented, including photocopying and recording, or in any information storage or retrieval system, without permission in writing from the publishers.

Trademark notice: Product or corporate names may be trademarks or registered trademarks, and are used only for identification and explanation without intent to infringe.

Library of Congress Cataloging-in-Publication Data
A catalog record for this title has been requested

ISBN: 978-0-8153-8354-3 (hbk)
ISBN: 978-0-8153-8355-0 (pbk)
ISBN: 978-1-351-20583-2 (ebk)

Typeset in Times New Roman
by codeMantra

 Printed in the United Kingdom by Henry Ling Limited

Francois Debrix
friend, husband, colleague

Contents

Acknowledgments   x

1   The Battlefield of Foreign Aid as Foreign Policy   1
Presidential-Congressional Struggle over Foreign Aid 2
The Conflict within Congress over Foreign Aid 4
Bureaucratic Politics in Foreign Aid Allocations 6
Administering Foreign Policy: Who Is in Charge of the Bureaucracy? 9
Inception of Contemporary Human Rights Policy: The Fraser Committee 13
    Bureau of Human Rights and Humanitarian Affairs (HRHA) 16
    Country Reports on Human Rights Practices 17
    Human Rights Legislation 18
Foreign Aid 21
    Bilateral Economic Aid 22
    Bilateral Security Assistance 23
    Multilateral Aid 24
The Prevaricator Who Set the Bar: Richard Nixon (1969–August 1974) 25
Notes 29
References 29

2   U.S. Human Rights Policy during the Cold War: A Historical Overview   34
The Ford Administration (August 1974–1977) 35
The Carter Administration (1977–1981) 40
The Reagan Administration (1981–1989) 44
Conclusion 49
Notes 50
References 51

3 U.S. Human Rights Policy in the Post-Cold War Era:
   A Decade of Lost Opportunities   54
   The Bush, Sr. Administration (1989–1993) 55
   The Clinton Administration (1993–2001) 61
   Conclusion 71
   Notes 72
   References 73

4 The Prevaricator in Chief: George W. Bush (2001–2009)   76
   *Torture (and Other Violations of Human Rights)
     and Its Justification 77*
   Bush's Wars on Terror 81
     Coalition of the Willing 84
     Women's Rights as Validation for the Global War
       on Terror 85
   Foreign Aid as a Tool in the Global War on Terror 87
     Economic Aid 88
     Military Aid 90
     DOD's Increasing Role in Foreign Aid 93
   Congressional Actions and Inactions 95
   Bureaucratic Policymaking and the Presidential Agenda 98
   Conclusion 100
   Notes 101
   References 102

5 The Prevaricator of Change: Barack Obama (2009–2017) 109
   *Similarities and Continuities with George W. Bush's
     Human Rights Policies in the War on Terror/
     Overseas Contingency Operations 110*
     Permanence of Terror Policy: Guantánamo, Military
       Commissions, and Rendition 112
     Foreign Aid Remains a Tool of Counterterrorism 115
   "Things Are Going to Get Worse" 119
     Traitors or Whistleblowers: The Government's Desire
       for Secrecy versus the Public's Right to Know 119
     Bagram: Obama's Gitmo 121
     Drones and Targeted Killing 122
     Failure to Prosecute 127
   Improvements in Human Rights Policies 128
     Interrogation Methods 128
     LGBTQ Rights 130

    Congressional Actions and Inactions 132
    Bureaucratic Resistance 135
    Conclusion 136
    Notes 137
    References 138

6   A Prevaricator Who Told the Truth: Donald Trump (2017–)   145
    A Billionaire as the Voice of the Everyman (and Perhaps Woman) 146
    Governmental Policies toward Socially Constructed Groups 149
    The Deviants 151
        Scapegoating Muslim Refugees and Mexican Immigrants 151
        The Nasty Women: Dismantling Women's Reproductive Rights 156
        LGBTQ Community 159
        Terrorists: Continuity with the Policies of Torture and Assassination 160
    Foreign Aid as a Discarded Tool of Foreign Policy 163
    Military Aid and Arms Sales Making America Great Again 166
    Congressional Push Back to Trump's Agenda 169
    Bureaucratic Resistance to Trump's Agenda 171
    Use of Loyalty Oaths and the Presidential Pardon 173
    Conclusion 174
    Notes 176
    References 177

7   The Future of U.S. Human Rights Policy   185
    Complying with Human Rights Norms 186
    The Populist Turn 188
    Apocalyptic Predictions: Sikkink vs. Hopgood 190
    Prevaricating Policy 191
    Notes 195
    References 195

Index   197

Acknowledgments

My thanks to all those many people who have sustained and loved me no matter what: Francois, Jeremy, Elizabeth, and Ethan. I would also like to acknowledge Natalja Mortensen, Senior Editor, for her support of my work.

1 The Battlefield of Foreign Aid as Foreign Policy

Prevarication denotes a lie. However, the connotation of prevarication softens to a half-truth or convoluted falsehood. Prevarication is about using ambiguity, omissions, or evasion to bend the truth and to mislead. In 1823, Clarke wrote that

> prevarication is the giving of contradictory or inconsistent evidence, which affects the credibility of the evidence, though neither the extent of the witness's falsehood, nor the precise points in which he has departed from the truth be capable of ascertainment.
> (Clarke 1823 as quoted in Schneider 2007: 316)

Thus, while to prevaricate means to lie, it also implies making it difficult to discern exactly what the lie is through the use of ambiguous language and the withholding of information. Since the inception of U.S. human rights policy, presidents have attempted to tell only part of the truth or to reformulate the truth by redefining the meaning of the terms human rights, democracy, or torture, for example. In this way, human rights policy has been about prevarication.

Presidents prevaricate for any number of reasons, but the primary reasons are convenience, self-promotion, and to further their political agenda. The aim of policy prevarication is to ensure that Congress and the public view the president's agenda favorably. In order to do so, the president will shade the truth, cherry-pick facts and circumstances that favor his position, while neglecting inconvenient evidence that may derail his program. Presidents, in the words of Cannon, have "a difficult time resisting the short-term gain a lie can afford them" (2007: 65). This suggests that presidents have both a capacity and a disposition to lie.

Before reviewing the prevarications associated with U.S. human rights policy, we will review the Congressional and bureaucratic structure and conflict associated with foreign aid. After all, Congress and executive bureaucracy either assist or resist the deception. It is possible that the Congress and the executive bureaucracy are complicit in presidential prevarications. On the other hand, it is also possible that Congress and the career bureaucrats harbor misgivings regarding the president's agenda and actively subvert and resist its implementation.

Presidential-Congressional Struggle over Foreign Aid

The foreign aid budget is subject to the budgetary process of bargaining and negotiating between the President and Congress (Brady and Volden 2005). The two-president thesis stipulates that the president's ability to direct policy differs between domestic and foreign affairs. The president enjoys certain advantages in foreign policy such as greater agenda-setting powers, with little interference from Congress. And the public tends to be less knowledgeable or concerned with foreign policy and relies heavily on presidential messages to mold their opinions (Meernik and Ault 2001). However, on domestic matters, the president is restrained by Congressional prerogative. Foreign aid blurs the distinction between domestic and foreign affairs. Foreign aid concerns domestic economic and commercial interests and the U.S. budget, with the resources directed at influencing foreign nations and people while supporting U.S. national interests. Congress funds program accounts, but the president can redirect funds within the program account to his desired countries, unless Congress earmarks the aid (Caddel 2013).

Congress and the President both use the foreign aid budget to impose their view and direction on foreign policy. However, it is generally assumed that, in foreign policy, the president holds the upper hand. The president is proactive by setting the foreign aid agenda while Congress is reactive and often follows the lead of the executive. The president has what is known as first mover advantage in aid allocations. The president, not Congress, initiates the foreign aid budget, and Congress can only consider the allocations once the president has submitted his budget proposal. Research by Canes-Wrone et al. (2008) found that, generally, the president has considerable success in attaining his requested budget levels for foreign policy and even greater success if his party controls Congress. The president's ability to set the agenda or blueprint for aid allocations, which Congress then increases, decreases, or accedes to, provides the president with considerable influence in foreign policymaking. However, the president cannot act—and can be completely stymied—until Congress appropriates the funds necessary to implement his policies. Thus, the budget is the battleground where Congress attempts to maximize control over U.S. foreign policy.

Congress can support the executive's policy program by heavily funding it, reject the program by starving it of resources, or attaching rigid conditions and exhaustive stipulations onto the legislation, or provide policy direction by earmarking funds. Human rights legislation, specifically the foreign aid budget, became an important tool for Congress to supervise and monitor presidential behavior. The threat to withhold funding "remains one of Congress's few effective legal tools to regulate presidential initiatives in foreign affairs" (Koh 1990: 131). Moreover, according to Liang-Fenton, the Congressional threat of aid termination can "prod the White House into action on issues that it may be reluctant to address and send a strong signal to foreign governments about the seriousness with which the United States regards particular human rights issues" (2004: 441). If Congress does not monitor human rights compliance, the more inclined the executive branch will be to ignore congressional preferences (Lindsay 1994). In the realm of human rights, Congress can also count on nongovernmental organizations (NGOs) to assist in the surveillance.

The inclusion of human rights into the Foreign Assistance Act (FAA) was a crucial procedure in Congress' effort to restrain Presidential powers. Congress wrote into the FAA provisions linking foreign aid and trade benefits to the status of human rights in foreign countries thereby regulating presidential and bureaucratic activities. Furthermore, Congress can earmark foreign aid funds, managing which states and programs may receive funds. In protecting and promoting human rights, Congress has on occasion refused to provide aid to those countries that violate the human rights of their citizens. Congress can constrain the executive's ability to use foreign aid as a tool of diplomacy or coercion by refusing to fund programs or by earmarking aid dollars. Thus in effect terminating any activity that Congress does not approve. An active Congress can thwart the President's ability to pursue his foreign policy strategy through the foreign aid allocation process. Congressional members are often divided on many issues, yet they frequently find common ground when it comes to opposing the President.

Congress has several other tools at its disposal to direct foreign policy and restrain executive choices and behaviors. Congress can also hold investigative hearings to examine and publicize foreign aid issues and events. Hearings are a commanding device that can shape the landscape of Congressional-Presidential relations by shifting the balance of power between the Hill and the White House. The Fraser Committee hearings in the 1970s are credited with establishing human rights as a policy concern in foreign aid allocations against the wishes of the executive. Congressional hearings are powerful tools to expose incidents, formalize congressional opinion, and shape foreign policy objectives. Another key method of Congressional oversight is the reporting requirement placed on the executive branch. For example, the Department of State (DOS) is responsible for compiling the annual public reports on the human rights conditions of every United Nations (U.N.) member state. Hearings and reports can also keep Congress informed regarding bureaucratic activity, thereby helping to prevent renegade behavior. And, perhaps most importantly, hearings and reports keep the executive branch accountable.

The Conflict within Congress over Foreign Aid

The foreign aid budget reflects the preferences of domestic decision-makers (Greene and Licht 2018). Legislators anticipate their constituents' preferences and act accordingly in order to maximize their chances of reelection. Although the majority of the American public think the United States spends too much on foreign aid, that it is simply a giveaway program producing few foreign policy benefits, and that the aid is often misused, Americans do support providing humanitarian, health, and disaster assistance to foreign people. Foreign aid may not have a formal interest group, but there are certainly supporters, as well as opponents, among the American public. Foreign policy issues, including foreign aid allocations, do have a constituency. Aldrich et al. (1989) determined that the influence of foreign policy issues varied substantially depending on the salience of the issues. American voters are concerned with where tax dollars are going and thus the issue of foreign aid influences voting choices. Political leaders do not necessarily "waltz before a blind audience" (Aldrich et al. 1989), although the audience may be severely nearsighted. In addition, human rights interest groups are perhaps among the best organized and persuasive, thus playing an important factor in Congressional foreign policy decision-making (Milner and Tingley 2011).

A Congressional member's support for foreign aid is a reflection of how her constituents are affected by foreign aid disbursements (Milner and Tingley 2010). Members who represent districts that have high-skilled workers, businesses, universities, nongovernmental organizations, or individuals holding contracts with U.S. Agency for International Development (USAID) or any other aid agency are significantly more likely to support foreign aid legislation than are members from districts with lower-skilled workers and fewer contractors and businesses. Milner and Tingley (2010) show that although the U.S. economy benefits from the allocation of aid, not every individual benefits equally. Each individual American has to pay higher taxes to finance the aid, but "due to the terms-of-trade effect, each individual receives a different amount of factor income... relatively unskilled labor in the donor are likely to lose from aid" (Milner and Tingley 2010: 207–208). In other words, lower- and working-class citizens do not benefit from generous allocations of economic aid. Highly skilled workers and businesses benefit substantially from foreign aid contracts, manufacturing opportunities, and shipping agreements due to procurement tying.

Procurement tying is a method of ensuring that U.S. foreign aid has a direct benefit to U.S. citizens and businesses. Tied aid is when a country binds its aid to the procurement of goods and services from the donor country. For example, tying aid occurs when the United States requires that aid recipients purchase the equipment, arms, materials, supplies, parts and services, or other commodities made in the United States or from the U.S. corporations, that they use contractors or consultants from the United States, or that the equipment be shipped via ships or airplanes flagged in the United States. The intent is to increase market opportunities for American businesses. Radelet (2006) reports that, historically, the United States has tied approximately 75 percent of its aid. Naturally, there is a struggle over foreign aid allocations between Congressional members whose districts benefit from large disbursements and those Congressional members whose constituents lose (that is, foot the bill), as a result of generous foreign aid programs.

Moreover, Congress, with its structure of committees and subcommittees, falls prey to a form of bureaucratic politics. Halperin et al. (2007) explain that Congressional committees, along with committee staff, behave much like bureaucracies in the desire to protect and advance committee interests. Each committee has a specific mission to perform and must jockey with one another for jurisdiction over policy and control over resources. Committees seek to expand their jurisdiction over policies and the agencies tasked with carrying out those policies. Legislation is often considered simultaneously in multiple committees due to increased issue and procedural complexity that crosses over committee boundaries, thus increasing tension between committees. For example, Arel-Bundock et al. (2015) report that, during the 111th Congress (2009–2010), 18 different committees and 44 separate subcommittees held hearings related to international affairs or foreign aid. Each Congressional committee and subcommittee seeks greater policy jurisdiction in order to enhance its prominence and stature in Congress. Some in Congress wish to reduce foreign aid allocations; others want to increase expenditures.

When Congress is polarized, it is more difficult for the legislative branch to reach a consensus on possible alternative foreign policies different from those put forward by the president. In this case, it is often easier for Congress to simply accept the president's agenda. Legislators' ideological leanings influence their support for foreign aid too. There is a continued ideological polarization in Congress over foreign aid, particularly when foreign aid packages include funding for family planning and reproductive health issues. Research has shown that the traditional left-right political spectrum often identifies which political leader will support foreign aid. Liberals are thought to favor foreign aid more generally. The granting of foreign aid serves basic humanitarian purposes: to eradicate poverty and hunger, to save the lives of children, or to improve the health of the poor. Social justice is an important but not primary rationale for aid allocations. For conservatives, on the other hand, foreign aid is often considered a give-away program at the expense of U.S. taxpayers. Individual effort, rather than welfare for foreign nations, and the free market are seen as the key to economic growth and to the betterment of citizens in developing countries. Unless, of course, foreign aid is a foreign policy tool supporting U.S. national interests. In such cases, for conservatives, foreign aid can be a useful tool of foreign policy that ought to be concentrated in nations that are economically and militarily important to the United States and further U.S. national interests. Although liberals and conservatives may both support aid, they have different objectives for that aid.

Bureaucratic Politics in Foreign Aid Allocations

The competition between the President and Congress in foreign policy is further complicated by the bureaucratic politics of the foreign policy bureaucracies, the Department of State (DOS), the Department of Defense (DOD), the Department of the Treasury, and the USAID, that implement foreign aid programs. The President initiates foreign policy, Congress legislates foreign policy, but they have to rely on a vast bureaucracy to implement it. The executive bureaucracy is officially under presidential authority, but Congress appropriates funds for the establishment, maintenance, and salaries of the foreign policy bureaucracy, thus defining its missions and goals. In addition, Congress has considerable influence on the kind of policies the bureaucracies will implement due to its oversight authority.

However, bureaucracies have their own agenda, too. When Congressional or executive mandates are viewed as detrimental to the bureaucracy, they are often delayed or simply ignored. Thus, there is often a significant difference in policy outcomes from the President's agenda or Congressional legislation. The bureaucracy's ability to resist, reform, or remake unpopular legislation is higher when there is disagreement between the executive and Congress on the purpose and function of the policy. As Norton Long states, "the bureaucracy is likely, day in and day out, to be our main source of policy initiative" (1952: 810). Foreign policy outcomes are more often the result of bureaucratic cooperation and rivalries than congressional legislation or Presidential directive.

A principal-agent framework adds to our understanding of bureaucratic conflict in the allocation of foreign aid. Political leaders delegate authority to a bureaucracy to implement, monitor, administer, and supervise government policy. The principal hands over control to the agent because the agent has expertise over a complex issue and the principal lacks the knowledge or time to oversee the issue. This gives the bureaucracy a great deal of power in determining policy. Because the principal entrusts the agent with power over the program, the agent is able to substitute its own preferences for the principal's directives. The ease of substitution is intensified when the agent has multiple principals (the President, Congress, powerful individual members of Congress, or even the American taxpayer) and when the agent has a greater level of autonomy. Hawkins et al. (2006) define autonomy as the degree of discretion and freedom of action available to the bureaucratic agent. The greater the autonomy, the simpler it is for the agent to pursue its own preferences in creating foreign aid policy. With several principals, each will attempt to persuade the agent to follow their dictates while ignoring the other principals. Conflict is compounded when the several agents (DOS, USAID, DOD) have overlapping authority. Thus, having multiple principals increases the ability of the multiple agents to substitute their own preferences while having competing agents increases bureaucratic infighting, which further lowers the efficiency of the aid.

The bureaucracy, as bureaucratic politics theorizes, is fragmentary and jockeys for power, influence, and turf. Thus, the bureaucracy is an agent of neither the president nor Congress. Bureaucrats are purposeful actors seeking to maximize their autonomy in pursuing their organization's interests. The bureaucratic politics model recognizes the conflicts over resources among multiple organizations where personal and political agendas are played out. Powerful bureaucracies and powerful individuals determine the likelihood of foreign aid allocation and relevant policy implementation. Bureaucrats are motivated by prospects of career advancement too, and they have an affinity for the bureaucracy to which they are attached. As Kissinger reveals, foreign service officers in the DOS bureaucracy "will carry out clear-cut instructions with great loyalty, but the typical Foreign Service officer is not easily persuaded that an instruction with which he disagrees is really clear-cut" (1979: 31). A bureaucracy's mission and values dictate its foreign aid preferences.

Bureaucratic rivalries and infighting are typical of the "internecine bureaucratic strife between DOS and USAID over the priorities and direction of U.S. foreign assistance," because of their overlapping and competing authority in development issues (Burton and Lord 2011: 118). The DOS views foreign aid as a tool of diplomacy while the USAID is narrowly focused on need-based aid rather than on the greater foreign policy picture (Gibson et al. 2005). The DOS and USAID have, in the opinion of Miles, different and conflicting cultures. The DOS has "an emphasis on analytical reporting skills over action or management... Conversely, USAID has an action-oriented, field-focused culture; however, it mirrors the development community's culture and rejects missions closely aligned with political agendas" (2011: 41). The State Department's culture is one of diplomacy and negotiation. This requires developing long-term friendly relations with foreign countries. Broadcasting a country's violations of human rights could undercut diplomacy and cordial relations with foreign leaders. Publicizing a country's human rights abuses may prompt Congress to terminate the DOS's number one tool of diplomacy—foreign aid. USAID culture is based on fieldwork, a deep understanding that poverty alleviation, the empowerment of women, and development as a long uphill battle. USAID has developed a culture of disbursement, not only to aid the poor and disadvantaged but also to increase the importance of its agency. The dispersing of aid maximizes USAID's budget and creates a demand for its services, thus requiring even more personnel and other resources.

The DOD, on the other hand, uses foreign aid to prop up national security concerns. The DOD plans, budgets, and implements U.S. security assistance programs (in consultation with the DOS). But the DOD has sought and been given funds to direct its own military assistance programs free of the policy leadership of State or the assistance of USAID. In addition, DOD now funds its own "post-conflict stabilization and reconstruction operations which overlap substantially with both State and USAID programs" (Adams 2007: 4). Although the DOD has the funding and personnel, it lacks the expertise, experience, knowledge, and patience to implement U.S. diplomatic and development goals.

To demonstrate the clash of bureaucratic cultures, Natsios (2010) uses the example of the USAID and the DOD reconstruction programs in Afghanistan. When the United States was asked to build schools, the DOD simply pulled out construction material and built a physical building labeled a school. The process was quick and efficient. The USAID, on the other hand, sought community input on the location and plans for the building. USAID would also take measures to increase the Education Ministry's capacity to staff, equip, and meet recurring costs. Without teachers, textbooks, and other essentials, the school was not a school but merely a building. The USAID projects took time and caused delays for DOD construction. The differing understanding of what a school was cause significant frustration and accusations of obstructionism between the two agencies.

DOD's short-term goal of pacifying the population, or winning hearts and minds, is different than USAID's long-term mission of funding development and poverty alleviation strategies. A 2010 report from the U.S. Government Accountability Office, the investigational arm of Congress often called the congressional watchdog, details many of the shortcomings of DOD development programs. The DOD does not develop detailed plans to accomplish its objectives, fails to use interagency expertise, and lacks coordination with other agencies to promote effective use of resources, which leads to activities that overlap, duplicate, or countervail those of USAID. However, development assistance (DA), and foreign aid in general, is becoming militarized.

Anderson (2014) reports that even the language of foreign aid means different things to different bureaucracies. The phrase "humanitarian assistance" to the USAID refers to short-term assistance given after a natural disaster or other crisis. But for the DOD, it means "civic assistance projects, such as schools, health clinics, water, and sanitation projects, which for USAID are often part of longer-term development assistance programs in education and health" (Anderson 2014: 113). The different understanding of the phrase leads to dissimilar and diverse implementation of programs and divergent measures of program success.

In this constrained budget environment, DOD has the upper hand over USAID and the DOS since "the economic scale of aid spending is similarly dwarfed by defense contracting; the total value of USAID-administered assistance is less than one tenth of DOD budgets for procurement, research, and development" (Adams 2007: 6). But it is not just about money. Lieutenant Colonel David Kilcullen, a senior advisor to General David Petraeus (former commander of the Multinational Force in Iraq), stated with regard to the level of personnel: "the Department of Defense is about 210 times larger than USAID and State combined" (as quoted in Patrick and Brown 2007: 3). According to Patrick and Brown (2007), 20 percent of aid is channeled through the DOD, with the majority of that aid targeted to Iraq and Afghanistan. Thus, the DOD's security and strategic concerns could easily overshadow or undermine USAID's authority in development programs.

Administering Foreign Policy: Who Is in Charge of the Bureaucracy?

The question of who controls the bureaucracy is important because the president will use the executive bureaucracy to assist in his prevarication while Congress will use the bureaucracy to resist the deception. The U.S. Constitution does not explicitly grant either the president or Congress with clear authority over the bureaucracy. To answer the question of who's in charge, Davidson and Oleszek conclude, "both the president and Congress are responsible for the fourth branch of government—the bureaucracy" (2004: 320). Congress and the president must compete for control over the bureaucracy and the implementation of foreign policy because each has a constitutional prerogative to dictate bureaucratic actions and policy. However, the bureaucracy, due to its size, complexity, expertise, not to mention its ability to play one side against the other, has allowed it a significant level of autonomy. Both Congress and the President attempt to constrain the actions and activities of the bureaucracy in order to retain control over policy outcomes.

The President, as the chief executive, holds the power to control policy and its bureaucratic enactment when he appoints loyalists and team players to lead the executive agencies. Lewis (2008) reports that the modern president has over 3,000 political appointments to make. These appointees, peppered throughout the bureaucracy, help ensure his control over the bureaucracy and the implementation of his policies and programs. The president can also demote or fire appointees, thereby ensuring that their loyalties remain with him. Among the institutional constraints to presidential action Stephens lists "the policies and practices developed by career civil servants and military personal," or what is known as the permanent bureaucracy (2012: 490). Career bureaucrats, those who do not serve at presidential whim, look to precedent rather than presidential proclamations for guidance in policy implementation, often resulting in policy inertia (Stephens 2012). Career bureaucrats tend to protect and support the interests of their agencies more willingly than those of the current administration. Presidents and policies come and go, but bureaucratic agencies are perpetual (they may be renamed or reorganized, but they are rarely disbanded).

A politically savvy president can use the Congress committee system to "fend off congressional efforts to control the agencies he wants to control himself" (Hammond and Knott 1996: 124) by playing the committees off against each other. With each Congressional committee and subcommittee working to protect and advance its interests and stature, the President can choose among them to find one sympathetic with his wishes. The bureaucratic politics model explains how the committee system can systematically advantage an astute president. Yet, the committee system can also constrain a president's ability to control the foreign policy bureaucracy because the bureaucracy can also find a sympathetic and amenable committee. By deferring to the views of one Congressional committee, the bureaucracy can fend off the competing demands of the President or other committees within Congress. In a situation where the bureaucracy is accountable to multiple agents, the bureaucracy can easily ignore the wishes of outside agents by playing them against each other. Bureaucratic agencies can maneuver between competing Congressional members or committees to align themselves with the one that best serves their interests, allowing greater autonomy in making policy choices. The range of policy options available to the bureaucratic agency and its greater autonomy to choose are broadened by the number of politicians involved and the degree of policy disagreement between them. The bureaucracy's ability to redefine and reformulate U.S. policy is higher when there is dissension between the executive and Congress over the purpose and function of the policy. The bureaucracy often forms strategic alliances with Congressional committees in order to weaken Presidential control and advance its own agenda.

Although Congress has become more assertive in foreign policy matters, it grants the president and bureaucracy great leeway in implementing policy. Lindsay finds that "in passing legislation Congress typically delegates tremendous power to the executive branch" (Lindsay 1992: 611). Congress typically provides the president a sufficient amount of flexibility in conducting foreign policy to meet unexpected or exceptional events. Human rights legislation contains "needy people" and "extraordinary circumstances" loopholes or exemptions allowing foreign assistance to be granted to gross human rights violators as long as it benefits needy people or if the United States has strategic, economic, or other interests in the recipient country. In addition, because Congress lacks the knowledge and expertise to direct the complexities of foreign policy, Davidson and Oleszek admit that Congress also allows the bureaucracy "considerable discretion in interpreting and implementing the laws it passes" (2004: 336). Laws by necessity have to be drawn with some level of vagueness and ambiguity to allow the President and the bureaucracy to handle unforeseen situations.

Clinton et al. (2014) determine that Congressional members want to be involved in oversight committees and important policy debates in order to secure potential media attention and resultant electoral benefits that committee membership may bring. But, more often, the purpose of grandstanding is to influence policy, as Congressional members understand that "playing to the galleries is an essential tool of policy entrepreneurs" (Lindsay 1992–1993: 623). Media attention can be a valuable tool to build public support for new policy. It can also force the President to reverse a course of action. The Fraser Committee and the human rights legislation, reporting requirements, and bureaucratic reorganization that followed were one such event. In the realm of human rights, Congress took the initiative in setting the agenda and steering foreign policy. Fraser and his supporters believed that the hearings would force the President and executive bureaucracy to consider the human rights implications of foreign policy actions and foreign aid allocations.

Congress exerts considerable influence over the bureaucracy through its funding responsibilities. Congress can control policy because it holds the power of the purse and thus can reward or sanction a bureaucracy for the policy it implements. And, as Daugirdas (2013) argues, executive branch agencies understand who pays their salaries and funds their organization and are careful to implement Congressional mandates. Congress can increase or decrease agency budgets or eliminate the agency altogether. Congress also controls personnel matters, such as retirement plans, special requirements needed to hold a certain position, performance standards, and, of course, wage rates. In addition, Congress can require the bureaucracy to hold hearings or publish reports on policy options and probable outcomes involving testimony from experts and gathering public viewpoints, thereby limiting an agency's discretion. For example, by requiring the DOS to publish accounts of the human rights conditions in foreign aid recipient states, human rights NGOs and the American public could mobilize to influence aid allocations. The *Country Reports on Human Rights Practices* also put recipient states on notice that their abuses would not go unnoticed. Hearings and reports reduce the bureaucracy's "hidden information" (technical expertise) and an agency's ability to engage in "hidden action," that is to say, an action that is not easily observable or measureable (Arrow 1985).

Lindsay (1992–1993) states that Congress will also create agencies in an attempt to shape foreign policy. An example, relevant to this study, is the creation of the Bureau of Human Rights and Humanitarian Affairs. In 1976, policy entrepreneurs in Congress created and funded the Coordinator for Human Rights and Humanitarian Affairs (HRHA), later upgraded to Assistant Secretary of State for Human Rights and Humanitarian Affairs, with an increased staff, because Congress felt that insufficient attention had been given to human rights considerations in foreign policy. After all, Congress was aware that "policies that don't have champions in the bureaucracy are doomed" (Lindsay 1992–1993: 617). The President may be supreme in foreign policy generally, but in foreign aid the President is reliant on Congress to allocate funds and on the bureaucracy to implement his programs.

Nevertheless, foreign policy bureaucracies do enjoy a significant level of autonomy and independence. Civil servants who work in the bureaucracy and implement foreign policy can only be fired for neglect of duty or malfeasance, but cannot be replaced by presidential whim or political patronage. Bureaucracies "establish political legitimacy—a reputation for expertise, efficiency, or moral protection and a uniquely diverse complex of ties to organized interests and the media—and induce politicians to defer to the wishes of the agency even when they prefer otherwise" (Carpenter 2001: 4). The range of policy options from which bureaucrats can choose is constrained by the policy preferences of political leaders. After the political leader sets the broad goals, the bureaucracy is left to fill in the policy details. The design of the program will greatly influence the policy outcomes. Because the agency is charged with monitoring the program, collecting technical data, and evaluating policy outcomes that will be transmitted to political leaders and the public, it has control over the evaluation, continuation, or modification of the program. Thus, the bureaucracy plays a vital role in influencing the direction of foreign policy.

In sum, U.S. foreign policy and foreign aid allocations are the outcome of pulling and hauling, a complicated annual "dance," between the major actors in the foreign policy decision-making process. Irwin explains that "the foreign aid process was marked by an elaborate public and private dance between the administration, the respective chamber leadership, and the committee and subcommittee leadership" (2000: 46). Presidents may have first-mover advantage, but they do not dominate foreign aid policy. Legislators must allocate the aid requested by the President, thus giving that branch significant power to direct presidential policy. Before aid can be used as a foreign policy tool, Congress and at least some segments of the American public must first approve of it. However, once funded, each bureaucratic agency "conducts its own foreign policy with little or no attachment to a central core of principles and interests" established by the President and Congress (Wiarda 2000).

Domestic political and economic issues continue to impact foreign aid allocations. Legislators understand the distributional effects of aid on their districts; the public responds to foreign events and holds preferences on aid allocations; and bureaucracies implement aid programs that favor the status and power of their organizations. Interests matter, but as Milner and Tingley (2010) and Greene and Licht (2018) demonstrate, so does ideology. Liberals support generous aid packages to ease human suffering while conservatives favor granting aid to reinforce U.S. geopolitical and security interests. Since any human rights restriction would be detrimental to future funding, the DOS and the foreign assistance bureaucracies were initially resistant to the inclusion of human rights requirements. The DOS objected to the restriction of foreign aid since foreign aid was an extremely important tool of diplomacy. The USAID had a vested interest in a well-funded foreign aid program because high levels of funding increased its resources, authority, and turf.

Inception of Contemporary Human Rights Policy: The Fraser Committee

Human rights have always been a key component of U.S. identity. Although human rights have a long theoretical tradition in U.S. political thought and policy, contemporary human rights policy originated in the 1970s. The U.S. government's immoral and ruthless policies around the world shocked members of Congress, the American public, and NGOs. The development of a human rights policy arose from the scandal of Vietnam, Watergate, the disillusion with U.S. support for dictatorial regimes in Rhodesia, South Africa, Brazil, Greece, Chile, and Uruguay, as well as to the efforts of the civil rights movement (Sikkink 2004). Cmiel (1999) credits the vibrant human rights movement of the 1970s to the growth of human rights nongovernment organizations, populated by anti-Vietnam peace activists, the new-found interest of churches, foundations, and universities in the topic, and, most importantly, the work of certain Congressional members and their staffs to challenge the cynical realpolitik of Nixon and Kissinger. At this time, Donald Fraser (D-MN), and other like-minded Congressional colleagues, saw an opportunity to regain a larger Congressional role in American foreign policy. Nixon was unable to challenge the growing human rights movement due to his political insecurity and the public's growing opposition to his presidency and policies. Congress and the public wanted a return to what they imagined was America's cultural values and identity—a country built on the protection of human rights and democratic freedoms. The U.S. commitment to human rights, using the famous words of Abraham Lincoln, "shall nobly save, or meanly lose, the last best hope of earth" (1862).

Established foreign policy practice is stable and consistent until and unless circumstances create a crisis of confidence. The Cold War policies were likely to continue with only minor modifications until Congress and the American public reacted to the trauma of Vietnam, the shock of Watergate, and the distress of learning of Nixon's support for brutal regimes. Jackson (2011) believes that an overarching principle or doctrine, such as the inclusion of human rights into U.S. foreign policy, is the result of two mutually constitutive elements. First, political leaders socially construct the principle primarily through the use of language. Fraser and other human rights advocates in Congress gave speeches, did interviews, and held televised hearings to provide the "explanation, rationale, justification and necessary social consensus" for developing and implementing a human rights policy (Jackson 2011: 392). Second, a new principle requires material resources to be able manifest itself. Examples of material resources needed to institutionalize a new doctrine include legislation, the reorganization of bureaucratic agencies, and the expansion of foreign assistance programs. The 92nd and 93rd Congresses provided the material resources necessary to institute human rights as a component in U.S. foreign policy.

The theory of policy entrepreneurs suggests that highly motivated and well-placed individuals can change government policy. Policy entrepreneurs "distinguish themselves through their desire to significantly change current ways of doing things in their area of interest" (Mintrom and Norman 2009: 650). Fraser had been an activist in the civil rights and anti-war movements before entering the House of Representatives. Entrepreneurs look for opportunities to bring attention to a specific problem and advocate their policy choices. Kingdon (1981, 1984) has shown that entrepreneurs look for a policy window of opportunity to make policy change. The political and economic environment is important, too once again and the country's discontent with Nixon, Watergate, and Vietnam provided that window. Yet, legislative "success comes only after subject matter experts [policy entrepreneurs] at the committee and subcommittee levels had done the heavy lifting of building support for a measure one legislator at a time" (Irwin 2000: 47). Fraser was not alone in the campaign to move human rights into a prominent place in U.S. foreign policy. In order to take advantage of the window of opportunity, Fraser built a tight-knit team composed of Congressional members and staffers, such as John Salzberg, with knowledge and a deep commitment to create human rights policy. In addition, Fraser developed an advocacy coalition within Congress encompassing Republicans and Democrats, conservatives and liberals, NGOs, and the American public. Congress contained a number of like-minded entrepreneurs: Tom Harkin (D-Iowa) and Edward Koch (D-NY) in the House of Representatives, and Ted Kennedy (D-MA), Hubert Humphrey (D-MN), and Alan Cranston (D-CA) in the Senate. However, human rights were not only a liberal democratic issue. Cmiel (1999) reports that John Ashbrook (R-OH) and conservative anti-communist Henry "Scoop" Jackson (D-WY) were also concerned with human rights, at least in the communist world.

In 1973, as a response to Nixon-Kissinger's immoral policies, Representative Donald Fraser (D-MN), then chair of the Subcommittee on International Organization and International Organization[1] of the House Foreign Relations Committee, began a series of hearings to examine and make recommendations on the international protection of human rights and to increase the priority given to human rights by the United States. Congressional hearings are a primary tool for committees to gather information, hear and question witnesses, and publicize issues of Congressional concern. In the words of Weissbrodt, "congressional hearings have a significant visibility and respect," making them "one of the most potent weapons in the human rights arsenal of the United States during a period when the Administration refused actively to pursue human rights" (1977: 239). Foreign policy issues are not normally salient with the American public. However, after the Vietnam War and Watergate, human rights captured the public's attention.

At the conclusion of its hearings, the Subcommittee issued a report titled *Human Rights in the World Community: A Call for U.S. Leadership* (March 27, 1974).[2] The Subcommittee's human rights hearings proved to be an important forum for witnessing human rights abuses around the world and in keeping human rights concerns in the forefront of U.S. foreign policy. In addition to investigating and publicizing U.S. policy toward nations that violate human rights, the Fraser hearings had a significant impact on foreign aid legislation, and bureaucratic organization and procedures too.

Three important pieces of legislation resulted from the Fraser's Subcommittee hearings that "all future U.S. human rights policies flow from and are based on these three early pieces of legislation" (Sikkink 2004: 70). First was the creation of the Office for Human Rights in the State Department, to be headed by an Assistant Secretary of State.[3] The Assistant Secretary of State would exercise jurisdiction over matters relating to human rights, advise the DOS on all matters having human rights implications, and prepare a human rights impact memorandum for governmental policies.

Second was the mandate that the State Department gather information on human rights situations around the world and publish an annual *Country Reports on Human Rights Practices*. Fraser (1979) believes this was the best innovation following his hearings. Prior to the *Country Reports*, accounts of human rights violations were reported through State Department cables marked "confidential," thus leaving Congress and the American public blind to the human rights conditions in countries the United States was giving assistance to. Today, the State Department's *Country Reports on Human Rights Practices* are the most widely used sources of information on human rights, and they are relied upon by scholars to create measures of the scope, intensity, and range of human rights violations.

And third was the inclusion of language denying military aid to those countries that violate the human rights of their citizens (Humphrey-Cranston Amendment, or Section 502B of the FAA). In formulating human rights legislation, Fraser (1979) acknowledges that his first priority was to focus on the most egregious human rights violations, torture, and summary execution. The second priority was to limit military assistance since it was the assistance most directly related to government repression. Fraser regrets include an exception to the prohibition of providing assistance to repressive regimes. The inclusion of the "extraordinary circumstances" allowance in 502B was pragmatically intended to cover unforeseen events, but was viewed by presidential administrations as an unrestricted license to pursue their foreign policy agenda.

Bureau of Human Rights and Humanitarian Affairs (HRHA)

As a result of the Fraser Committee's recommendation, Congress established a bureaucratic office in the DOS to monitor and report on the human rights situation in countries receiving U.S. aid.[4] Deputy Under Secretary of State for Management, Lewis Dean Brown, when laying out the various options of reforming the DOS to better include human rights as requested by Congress, warned that "some see this Bureau as a kind of 'conscience of the Department' and this could cause substantive problems" (Brown 1974). A bureau within the State Department whose purpose was to call out human rights abuses in a foreign country is contrary to the State Department's traditional function as diplomat and mediator.

James Wilson, a career diplomat, was the first coordinator of the newly created Bureau of Human Rights and Humanitarian Affairs (HRHA) in 1974.[5] Wilson was an unlikely candidate for the office as he admitted he "knew nothing about human rights beyond an acquaintanceship with the U.N. Universal Declaration of Human Rights during my law school days" (as quoted in Keys 2010: 833). Wilson, unfortunately, was caught between the enthusiasm of Congress for human rights and the disdain for human rights of the executive branch. Consequently, Mr. Wilson had very little impact on human rights policy. The Secretary of State at the time, Henry Kissinger, was unreceptive with regard to human rights as a foreign policy objective and hostile to Congressional initiatives that targeted foreign governments allied to the United States. Kissinger rejected virtually all of Wilson's human rights memoranda.

In 1977, the position of coordinator of HRHA was upgraded to the rank of Assistant Secretary of State, nominated by the President subject to Congressional approval. Maynard (1989) suggests that the lack of respect the Bureau of Human Rights and Humanitarian Affairs initially received from both the executive and career Foreign Service officers was due to the fact that Congress "thrust a human rights office upon the diplomatic and bureaucratic decision-making process of the executive branch" led by a lowly coordinator not a leader with Assistant Secretary status (1989: 179). In fact, before the institutional establishment of human rights within the executive branch, "the best guarantee of an aborted career in the defense and foreign policy establishments is a marked concern for the humanitarian consequences of national behavior" (Farer 1974: 623).

In 1994, the bureau was reorganized and renamed Bureau of Democracy, Human Rights, and Labor (DRL) to emphasize the importance of workers' rights and democracy in securing human rights. Since its creation, DRL's responsibilities and duties have grown. In addition to the *Country Reports on Human Rights Practices*, the DRL presently administers the U.S. Human Rights and Democracy Fund (established in 1998) and prepares *The Report to Congress on International Religious Freedom* (legislated in 1998), *The Trafficking in Persons Report* (initiated in 2000), and the *United States Universal Periodic Review* (first reviewed in 2011).

Country Reports on Human Rights Practices

The mandate that the DOS collect and publish details on the human rights situations in foreign aid recipient countries was intended to provide Congress with an accurate picture of the human rights condition globally. It also had the purpose of countering Nixon's contention that human rights violators could not be determined. Nixon argued that Congressional attempts to link a government's human rights record to the provision of U.S. foreign assistance was impractical and unfeasible since there was no objective way to distinguish between good and bad countries (he furthered claimed that human rights abuses were widespread and hidden). Robert Ingersoll, Assistant Secretary of State for East Asian and Pacific Affairs, testified before Congress explaining that the Nixon Administration could not define "political prisoner," and, therefore, could not objectively determine who was or was not a political prisoner (June 1974).

The State Department, under Kissinger, obstructed the collection and publication of the human rights conditions of foreign countries on the grounds that doing so would interfere with the diplomatic purposes of U.S. embassies. Reporting on a country's human rights abuses contradicts the State Department's perceived mission of diplomacy and building friendly relations with foreign governments. Accordingly, the collection and publication of the brutal abuses of human rights and fundamental freedoms by U.S. friends and allies was viewed as a violation of the State Department's *raison d'être*. Kissinger, as Secretary of State, attempted to evade the Congressional mandate to collect and publish accurate and factual information on human rights in U.S.-allied states. Weissbrodt notes that the State Department "protested vigorously against violations of human rights by Communist governments" but "fell strangely silent about massacres and other grave human rights violations" (1977: 234–235) in countries friendly to the United States. Thus, the initial reports were biased, downplaying the violations in friendly states while targeting on the violations in anti-American states.

In order to get an accurate picture of the human rights situation, Congress mandated that the State Department had to present "all the available information" regarding human rights practices in the foreign country and to describe the steps the State Department had taken to promote respect for human rights. Furthermore, the reports were required to give "due consideration" to information provided by "appropriate international organizations," like the Red Cross or Amnesty International. In fact, Human Rights Watch was founded to counter "all the lies" presented in the early *Country Reports* (Cmiel 1999). The *Human Rights in the World Community: A Call for U.S. Leadership* also recommended that a human rights officer be appointed for each of the five regional bureaus within the DOS (Europe, Latin America, Africa, the Near East, and East Asia). The human rights officers would assist in the collection of information and evidence on human rights practices for the annual country reports.

The *Country Reports* are used by the U.S. Congress to determine the level of foreign aid to be granted or whether to impose sanctions upon an abusing country. The *Country Reports* now cover all countries receiving assistance and all U.N. member states. The *Country Reports* are the result of a detailed and time-consuming investigation. The human rights office in each U.S. embassy around the world gathers the information from the foreign government, NGOs, news agencies, opposition groups, etc., and then transmits a draft report based on the collected information to the DRL. DRL's regional desk officer examines the draft reviews and edits the draft to ensure that it follows the specific guidelines for a given year's report. The reports must consider the extent to which the foreign government allows or impedes U.S. or independent investigation and reporting of their human rights conditions. Finally, if aid is to be offered or continued to a human-rights abusing recipient government, the State Department must describe the extraordinary circumstances that necessitate continued assistance. If, at any point in the review process, an official questions the accuracy or legitimacy of the information contained in the report, the report is sent back to be reinvestigated and rewritten. Once the reports have been reviewed and approved, they are submitted to Congress by January 31 of each year. Although initially considered weak and biased, the *Country Reports* have evolved to a primary source of accurate, balanced, and truthful reflections on human rights conditions.

Human Rights Legislation

Congress attempted to restrain presidential foreign initiatives by legislating human rights mandates in order to curb the immoral if not illegal behavior of President Nixon. The early human rights legislation passed by Congress in the 1970s did not include binding directives forcing the President to consider human rights when allocating foreign aid or making trade deals. A "Sense of Congress" amendment allows Congress to go on the record to support or oppose a particular policy, send a stern message to the President regarding Congress' strong opinion of the policy, and give a warning to the President that Congress expects a change in policy. What a "Sense of Congress" is not, however, is a binding or enforceable law. Congress would later amend the human rights legislation mandating Presidential adherence to human rights conditionalities as a direct consequence of the executive branch's persistent noncompliance with the "Sense of Congress."

Congress first attempted to establish a human rights policy by including Section 32 into the 1973 FAA. The 1973 FAA included Section 32 as a "Sense of Congress," advising (though not mandating) the President to deny economic and military aid to governments that violate human rights. The initiative, introduced by Senator James Abourezk (D-SD), instructed denial of economic and military aid to governments that imprison or intern their citizens for political reasons.

As a consequence of the Nixon Administration's noncompliance with Section 32, Congress expanded and amended the human rights legislation (S. Cohen 1982). In 1974, Section 502B was added to the FAA to prohibit security assistance to governments that grossly violate human rights. The amendment was stronger, less ambiguous, and sharper in focus, but it still remained a "Sense of Congress." However, the new amendment is notable for two reasons. First, Section 502B restricts the allocation of security assistance not just military aid. The modification in the language of the legislation, from military assistance found in Section 32 to security assistance in 502B, reflects Congress' intention to limit not only military aid, but also arms sales and police equipment (S. Cohen 1982). Second, Congress expanded and detailed what constituted human rights violations to include torture or cruel, inhuman or degrading treatment or punishment; prolonged detention without charges; or other flagrant denials of the right to life, liberty, and the security of the person.

The Ford Administration, like the Nixon Administration before, ignored Section 502B. Carlyle Maw, Under Secretary of State for Security Assistance, testified in a hearing, before the House Committee on International Relations, that no security assistance was denied based on a country's human rights record (1976). Congress then legislated a binding provision in 1976. The Humphrey-Cranston Amendment, as it was known, removed the "Sense of Congress" language and replaced it with an explicit mandate for the termination of security aid to gross violators of internationally recognized human rights. This was followed by Section 301 of the International Security Assistance and Arms Export Control Act of 1976 requiring the President to formulate military assistance programs to promote human rights and to avoid identification with repressive regimes.

U.S. economic assistance was often used to support pro-American repressive regimes. Thus, in 1975, the Harkin Amendment was included in the FAA (Section 116). The Harkin Amendment prohibits economic assistance to any country that commits gross human rights violations unless it can be shown that the aid will directly benefit needy people. Section 116 of the FAA stipulates that no assistance may be provided to any country that engages in consistent pattern of gross violations of internationally recognized human rights unless such assistance will directly benefit the needy people in such country. The denial of economic aid would, in the words of Fraser, inform offending countries that "human rights violations will cost them something in their relationship with the United States" (1977: 147). Learning from its mistakes, Congress legislated Section 116 as a legally binding mandate.

Along with sections 502B and 116 of the FAA, Congress passed several other amendments protecting human rights.

- The Jackson-Vanik Amendment to the Trade Act of 1974[6] denied most favored nation status to countries with nonmarket economies that denied their citizens the right or opportunity of emigration. The Jackson-Vanik Amendment was passed in response to emigration restrictions and limitations posed by the Soviet Union. The Jackson-Vanik Amendment "constituted a political setback to détente since it affirmed that human rights should have prominence in guiding the policy of détente" (Tulli 2012: 586)
- The Nelson-Bingham Amendment (1974) tightened the restrictions of arms sales to foreign countries by requiring all foreign arms sales of more than $25 million to be reviewed by Congress. The sale was subject to Congressional veto. The Amendment was in response to the revelation that President Nixon secretly sold weapons to the repressive governments of Iran and Saudi Arabia (Tompa 1986). Human rights activists and sympathetic members of Congress were not only disturbed that lethal weapons were sold to repressive governments, but also that sooner or later the sale of sophisticated weapons would draw the United States into Middle East conflicts.
- The Hughes-Ryan Amendment (1974) curtailed the power of the Central Intelligence Agency (CIA) to engage in covert action. In response to the Nixon Administration's secret wars in Cambodia, Laos, and North Vietnam, Congress enacted the Hughes-Ryan Amendment. The Amendment disallowed funding for CIA covert operations unless the President determined that the operation was important to U.S. national security and provided the eight Congressional oversight committees with a description and scope of the operation.
- The 1974 addition of Section 660 to the FAA had banned all U.S. aid to foreign police forces that engage in gross human rights violations.

Because of the widespread allegations that the USAID's Office of Public Safety advocated, or even taught, torture techniques to foreign police officers in South Vietnam, Chile, Guatemala, Brazil, and other countries, Congress introduced Section 660 in the 1974 FAA. However, there were numerous exceptions to this prohibition including aid that was given under the authority of the Drug Enforcement Administration or the Federal Bureau of Investigation. This act further exempted aid if it were to be used to fight terrorism, narcotics trafficking, and maritime law enforcement, or if the country was without a standing army.

- Section 111 of the Agricultural Trade Development and Assistance Act (1977) forbids any agreement to finance the sale of agricultural goods, commodities, or items to any state that consistently practices gross human rights violations.

Congress also passed country-specific human rights legislation. Country-specific legislation is commonly used to deny or reduce security assistance to named countries on human rights grounds. Congress resorts to country-specific legislation when it feels the President has failed to apply general human rights legislation to a particular country (S. Cohen 1982).

Later, during the Carter Administration, Congress would enact Section 701 of the International Financial Institutions Act of 1977 to prohibit U.S. support for World Bank or International Monetary Fund (IMF) loans to governments that engage in a systematic pattern of gross violations of internationally recognized human rights, unless the loan addresses basic human needs.

Weissbrodt (1977) credits individual members of Congress and their staffs for generating the political will needed to pass human rights legislation, while human rights NGOs worked to raise public awareness and generate popular opposition to U.S. support of dictators and despots abroad.

Foreign Aid

Since its inception, foreign aid has been an essential instrument of U.S. foreign policy and the primary tool available to foreign policy decision-makers to implement U.S. human rights policy. Tarnoff and Lawson affirm that U.S. leaders and policymakers view foreign assistance as an "essential instrument of U.S. foreign policy," which has "increasingly been associated with national security policy" (2016: 1). Foreign aid promotes moral principles while preserving the national security of the United States. As a tool of foreign policy, foreign aid can be provided to a recipient country either as a reward for some behavior or as an inducement to change behavior. The provision of foreign aid is the carrot that influences the recipient's policy choices or other behaviors.

The termination of aid, the stick, can also be used in an attempt to alter a recipient country's behavior. This fact is explicitly recognized by Tarnoff and Lawson when they write: "Foreign aid is a particularly flexible tool—it can act as both carrot and stick, and is a means of influencing events, solving specific problems, and projecting U.S. values" (2016: 1).

When pursuing foreign policy, including foreign aid policy, states can choose between bilateral or multilateral actions. Bilateral aid is resources that flow directly from one country to another. With bilateral aid, the United States retains control over the funds, thus preserving the U.S. freedom in deciding which countries will receive aid, the amount of aid provided, the time frame for which aid is given, and under what conditions the recipient will be favored with aid. The provision of bilateral foreign assistance leaves the recipient obligated to the United States.

Aid that is channeled through intergovernmental organizations such as the World Bank, regional development banks, the International Monetary Fund, U.N. agencies, or the Organization for Economic Co-operation and Development (OECD) is known as multilateral aid. The aid becomes the development asset of the multilateral institution, which it then disperses based on the multilateral institution's own decision-making process.

Bilateral Economic Aid

U.S. bilateral economic aid is complex and has been used to fulfill multiple objectives. Economic aid includes cash or credits, food, medicine, commodities, funding projects for democracy building, emergency relief activities, debt relief, and technical advice and training. The purpose of U.S. economic aid is to promote democracy and assist the poor. The United States provides economic aid to help economies prosper and to raise the living standard of the poor. The promotion of democracy and the protection of human rights remain core objectives of economic aid. But economic aid has other uses too. Aid can be used to support a friendly authoritarian regime, to increase economic trade, to encourage economic liberalization, or to reward backing of the United States. It can also be withdrawn to destabilize or punish an unfriendly regime.

There are three major categories of U.S. economic aid: Bilateral DA, Humanitarian Assistance, and Economic Support Funds (ESFs). Humanitarian aid programs include disaster relief and humanitarian crises. Humanitarian aid is meant to "alleviate human suffering caused by natural and manmade disasters by providing assistance for the relief and rehabilitation of people and countries affected by such disasters" (USAID 2013). The purpose of DA is to sponsor advances in health, education, or agriculture development, in short, to invest in people. DA intends to promote conditions that enable developing countries to achieve self-sustaining economic growth with equitable distribution of benefits while ensuring rights are respected and enhanced. Another category of economic assistance is ESF. This funding is listed as economic aid since its purpose is to promote political and economic stability in recipient countries to further U.S. political and security interests. Funding decisions are made by the State Department but the programs are managed by the USAID (Tarnoff and Gill 2017). Its security component is evidenced by the fact that the State Department, not USAID, controls its allocation and disbursement. Provided as budget support, ESF allows recipient countries to use their own resources to build up their defense infrastructures.

Since it is classified as economic and not military assistance, ESF does not face the same level of scrutiny or limitations and can more easily be provided to human rights abusing regimes. ESF funding's primary purpose, since 9/11, has been to support U.S. strategically important countries in the war on terror. ESF resources are often allocated in lieu of military aid in order to avoid a congressional debate on the ethical, moral, or political consequences of providing military aid to certain countries or groups (Ruttan 1996).

Bilateral Security Assistance

Security assistance serves U.S. geopolitical concerns: strengthening the U.S. hard power, fortifying military alliances, buying permission to build and maintain foreign bases, sustaining pro-American regimes in power, or underpinning U.S. commercial interests through the sale of military equipment.

Security assistance consists of military and nonmilitary aid, military support equipment, military education and training, and anti-terrorist assistance. Proponents claim security assistance strengthens U.S. allies' legitimate self-defense capabilities while enabling them to participate in multinational military missions. Military assistance is administered by the DOD's Defense Security Cooperation Agency, in coordination with the State Department's Political-Military Affairs bureau. The Defense Security Cooperation Agency recommends the appropriate level of country funding, determines what military equipment is suitable and available, procures the equipment, provides overall policy guidance, and implements the U.S. security assistance programs.

Military assistance includes the Foreign Military Financing (FMF) and the International Military Education and Training (IMET) program. FMF is a grant program that provides military equipment to foreign governments. In an FMF arrangement, the U.S. government either buys the requested military equipment from U.S. manufacturers at market price and gives the equipment to the recipient government, or simply loans the funds at lower than market rates to the recipient country so that it can purchase the arms directly. IMET trains foreign soldiers in the use of U.S.-supplied military equipment, advanced military tactics, and the rules of war. The DOD manages the IMET program, and the State Department determines the political advisability of its recipients. The Transfers of Excess Defense Articles program is administered by the DOD. Articles designated as surplus military equipment and supplies are given at no cost to the allied government.

Nonmilitary security assistance provides money to counterterrorism, illicit narcotics production and transportation, transnational organized crime, and weapons proliferation. The funds aim to detect and dismantle terrorist networks, create watch lists, and build country anti-terrorist capacities, all activities that carry a high risk of violating the basic human rights of criminals and noncriminals alike.

Multilateral Aid

Multilateral foreign aid is assistance provided by donor governments to international organizations, such as the World Bank, regional banks, or the IMF, to alleviate poverty. Multilateral aid may contribute to the efficiency and effectiveness of aid by joining forces with other donors to improve coordination of policies, avoiding duplication, and sharing development knowledge (USAID 2013).

The Department of Treasury manages multilateral development bank funding. The President of the United States, through the Treasury Department, serves as the U.S. Executive Director of the World Bank, and votes in the positive or in the negative for countries requesting loans from the World Bank or one of the regional multilateral development banks. Congress became aware of the fact that several countries were being provided with unusually large World Bank and regional multilateral bank loans to make up for the fact that Congress was restricting U.S. bilateral aid due to human rights concerns. Congress then enacted legalization instructing the U.S. representative how to vote in the international financial institutions (IFIs) or when to negotiate a policy. U.S. votes in multilateral lending institutions are governed by Section 701 of the International Financial Institutions Act of 1977 which prohibits U.S. support for loans to governments that engage in a systematic pattern of gross violations of internationally recognized human rights, unless the loan addresses basic human needs.

The U.S. Treasury Department, an executive branch bureaucracy, not only votes on IFI loans but also collaborates with the IFIs and other shareholders to work out deals for loans prior to the vote. This behind-the-scenes negotiation process makes multilateral loans a foreign policy tool of the executive branch without the involvement of Congress.

There are several reasons why a president may choose to channel foreign aid through multilateral institute. Headey (2008) determined that, often, donors tend to channel their anti-poverty, development-motivated assistance through multilateral institutions, and they use their bilateral aid to pursue geopolitical objectives. Multilateral aid is believed to be politically neutral and more needs-based driven. Second, multilateralism is cheaper due to the saving of monitoring and surveillance costs. Multilateralism is, in the opinion of Thompson and Verdier (2014), the solution to transaction costs, that is, the costs of negotiating (and renegotiating), monitoring, and enforcing a foreign aid agreement.

Third, burden sharing is another important reason to turn to multilateral institutions. The costs and responsibilities for resolving global issues of poverty or disease eradication are not the burden of any one country but are based on the ability to pay. Small donations can be combined with donations from other countries, thus amplifying their significance and providing help to recipient countries. Finally, using a multilateral aid agency allows the President a certain degree of plausible deniability. Presidents realizes that aid is an important tool of foreign policy but may wish to distance themselves from politically controversial programs that may upset their domestic constituencies. Over the years, multilateral institutions have provided funding to North Korea, Iran, Cuba, and Russia. The United States may direct its aid through multilateral venues when conditions in the recipient country are politically sensitive or fragile, dangerous for American staff members, or if the President simply wants to diffuse accountability.

The Prevaricator Who Set the Bar: Richard Nixon (1969–August 1974)

The inception of U.S. human rights policy was due to a configuration of events, what Haas (2012) refers to as a perfect storm of events, and not a calculated or planned strategy. This storm was the result of the backlash with the realpolitik of Kissinger, the scandal of Watergate, the humiliation of Vietnam, the disgrace of Nixon's involvement in the coup that killed President Salvador Allende in Chile, the outrage of the U.S. bombings in Cambodia[7] and Laos, drug experiments on unwitting American citizens, the use of assassins to kill foreign leaders, and the revelation of the unlawful surveillance of U.S. citizens, particularly anti-war activists and the media. Indecorously, Nixon usurped Congress' constitutional grants of powers and prerogatives. Schlesinger claimed that there was a significant "shift in the constitutional balance" between the Congress and the President marked by "the appropriation by the Presidency, and particularly by the contemporary Presidency, of powers reserved by the Constitution and by long historical practice to Congress" (1973: viii). Nixon impounded funds authorized by Congress; he claimed executive privilege thus denying Congress' right of oversight; he secretly funded military operations in Thailand and Ethiopia; and he extended war into neutral countries without consulting Congress (Schlesinger 1973).

Furthermore, Nixon claimed that the President was not under any obligation to follow the law. In response to the imperial presidency of Richard Nixon, Congress moved to reinstate its constitutional authority in foreign policy and to restore the balance of power between the legislative and executive branches. Congress also wished to restore morality in U.S. foreign policy. Against the wishes of Nixon and Kissinger, Congress pushed human rights considerations on a reluctant executive bureaucracy. Nixon believed the bureaucracy was subverting his policies and programs. Congress imposed human rights mandates onto foreign policy initiatives, redirected foreign aid allocations, and restructured the bureaucracies in order to redress illicit presidential activities. Thus, as I have argued elsewhere, the development of the U.S. human rights policy was a matter of unintended consequences resulting from Congressional attempts to restrain an imperial president and regain control of an unbridled foreign policy that resulted in U.S. support for brutal dictatorial regimes (Apodaca 2006). The U.S. human rights policy, during the Nixon Administration, was established by Congress, discounted by the executive branch, and hindered by the agency directed to implement the policy (the State Department).

Although Nixon won the 1972 presidential election by a landslide, by the time of the Fraser Committee hearings in 1973, Congress and the American public were well aware of Nixon's misdeeds. Nixon's reputation and political support were greatly weakened by then as he faced increasingly negative public opinion and mistrust from Congress. Generally, a president can count on the support of his party, those Congressional members that hold similar ideological leanings even if they are of the opposite party, and the political bump provided by the level of his public popularity and approval. However, a scandal can greatly weaken a president's political capital and leverage, thus destroying his political base, allowing weaker supporters to defect, and encouraging opponents to promote their own agendas (Meinke and Anderson 2001). The scandals, along with Nixon's adversarial and contemptuous behavior, left him with few allies or supporters in Congress. The revelation of a sequence of scandals contributed to a decline in Presidential legitimacy and an upsurge in Congressional authority. This situation allowed members of Congress to advocate for and implement a U.S. human rights policy.

The Nixon Administration supported pro-American dictatorships' use of death squads, secret police, and repression in order to maintain U.S. superiority in the Cold War. For Nixon, human rights were not simply irrelevant to U.S. foreign policy, but possibly dangerous as well. Kissinger believed that if human rights considerations go "on another two years, we are going to see a precipitant slide of American position in the world that is totally unprecedented... and all the other stuff is sentimental nonsenses" (1974: 16). U.S. security interests, primarily the containment of the Soviet Union, trumped human rights considerations. Foreign policy decisions had to be governed by considerations of national security, not morality, and certainly not about the human rights of foreign citizens.

Although Nixon and Kissinger fought to eliminate human rights concerns from foreign policy and foreign aid allocation decisions, the idea of human rights and morality as foundations for U.S. foreign policy resonated with many members in Congress and the American public during this time. Human rights policy produced a growing tension between not only Congress and the President, but also between Congress and the DOS during the Kissinger years. Nixon and Kissinger worked to actively "sabotage of human rights initiatives" (R. Cohen 1979: 225). Nevertheless, the dedication and commitment of individual members of Congress, their staffs, the American public, and NGOs led to the inclusion of human rights in U.S. foreign policy, specifically in foreign aid allocations. Still, it was the heat of political battle that wrought U.S. human rights policy.

Congressional action on human rights legislation was in direct response to the Nixon Administration's unscrupulous foreign policy behavior when reports surfaced "of CIA assassination programs in Vietnam, the use of torture by agents trained by U.S. police advisors in Latin America and Southeast Asia, and the American role in the overthrow of Chile's President Allende" (Doyle 2003). The amorality, perhaps immorality, of Nixon and Kissinger's ideology of realpolitik was the source of Congressional anger. In 1973, citing a concern "over the rampant violations of human rights and the need for a more effective response from both the United States and the world community," the U.S. House Foreign Affairs Subcommittee on International Organizations, chaired by Representative Donald Fraser (D-MN), began hearings on the human rights conditions in 15 countries. The Fraser Subcommittee hearings on human rights determined that the Nixon Administration was at fault for "embracing governments which practice torture and unabashedly violate almost every human right....Through foreign aid and occasional intervention—both overt and covert—the United States supports these governments" (United States Congress 1974: 9).

As a result, Congress charged the State Department to create a Bureau of Human Rights and Humanitarian Affairs to monitor human rights and assemble annual public reports on the human rights conditions in aid recipient states. The reports for countries receiving economic aid must contain specifics of how the aid will benefit needy people, while military aid reports must establish that the aid is justified by extraordinary circumstances and the national interest of the United States. The reports must also detail the steps the administration has taken to promote human rights. Fraser's committee also recommended the assignment of a human rights officer to each regional bureau in the State Department.[8] The DOS complied, but these new human rights officers were simply overworked Foreign Service officers who were simply assigned additional tasks. Few were receptive to human rights, and more were skeptical about including human rights into issues of diplomacy (Lister 1987, Wilson 1999). The collection and publication of unfavorable information on friendly regimes were seen by the State Department as conflicting with its duty to promote cordial relations. Accusations of human rights abuses would undoubtedly offend the client government and make diplomacy more difficult.

Nevertheless, in response to the unprincipled behavior of the Nixon Administration, the U.S. Congress wrote into law formal requirements for the restriction or denial of foreign aid to countries that consistently violate the human rights of their citizens. However, Nixon was forced from office on August 9, 1974, and the Ford Administration became the initial addressee of Congress's binding human rights legislation.

Nixon and Kissinger's dismissal of human rights had significant consequences for foreign aid allocation. A country's human rights record would be overlooked, in an effort to secure U.S. geopolitical and strategic interests. Nixon's use of foreign aid was directly related to the containment of communism and put to the service of his military campaigns. To deny a state foreign aid due to its human rights record would alienate U.S. allies and thwart the struggle to contain the Soviet Union. The Nixon Administration further argued that neither U.S. interests nor the cause of human rights would be furthered by public humiliation and damaged relations with aid recipient countries.

Although the Nixon Administration's immoral behavior may have initiated the policy shift to include human rights considerations in American foreign policy, he was forced from office under as shadow of dishonor before congressional efforts took effect. President Ford would be the first president to face the newly legislated human rights policies.

In sum, funding is a clear measure of the U.S. commitment to human rights, humanitarian assistance, and poverty reduction. Governmental priorities are reflected in the allocation of government resources (government budgets) and staffing levels. How the government spends its scarce resources is important because, as Apodaca suggests, "United States human rights policy assumes its most tangible consequence with the granting or restricting of economic and military foreign assistance" (2006: 42).

Donald Fraser, along with his like-minded colleagues in Congress and with support from human rights NGOs, contributed to a new human rights policy against the intense opposition of Nixon and Kissinger. During the Nixon presidency, Congress held groundbreaking hearings and legislated human rights conditionalities for foreign aid allocations. Nixon and his bureaucracy actively opposed Congressional efforts to impose human rights concerns in foreign policy matters. However, as the next chapter will verify, human rights supporters prevailed and human rights considerations were now to be included in decisions to grant or deny foreign aid to abusive states. During the Cold War, foreign aid was a tool used to contain the spread of communism and to keep the power of the Soviet Union in check. Nonetheless, during the Cold War human rights remained a core moral value and legislated foundation of U.S. foreign policy whether neglected by Ford, supported by Carter, or usurped by Reagan.

Notes

1 The Committee on Foreign Affairs first created the Subcommittee in 1947 to monitor "the development of the United Nations and other major forms of international organization and the development of international law" (80th Congress 1948).
2 Committee members H.R. Gross (R-Iowa) and Edward Derwinski (R-IL) denied making any contribution to the report, while L.H. Fountain (D-NC) dissented with the report's conclusions and recommendations.
3 The original position was "coordinator," a full-time human rights officer with two staff members.
4 Prior to that time, there was a single human rights officer in the executive bureaucracy. This officer was banished to an obscure office in the State Department and deprived of operating resources or access to the President (R. Cohen 1979).
5 In 1976, the position changed to Assistant Secretary of State and became subject to Congressional approval.
6 The Magnitsky Act (2012) repealed the Jackson-Vanik amendment.
7 The Cambodia bombings from March 18, 1969 to May 26, 1970 resulted in an estimated 100,000–500,000 civilian deaths (the exact number of casualties remains unknown), with another two million becoming homeless. The United States dropped approximately 2.5 million tons of bombs.
8 The State Department assigned an Officer for Human Rights Affairs in each regional bureau (Julius Walker, Africa Bureau; Robert Walkinshaw, East Asian and Pacific Affairs Bureau; and George Lister, Bureau of Inter-American Affairs) and appointed an Assistant Legal Advisor on Human Rights (Charles Runyon).

References

Gordon Adams. 2007. *The Politics of National Security Budgets*. Muscatine, IA: The Stanley Foundation.

John Aldrich, John Sullivan, and Eugene Bordiga. 1989. "Foreign Affairs and Issue Voting: Do Presidential Candidates Waltz before a Blind Audience?" *American Political Science Review* 81(1): 123–141.

G. William Anderson. 2014. "Bridging the Divide: How Can USAID and DOD Integrate Security and Development More Effectively in Africa?" *Fletcher Forum of World Affairs* 38(1): 101–126.

Clair Apodaca. 2006. *Understanding US Human Rights Policy: A Paradoxical Legacy*. New York: Routledge.

Vincent Arel-Bundock, James Atkinson, and Rachel Potter. 2015. "The Limits of Foreign Aid Diplomacy: How Bureaucratic Design Shapes Aid Distribution." *International Studies Quarterly* 59(3): 544–556.

Kenneth Arrow. 1985. "The Economics of Agency," in *Principals and Agents: The Structure of Business*. John Pratt and Richard Zeckhauser, eds. Boston, MA: Harvard Business School Press.

David Brady and Craig Volden. 2005. *Revolving Gridlock: Politics and Policy from Carter to George W. Bush.* New York: Routledge.

Lewis Dean Brown. 1974. "Briefing Memorandum from the Deputy Undersecretary for Management (Brown) to Secretary of State Kissinger." Washington, 8 August, in Foreign Relations of the United States, Volume E-3. https://history.state.gov/historicaldocuments/frus1969-76ve03/d241

Brian Burton and Kristin Lord. 2011. "Did the State Department Get the Quadrennial Diplomacy and Development Review Right?" *The Washington Quarterly* 34(2): 111–123.

Jeremy Caddel. 2013. *Domestic Political Institutions in U.S. Foreign Policy Decision Making.* https://openscholarship.wustl.edu/etd/1126/

Brandice Canes-Wrone, William Howell, and David Lewis. 2008. "Toward a Broader Understanding of Presidential Power: A Reevaluation of the Two Presidencies Thesis." *Journal of Politics* 70(1): 1–16.

Carl Cannon. 2007. "Untruth and Consequences." *The Atlantic* (January/February) 56–67.

Daniel Carpenter. 2001. *The Forging of Bureaucratic Autonomy: Reputations, Networks, and Policy Innovation in Executive Agencies, 1862–1928.* Princeton, NJ: Princeton University Press.

Joshua Clinton, David Lewis, and Jennifer Selin. 2014. "Influencing the Bureaucracy: The Irony of Congressional Oversight." *American Journal of Political Science* 58(2): 387–401.

Kenneth Cmiel. 1999. "The Emergence of Human Rights Politics in the United States." *The Journal of American History* 86(3): 1231–1250.

Roberta Cohen. 1979. "Human Rights Decision-Making in the Executive Branch: Some Proposals for a Coordinated Strategy," in *Human Rights and American Foreign Policy.* Donald Kommers and Gilbert Loescher, eds. Notre Dame, IN: University of Notre Dame.

Stephen Cohen. 1982. "Conditioning U.S. Security Assistance on Human Rights Practices." *American Journal of International Law* 76(2): 246–279.

Roger Davidson and Walter Oleszek. 2004. *Congress and Its Members.* 9th ed. Washington, DC: CQ Press.

Kristina Daugirdas. 2013. "Congress Underestimated: The Case of the World Bank." *American Journal of International Law* 107(3): 517–562.

Kate Doyle. 2003. "Human Rights and the Dirty War in Mexico." *National Security Archives.* George Washington University, May 11. www.gwu.edu/~narchives/

Tom Farer. 1974. "United States Foreign Policy and the Protection of Human Rights: Observations and Proposals." *Virginia Journal of International Law* 14(4): 623–651.

Donald Fraser. 1979. "Human Rights and U.S. Foreign Policy: Some Basic Questions Regarding Principles and Practice." *International Studies Quarterly* 23(2): 174–185.

Clark Gibson, Krister Andersson, Elinor Ostrom, and Sujai Shivakumar. 2005. *The Samaritan's Dilemma.* Oxford: Oxford University Press.

Zachary Greene and Amanda Licht. 2018. "Domestic Politics and Changes in Foreign Aid Allocation: The Role of Party Preferences." *Political Research Quarterly* 71(2): 284–301.

Lawrence Haas. 2012. *Sound the Trumpet: The United States and Human Rights Protection.* Lanham, MD: Rowman & Littlefield Publishers.

Morton Halperin, Priscilla Clapp, with Arnold Kanter. 2007. *Bureaucratic Politics and Foreign Policy*. Washington, DC: Brookings Institution Press.
Thomas Hammond and Jack Knott. 1996. "Who Controls the Bureaucracy?: Presidential Power, Congressional Dominance, Legal Constraints, and Bureaucratic Autonomy in a Model of Multi-Institutional Policy-Making." *Journal of Law, Economics, and Organization* 12(1): 119–166.
Darren Hawkins, David Lake, Daniel Nielson, and Michael Tierney. 2006. "Delegation under Anarchy: States, International Organizations, and Principal-Agent Theory," in *Delegation and Agency in International Organizations*. Darren Hawkins, David Lake, Daniel Nielson, and Michael Tierney, eds. Cambridge: Cambridge University Press.
Derek Headey. 2008. "Geopolitics and the Effect of Foreign Aid on Economic Growth: 1970–2001." *Journal of International Development* 20(2): 161–180.
Robert Ingersoll. 1974. Testimony. Fiscal Year 1975 Foreign Assistance Request: Hearing Before the House Committee on Foreign Affairs, 93rd Congress, 2nd Session, pp. 280–281.
Lewis Irwin. 2000. "Dancing the Foreign Aid Appropriations Dance: Recurring Themes in the Modern Congresses." *Public Budgeting & Finance* 20(2): 30–48.
Richard Jackson. 2011. "Culture, Identity and Hegmony: Continuity and (the Lack of) Change in US Counterterrorism Policy from Bush to Obama." *International Politics* 48(2/3): 390–411.
Barbara Keys. 2010. "Congress, Kissinger, and the Origins of Human Rights Diplomacy." *Diplomatic History* 34(5): 823–851.
John Kingdon. 1981. *Congressmen's Voting Decisions*. New York: Harper and Row.
John Kingdon. 1984. *Agendas, Alternatives, and Public Policies*. Boston, MA: Little, Brown & Co.
Henry Kissinger. 1974. 'Minutes of the Secretary's Staff Meeting', in *Foreign Relations of the United States, 1969–1976*, Volume E-3, October, 22.
Henry Kissinger. 1979. *The White House Years*. Boston: Little, Brown and Co.
Harold Hongju Koh. 1990. *The National Security Constitution: Sharing Power after the Iran-Contra Affair*. New Haven, CT: Yale University Press.
David Lewis. 2008. *The Politics of Presidential Appointments: Political Control and Bureaucratic Performance*. Princeton, NJ: Princeton University Press.
Debra Liang-Fenton 2004. "Conclusion: What Works?" in *Implementing U.S. Human Rights Policy*. Debra Liang-Fenton, ed. Washington, DC: United States Institute of Peace Press.
Abraham Lincoln. 1982. "Second Annual Message to Congress—Concluding Remarks." http://www.abrahamlincolnonline.org/lincoln/speeches/congress.htm
James Lindsay. 1992–1993. "Congress and Foreign Policy: Why the Hill Matters." *Political Science Quarterly* 107(4): 607–628.
James Lindsay. 1994. *Congress and the Politics of U.S. Foreign Policy*. Baltimore, MD: Johns Hopkins University Press.
George Lister. 1987. "U.S. Human Rights Policy: Origins and Implementation." *Current Policy* No. 973. https://law.utexas.edu/humanrights/lister/assets/pdf/Human%20Rights%20Bureau/originsandimplementation%20.pdf?id=txublac-glp-302
Norton Long. 1952. "Bureaucracy and Constitutionalism." *American Political Science Review* 46(3): 808–818.

Edwin Maynard. 1989. "The Bureaucracy and Implementation of US Human Rights Policy." *Human Rights Quarterly* 11(2): 175–248.

James Meernik and Michael Ault. 2001. "Public Opinion and Support for U.S. Presidents' Foreign Policies." *American Politics Research* 29(4): 352–373.

Scott Meinke and William Anderson. 2001. "Influencing from Impaired Administrations: Presidents, White House Scandals, and Legislative Leadership." *Legislative Studies Quarterly* 26(4): 639–659.

Renanah Miles. 2011. "The State Department, USAID, and the Flawed Mandate for Stabilization and Reconstruction." *PRISM* 3(1): 37–47.

Helen Milner and Dustin Tingley. 2010. "The Political Economy of U.S. Foreign Aid: American Legislators and the Domestic Politics of Aid." *Economics and Politics* 22(2): 200–232.

Helen Milner and Dustin Tingley. 2011. "Who Supports Global Economic Management? The Sources of Preferences in American Foreign Economic Policy?" *International Organization* 65(1): 37–68.

Michael Mintrom and Phillipa Norman. 2009. "Policy Entrepreneurship and Policy Change." *Policy Studies Journal* 37(4): 640–667.

Andrew Natsios. 2010. "The Clash of the Counter-bureaucracy and Development." Center for Global Development Essay. www.cgdev.org/content/publications/detail/1424271.

Stewart Patrick and Kaysie Brown. 2007. *The Pentagon and Global Development: Making Sense of the DOD's Expanding Role*. The Center for Global Development Working Paper No. 131.

Steven Radelet. 2006. *A Primer on Foreign Aid*. Center for Global Development Working Paper Number 92. Washington, DC: CGD.

Vernon Ruttan. 1996. *United States Development Assistance Policy: The Domestic Politics of Foreign Economic Aid*. Baltimore, MD: Johns Hopkins University Press.

Arthur Schlesinger, Jr. 1973. *The Imperial Presidency*. Boston, MA: Houghton Mifflin Co.

Kathryn Sikkink. 2004. *Mixed Signals: U.S. Human Rights Policy and Latin America*. Ithaca, NY: Cornell University Press.

Wendie Ellen Schneider. 2007. "Enfeebling the Arm of Justice: Perjury and Prevarication in British India," in *Modern Histories of Crime and Punishment*. Markus Dubber and Lindsay Farmer, eds. Stanford, CA: Stanford University Press.

Paul Stephens. 2012. "The Limits of Change: International Human Rights under the Obama Administration." *Fordham International Law Journal* 35(2): 488–509.

Curt Tarnoff and Marian Lawson. 2016. *Foreign Aid: An Introduction to U.S. Programs and Policy*. Congressional Research Service, CRS Report to Congress R40213. Washington, DC: Congressional Research Service.

Curt Tarnoff and Cory Gill. 2017. *State, Foreign Operations Appropriations: A Guide to Component Accounts*. Congressional Research Service, CRS Report to Congress R40482. Washington DC: Congressional Research Service.

Alexander Thompson and Daniel Verdier. 2014. "Multilateralism, Bilateralism, and Regime Design." *International Studies Quarterly* 58(1): 15–28.

Peter Tompa. 1986. "The Arms Export Control Act and Congressional Codetermination over Arms Sales." *American University International Law Review* 1(1): 291–330.

Umberto Tulli. 2012. "'Whose Rights are Human Rights?' The Ambiguous Emergence of Human Rights and the Demise of Kissingerism." *Cold War History* 12(4): 573–593.
United States Congress. 1974. *Human Rights in the World Community: A Call for U.S. Leadership*. A Report of the Subcommittee on International Organizations and Movements of the Committee on Foreign Affairs, House of Representatives, 93rd Congress, 2d Session. Washington, DC: U.S. Government Printing Office.
USAID. 2013. *U.S. Foreign Assistance Reference Guide*. Technical report U.S. Department of State. http://pdf.usaid.gov/pdf_docs/Pnadc240.pdf
U.S. Government Accountability Office (GAO). 2010. *Improved Planning, Training, and Interagency Collaboration Could Strengthen DOD's Efforts in Africa*, GAO-10-794. Washington, DC: Government Printing Office.
David Weissbrodt. 1977. "Human Rights Legislation and U.S. Foreign Policy." *Georgia Journal of International and Comparative Law* 7: 231–287.
Howard Wiarda. 2000. "Beyond the Pale: The Bureaucratic Politics of United States Policy in Mexico." *World Affairs* 162(4): 174–190.
James Wilson. 1999. *Interview by Charles Stuart Kennedy*. The Association for Diplomatic Studies and Training Foreign Affairs Oral History Project. https://cdn.loc.gov/service/mss/mfdip/2004/2004wil14/2004wil14.pdf

2 U.S. Human Rights Policy during the Cold War
A Historical Overview

Human rights is a powerful concept. In the words of Moyn, human rights "evoke hope and provoke action" (2010: 1). The idea of human rights challenges (although some would say it complements) the concept of national security in foreign policy and aid allocation. The U.S. version of Moyn's human rights as "last utopia" began with the transformative events of the 1970s. The events include the U.S. withdrawal from Vietnam, the American role in the brutal Chilean coup, the scandal of Watergate, the continued organization of civil rights activists looking for their next cause, and Andrei Sakharov's open letter to Congress in support of the Jackson-Vanik Amendment. Haas (2012) believes that the mid-1970s represented a dividing line, marking the commencement of a new human rights foreign policy.

Policy entrepreneurs—those wishing to change the status quo in foreign policy— can disrupt political constancy or inertia but only when conditions are favorable. In the mid-1970s, with the president distracted by the Watergate scandal and the resultant reduction in presidential legitimacy, Congressional members were poised to reassert their authority and fill the power vacuum in foreign policy decision-making. Congress created new bureaucratic institutions and enacted new legislation to protect and promote human rights. Human rights were to be an essential component of U.S. foreign policy. Using what McCubbins and Schwartz (1984) referred to as "police patrol" oversight, in 1973, Congress commenced hearings on the human rights consequences of President Nixon's foreign policy behaviors. Congress then established rules, procedures, and practices that enabled NGOs to monitor and sound the alarm in the event the executive branch fails to fulfill its legislated duties toward human rights. Human rights NGOs were also enthusiastic about taking advantage of a suddenly promising situation. The momentum for policy change during the 1970s becomes a torrent that forces a shift in foreign policy behavior.

Despite the historiographies of the origins of U.S. human rights policy, contemporary human rights policy began in the early 1970s, before the Carter Administration, when the United States began incorporating human rights in foreign policy. George Lister,[1] the first human rights officer in the State Department's Bureau of Latin American Affairs, and later a Senior Policy Advisor in the Bureau of Human Rights and Humanitarian Affairs (HA), credits the origins of U.S. human rights policy to the work of House of Representatives Donald Fraser (D-MN) and Tom Harkin (D-Iowa). Fraser's interest in human rights began with the realization that the tanks used by Greece's brutal military junta "were tanks made in the United States, and they were being used to suppress students who were protesting against the military junta's destruction of democracy in Greece" (Fraser 1979: 176). Harkin's interest in human rights began when, as a congressional aide, he was among the group that visited the prison on Con Son Island in Vietnam where he witnessed the use of underground tiger cages to incarcerate Vietnamese peasants suspected of sympathizing with the communists (Luce 2009). Keys believes that human rights, during the turbulent Nixon years, "emerged from a struggle for the soul of the country" (2014: 3). Human rights would redefine the identity of America and act as a salve to overcome the Nixon legacy.

The Ford Administration (August 1974–1977)

The scandal of the Nixon years lead to a reduction in Presidential authority and set the stage for a revitalization of Congressional control over foreign policy. President Gerald Rudolph Ford faced a motivated and dynamic Congress. President Ford came to office under a cloud: he was not elected to either the Presidency or Vice Presidency of the United States. He assumed his position as Vice President with the resignation of Spiro Agnew,[2] and later he became President with the resignation of Richard Nixon.[3] This unprecedented situation left Ford with no mandate to govern. Although Ford served 25 years as a U.S. representative (R-MI), the final nine years of which were as the House Minority Leader where he built a reputation as a person of honesty and integrity, Congress did not give Ford the benefit of the doubt, nor did it relinquish its newly restored power in foreign affairs. Kissinger wrote: "the irony that the Congress [Ford] genuinely loved and respected had harassed his presidency unmercifully from the beginning and encumbered it with unprecedented restrictions, crippling many aspects of this foreign policy" (1999: 1064). Congress was wary of Nixon's hand-picked successor. A newly invigorated Congress and the lack of support he received from the Republican Party hampered Ford's executive branch in the administration of foreign policy. As an example, scholars suggest Congress' refusal to continue sending U.S. military aid to the Nguyen Van Thieu regime for finally ending the devastating Vietnam War (officially April 30, 1975) against Ford's and Kissinger's wishes (Colby 1989, Lind 2002).

Although Ford was not responsible for Nixon's crimes, he was the first president to experience post-Nixon legislative checks on foreign aid restrictions. U.S. human rights policy, during the Ford Presidency, was a matter of continued Congressional efforts to restore the balance of power between the executive and legislative branches of government. Congress was not going to allow the Ford Presidency to become an imperial presidency that characterized the Nixon Administration. Ford was not Nixon, but Kissinger was still Kissinger. Ford's pardon of Nixon[4] and the American public's continued anger over Watergate led to the Democratic Party's overwhelming command of Congress. The 94th Congress sat 75 new first-term Democrats with no political experience. These Watergate Babies, as they were known, were activist, independent, contemptuous of traditional seniority norms in Congress, and held little allegiance to their party, believing instead that their loyalty belonged to the American people (Mieczkowski 2005).

Congress' Watergate Babies were active and energetic partners in foreign policy during the Ford years. In 1975, the Senate Select Committee on Intelligence Activities, known as the Church Committee (led by Frank Church (D-ID)), was set up to determine "the extent, if any, to which illegal, improper, or unethical activities were engaged in by any agency of the Federal Government," and specifically the use of assassinations of foreign leaders (United States Senate 1975). The House Select Committee on Intelligence, chaired by Otis Pike, also took up the investigation of U.S. intelligence agencies. The intelligence agencies had abused their powers, not only against foreign countries, but also against U.S. citizens within the U.S. borders. Ford, in an attempt to sideline a Congressional investigation, called for a special presidential commission to investigate domestic spying. The commission was to be co-chaired by Vice President Rockefeller, who by Olmsted's (2016) account approved CIA activities while serving on the Foreign Intelligence Advisory Board, and California Governor Ronald Reagan who was known as a fervent supporter of domestic spying. In response to the unflattering Congressional reports revealing the extent of intelligence agencies' involvement in illegal activities, President Ford was compelled to issue an executive order banning U.S. involvement in political assassinations.[5] Kissinger fumed in response: "It is an act of insanity and national humiliation to have a law prohibiting the President from ordering assassination" (as quoted in Prados 2003: 314). However, Ford's executive order banning assassinations did not end the government's use of political killings (Claburn 1994).

The three key human rights amendments enacted by Congress during the Ford Presidency are the Harkin Amendment (1975), the Humphrey-Cranston Amendment (1976) of the Foreign Assistance Act, and Section 301 (1976) of the International Security Assistance and Arms Export Control Act. The Harkin Amendment prohibits economic assistance to any country that commits gross human rights violations, unless it can be shown that the aid will directly benefit the poor and the needy within the recipient country. The Humphrey-Cranston Amendment directs that the President will be legally obligated to deny or restrict security aid to countries violating human rights, unless extraordinary circumstances can be proven. Section 301 affirmed the promotion of human rights standards as an explicit goal of U.S. foreign policy. The act instructed the president to formulate military assistance programs to promote human rights and to avoid identification with repressive regimes. Since early human rights legislation was merely an advisory "Sense of Congress," the Ford Administration was able to legally ignore both the spirit and letter of the law. Undersecretary of State for Security Assistance Carlyle Maw testified in a hearing before the House Committee on International Relations that no security assistance was denied based on a country's human rights record (1976). During the Ford years, Congress removed the "Sense of Congress" language and replaced it with an explicit mandate for the termination of security, economic, and multilateral aid to gross violators via these three amendments.

The Ford Administration largely ignored the Office of Human Rights and Humanitarian Affairs and attempted to subvert its mandate to report on the human rights situations in foreign aid recipient countries. The first *Country Reports on Human Rights Practices* was issued in 1975, but the Ford Administration attempted to prevent its release. Scholars and human rights advocates regard the report as generally weak in substance, rudimentary, and heavily biased (Weissbrodt 1977). Kissinger believed a previously prepared candid document was too inflammatory, and directed the State Department to whitewash the human rights conditions in allied repressive states. The result was a report that did not mention a single country as a human rights violator, nor did it record the "objective facts" on verifiable human rights abuses of aid recipient countries (Weissbrodt 1977: 244). Representative Fraser criticized the *Country Reports* as "primarily a defense of the State Department's apparent intention not to comply with the law" (Gwertzman 1975: 14). Kissinger intended to ignore, frustrate, or prevent the collection of human rights data for the *Country Reports* mandated by Congress.

Kissinger complained that the State Department should not "pretend that it is sort of a reform school for allies," correcting repressive allies' domestic behavior toward their own citizens (1974). Kissinger believed that even these whitewashed reports were too inflammatory and had them classified. He stated that "since all but a handful of countries committed human rights violations it served no useful purpose to specify for criticism American allies and friends" (cited in Weissbrodt 1977: 244). Consequently, the classified reports were unavailable to the public. Congressional pressure compelled declassification, making the reports open to the public. Before declassification, however, the State Department "responded by excising certain material but ultimately acceded to congressional pressure and, in December 1976, the [1976] reports were made public" (Weissbrodt 1977: 265).

Yet, the State Department did make some concessions to Congress. In order to prevent further regulatory measures by Congress, and in an attempt to safeguard its diplomatic mission, the State Department complied with some of the recommendations presented in *Human Rights in the World Community: A Call for U.S. Leadership*. Schmidli concludes that the "growing support for human rights in Congress stimulated a rear-guard action in the State Department to head off further legislative action" (2011: 365). The State Department created the Office of Humanitarian Affairs, but gave it minimal staff and resources. The State Departments' resistance to the creation of the new department is understandable since, as Drezner reports, "Preexisting bureaucracies will automatically resist the introduction of new actors into the policy mix and impose constraints" (2000: 733–734). It is particularly difficult for an "idea-infused" agency, such as one established to protect human rights, to withstand outside pressure if it is embedded within a powerful bureaucracy like the DOS.

The position of Coordinator for Humanitarian Affairs was established in 1975 and placed in the Office of the Deputy Secretary, Roger Ingersoll. The first Coordinator for HA, James Wilson, Jr. (1975–1977) "kept a low profile and had relatively little impact on policy" (Maynard 1989: 179). Wilson's Deputy Coordinator for Human Rights was Ronald Palmer. The duties of the newly created bureaucracy were to monitor decisions to provide foreign assistance to gross violators of human rights, to formulate U.S. foreign policy toward human rights, and to prepare the annual human rights reports. Wilson believed that the objectives of his office were laudable but that the topic of human rights "was obviously not going to be popular in the front office [meaning Kissinger]" (1977). Wilson believed the new Office of Humanitarian Affairs, which combined Missing in Action (MIAs), refugees, and human rights, "was to be a coordinating, not an operating function," except for the refugee section (1999: 58). In his interview with Kennedy, Wilson was clear that all chiefs of mission in the State Department viewed the human rights legislation as an obstacle to their work and would cause major problems with their foreign client states. Congressional mandates that are viewed as detrimental are often delayed or simply ignored. However, bureaucratic politics reveals that government actors often move to protect or promote their agency's interests, thereby entrenching and enhancing their agency status. HA was no different.

Bureaucratic politics played a significant role in enforcing the human rights requirements within Kissinger's State Department. Cmiel (1999) relates the story of Ronald Palmer's meeting with Amnesty International (AI) in order to prod the State Department into looking into human rights violations. Palmer, the deputy coordinator for human rights in the State Department, was frustrated that very little information on human rights violations was being passed from U.S. embassies to his office. He met with AI to have them ask questions of sympathetic members of Congress regarding human rights in different countries. The State Department could ignore questions from AI members but was bound by law to respond to inquiries made by Congress. Thus, the State Department would have to organize an investigation, utilizing the human rights bureau, to answer Congress' queries. The Office of Human Rights and Humanitarian Affairs was a weak and besieged unit with the Secretary of State actively attempting to undermine its work. Therefore, in 1977, Congress upgraded its principal to the rank of Assistant Secretary of State.

Many in Congress and in the American public believed that the Ford Administration was simply a continuation, albeit in a less criminal fashion, of the Nixon Administration. In many ways, this judgment was correct. Ford inherited and continued Nixon's foreign policy of realpolitik and détente with the Soviet Union, the predisposition to impound Congressionally allocated funds, the conduct of covert operations in foreign states,[6] lying to Congress, and retaining Secretary of State Kissinger. For example, in 1974, Congress enacted the Hughes-Ryan Amendment requiring the President to report all covert actions of the CIA to several Congressional oversight committees. Nevertheless, Ford provided covert aid to support the civil war in Angola, in violation of the Hughes-Ryan Amendment. When the Administration was caught in a lie, Congress enacted the Clark Amendment terminating all aid to Angola.

Under Kissinger's influence, Ford attempted to furnish foreign aid to countries against Congress' directives. In July 1974, Turkey invaded Cyprus, using U.S. supplied weapons (Turkey is a member of North Atlantic Treaty Organization (NATO) and had access to U.S weapons as a friend and ally). The use of American weapons violated the U.S. Foreign Military Sales Act that specified that the weapons could only be used for defensive purposes. Because Turkey allowed the United States to establish military bases and house missiles in its territory, the Ford-Kissinger Administration sided with Turkey. Congress, on the other hand, supported the Greek government, also a member of NATO, and passed legislation to cut off military aid to Turkey. Ford twice vetoed the legislation but Congress compelled the executive to follow the dictates of the Foreign Military Sales Act and to obey the law.

The Ford Administration's support of Indonesia's invasion of East Timor illustrates how the United States used its foreign aid during the Cold War to maintain a repressive murderous regime in power. After the setback in Vietnam, Indonesia became the most important non-Communist state in Southeast Asia. President Suharto of Indonesia was anti-communist, pro-American, and had control over vast oil reserves. In addition, the Ford Administration needed Indonesia's permission for U.S. nuclear submarines to pass through its territorial waters undetected (Simpson 2005). Thus, Suharto was able to leverage U.S. geopolitical concerns for increased military aid and overlooking its invasion of Timor. Notwithstanding Congressional restrictions on military assistance, the Ford Administration promised to double Indonesia's military aid after a six-month suspension (due to its invasion of Timor) (Simpson 2005). Recently declassified documents reveal that the Ford Administration actively hid and deliberately misled Congress on the extent of the brutal occupation of East Timor.

In communist countries, human rights were to be protected and monitored by the Helsinki Accords. The Helsinki Accords are regarded as one of the most important human rights resolutions of the Cold War and Ford's brightest accomplishment. At the time, Ford, Kissinger, and many anti-Soviet Congress members thought it was a mistake. Ford was sharply accused of giving away Eastern Europe and, consequently, many believe that the Helsinki Accords cost Ford the 1976 Presidential election. Ford's support of Kissinger's policy of détente at the expense of human rights in the Soviet Union put him at odds with conservative Congress members from both the Democratic (Henry Jackson) and the Republican (Ronald Reagan, Jesse Helms) parties. The issue of Helsinki split the Republican Party and undermined Ford's election campaign. Ford simply wanted Helsinki to be forgotten. Congress established a joint legislative-executive commission to be chaired by Congressman Dante Fascell (D-FL). Congress further required the executive office to produce a semiannual report on European compliance with the Accords. President Ford and Secretary of State Kissinger vigorously opposed the Congressional oversight. Ford reluctantly signed the bill creating the Helsinki Commission. Tulli (2012) reports that Ford-Kissinger engaged in delay tactics by failing to appoint representatives from the executive branch to the Commission in an attempt to obstruct Congressional will. Four months later, just a month before the presidential elections, Ford finally appointed James Poor, Monroe Leigh, and Mansfield Sprague to the commission.

Ford, like his predecessor, was constrained by an active Congress, a dynamic NGO network, and a concerned public that dictated a human rights policy on the unwilling administration. By supporting repressive governments that are unstable and dangerous due of their lack of popular support, the Nixon-Ford-Kissinger Administrations actually risked America's long-term interests.

The Carter Administration (1977–1981)

The election of James "Jimmy" Earl Carter as President of the United States brought a renewed hope for the restoration of morality to U.S. foreign policy and an opportunity for establishing human rights as a major tenet of U.S. foreign policy. U.S. foreign policy would now include a focus on human rights. Carter used human rights rhetoric to establish a tone for his administration, but he had a difficult time formulating a substantive policy on human rights. Regrettably, the promise of a balanced and encompassing U.S. human rights policy under Carter was not fulfilled. The Carter White House suffered from the bureaucratic strife between Secretary of State Cyrus Vance and National Security Advisor Zbigniew Brzezinski. Furthermore, a coherent and effective human rights policy was a casualty of the foreign policy bureaucracy infighting between the DOS and the newly created HA. Human rights policy during the Carter Administration was the victim of the disunity and dissention within the White House, of bureaucratic infighting, and of international power politics.

Initially Carter's absolute commitment to human rights would apply to both pro-U.S. and anti-U.S. regimes. Carter promised a single standard for U.S. human rights policy that would apply to friend and foe alike. However, the Carter Administration stealthily shifted to case-by-case implementation of its human rights policy resulting in the creation of a double standard. Countries that were politically and strategically important could violate human rights without penalization while periphery countries, those with little or no geopolitical importance to U.S. national security, faced U.S. condemnation or withdrawal of aid. Unfortunately, Carter, increasingly concerned with national security, distanced himself from his early pronouncements on human rights. He moved from an absolute standard to a case-by-case standard and, finally, to no standard at all.

However, Carter's human rights rhetoric was a long way from reality. The Carter Administration made substantial use of the "extraordinary circumstances" clauses written into human rights legislation, and thus rarely reduced or denied foreign aid (Carleton and Stohl 1985: 216). S. Cohen (1982) suggests that formally determining a country engaged in a consistent pattern of gross violations of internationally recognized human rights would have restricted the President's ability to provide military aid thereby limiting his foreign policy options.

Sikkink (2004) suggests that the Carter Administration can be divided into two distinct periods: an idealist or active phase, and a disenchanted phase. During the first two years of his Presidency, Carter was in an active idealist phase during which he sincerely attempted to implement a moral human rights policy. This was followed by two years of disenchantment. During the active phase, Carter appointed Patricia Derian, a renowned civil rights activist, to the post of Human Rights Coordinator and he increased her staff from the original 2 to 12. Carter also created the Inter-Agency Group on Human Rights and Foreign Assistance, commonly referred to as the Christopher Committee, to examine foreign aid proposals and coordinate the granting of U.S. bilateral foreign aid and to approve loans from multilateral development banks as a function of a recipient country's human rights practices. The Arms Export Control

Board, established in 1977, performed a function analogous to that of the Christopher Committee for military and security assistance. Carter declared that arms transfers were to be exceptional tools of U.S. foreign policy. Carter signed Presidential Directive 13 (PD-13) in May 1977. PD-13 reduced the two largest security assistance programs, the Military Assistance Program (MAP) and Foreign Military Sales (FMS), and it prohibited the retransfers of U.S. military equipment, with the exception of Israel, NATO, Japan, Australia, and New Zealand. Before arms transfers could be authorized, HA would have to determine the human rights consequences of the transfers (Carter 1977).

In 1979, with a series of foreign policy setbacks and a sluggish domestic economy Carter's disenchantment period began. Presidents have an overall agenda that they bring to the office, and they will attempt to implement it until other, more pressing, foreign policy issues develop. When faced with a foreign crisis that requires the president's immediate and undivided attention, the president's personal agenda (in Carter's case his legacy as the human rights president) stalls. Carter faced a series of foreign crises: the hostage crisis in Iran, a large Soviet military presence in Cuba, the Nicaraguan revolution, the Soviet invasion of Afghanistan, and gas shortages. Both U.S. military aid and U.S. commercial arms sales increased during the disenchanted phase. The link between human rights and military armaments was abandoned for security concerns. With every international crisis, U.S. foreign aid would shift from a focus on human rights to security concerns. Human rights, in both rhetoric and actuality, took a back seat to traditional power politics. Carter sharply increased defense spending and security aid allocations, created the Rapid Deployment Force, and lifted the restrictions placed on CIA covert activities. Countries with a consistent pattern of gross violations of human rights, such as the Philippines, South Korea, Iran, or Zaire, were found to fit the extraordinary circumstance criteria and consequently did not suffer a reduction of U.S. foreign aid allocations. Remarkably, the human rights president never formally found that any country was "engaged in a consistent pattern of gross violations of internationally recognized human rights." If a country was determined to be a gross human rights violator providing foreign aid would be highly controversial and a change in status, due to claims of improved human rights conditions, would be heavily scrutinized.

Congress, however, would not be lulled into passivity by Carter's words of goodwill and good intentions. Senator James Abourezk was quoted as saying: "While the President's words sound very beautiful, after the announcements nothing really happens" (from Drew 1977: 59). Congress was not willing to relinquish its hard-won partnership in the realm of foreign policy. Congress thrust the issue of human rights on the recalcitrant Nixon Administration, and it was not going to abandon its constitutional authority because the new president gave beautiful speeches. Congress enacted Section 701 of the International Financial Assistance Act (1977) that instructs U.S. representatives to the international financial institutions, such as the IMF and the World Bank, to use their voice and vote to oppose loans, grants, extensions, or technical assistance to any country that is a gross human rights violator, unless the aid is directed to programs that will fulfill the basic human needs of the country's citizens.

Congress would also upgrade the Bureau of Human Rights and Humanitarian Affairs in 1977. The Bureau was to be headed by the Assistant Secretary of State. This promotion in the bureaucratic structure institutionalized human rights issues in the DOS and in U.S. foreign policy. Carter's choice of Patricia Derian for Assistant Secretary of State for HA had no experience in foreign policy or diplomacy. Derian, a renowned civil rights activist, was a devoted and uncompromising champion of human rights. Derian was viewed as an interloper who had not paid her dues, had no diplomatic experience, and, perhaps worse of all, was a woman (Derian 1996).[7] However, given the climate within the State Department and the need to establish a power base, the new bureau needed an assertive and dynamic leader with a laser focus on human rights concerns. Because lives were on the line, Derian was unlikely to submit to the standard bureaucratic compromise procedures.

Derian's HA was the epicenter of human rights during the Carter Administration. HA coordinated the energy and activity of human rights advocates, Congressional members and their staff, and NGOs (Schmidli 2011). HA would routinely antagonize the regional bureaus by directly challenging their interpretation of the human rights conditions in a potential recipient country. Richard Holbrooke was reported as saying that Derian "was myopically fixed on human rights as the only plank in American foreign policy" while the other bureaus in the State Department must consider a variety of issues, purposes, and viewpoints in their work and incorporate economic, security, political, and diplomatic interests (quoted in Kaufman 1998: 54). HA had to directly counter the Foreign Service officers' tendencies to defend their client country by understating abuses and overstating positive human rights trends.

The State Department's bureaucracy thwarted attempts to incorporate human rights into diplomacy. Warshawsky suggests that the State Department resented the inclusion of human rights into foreign policy because human rights would "disrupt and possibly endanger the pursuit of more important and legitimate foreign policy goals" (1980: 195). Human rights were seen not only as an annoyance, but also as a hindrance to the work of the State Department. State Department Foreign Service officers traditionally support foreign aid, even to repressive governments, since "the diplomat without an aid program has to work much harder to advance U.S. objectives" (Zimmerman 1993: 14). The denial of aid could pose a serious threat to good relations, particularly if the denial is predicated on a condemnation of a country's human rights record.

In 1977, President Carter created the Inter-Agency Group on Human Rights and Foreign Assistance, commonly referred to as the Christopher Committee or Christopher Group, to examine foreign aid proposals and coordinate the granting of U.S. bilateral foreign aid with a recipient country's human rights practices. The Christopher Committee examined and approved U.S. foreign assistance decisions and it assessed if the human rights situation in the recipient country was good, if human rights conditions were genuinely improving, or if the project could directly benefit needy people. However, Franck and Weisband note that the number of negative votes on aid projects was "small in comparison to the number ... recommended for approval" (1979: 90). But this was to be expected. Several important aid programs were exempt from the committee's oversight. In a bureaucratic turf war, Undersecretary for Security Assistance Lucy Benson was able to exempt military assistance and Security Supporting Assistance from review by the Christopher Committee where HA had a strong voice. Moreover, most foreign aid, other than military aid, has a development or poverty elimination dimension, which by definition would benefit needy people. Finally, when a country expected that their human rights record would trigger a negative vote by the United States, they often withdrew their loan/aid request.

During the "human rights presidency" of James Earl Carter, U.S. human rights policy actually became incoherent, inconsistent, and even incongruous at times. The Bureau of Human Rights faced two major challenges during the Carter Administration. The first was its mission of calling out human rights abusing states for their violations, which clashed with the State Department's mission of diplomacy and negotiation. The second was the appointment of a civil rights activist not a career bureaucrat to head the Bureau. The result was an under-resourced agency in terms of funding, information, and personnel.

There was a significant gap between the Carter Administration's words and deeds. The hope for a human rights policy was thwarted. U.S. human rights policy was an unintended victim of bureaucratic squabbling and of Carter's ideological shift from idealist aspirations to realist behaviors.

The Reagan Administration (1981–1989)

With the election of Ronald Wilson Reagan as President of the United States, many people thought that human rights as a foreign policy issue was lost. Reagan attempted to abandon what he believed was the idealistic and perilous policy of human rights in foreign policy. When that failed, the Reagan Administration prevarication redefined human rights narrowly to exclusively mean democracy and anticommunism. Maechling (1983), a former State Department advisor, warned that Reagan's ill-chosen redefinition of human rights violations would equate the communist states of Poland and Czechoslovakia with the cold-hearted and murderous regimes in Guatemala or El Salvador. Yet, the Reagan administration sought to provide the security forces in El Salvador and Guatemala with millions of dollars in U.S. military aid.

However, when a president comes to office, his policy options are often narrowed by the choices made by his predecessor and legislation passed by Congress. Presidents are constrained by the work and legacy of their predecessors and take custody of an existing foreign policy agenda (Jones 1994). Reagan's foreign policy strategy was hindered by the human rights legacy he inherited from the Carter Administration. Policy burrowing, as it is known, along with bureaucratic inertia and entrenchment protected human rights policy during the Reagan Administration. Carter was out, but the belief that human rights ought to be a focus in U.S. relations with other countries was not. The Bureau of Human Rights and Humanitarian Affairs became an established fixture in U.S. foreign policy with its attendant career officers, its vested interests, and its funding.

Congress deliberately embedded human rights within U.S. foreign policy when it created HA, legislated 116 and 502B in the FAA, and required annual reports on the human rights conditions of countries around the world. Due to Congress' insistence on annual reports and oversight hearings, Foreign Service officers and bureaucrats became more professional, acquiring informational in-country networks, and developing procedures and routines in the collection and reporting of human rights data. Thus, the inclusion of human rights into foreign policy became institutionalized and normalized in the State Department as well as within American culture. By the time Reagan came to the Presidency, employees of HA had built careers in human rights that depended on the perpetuation and advancement of the Bureau and the continued commitment of resources directed to it. In addition, human rights were an integral part of American culture. Civil society, from church groups to grassroots NGOs, had taken up the cause of human rights. Congress, when necessary, could count on these organizations to provide "fire alarm" oversight (McCubbins and Schwartz 1984) to counter the Reagan Administration's attempt to reduce or eliminate human rights from policy concerns. Although Reagan attempted to jettison human rights from U.S. foreign policy, human rights "actually became more and more institutionalized in U.S. foreign policy" (Donnelly 1995: 239). Institutionalization means that human rights became a standard component in the foreign policymaking debate. Human rights concerns would have to be considered among a variety of competing issues, even if human rights concerns did not dominate the debate.

Sikkink (2004) believes that Reagan also experienced two phases in his administration with respect to human rights. The first phase was the active implementation of the Kirkpatrick's "Dictatorships and Double Standards." Kirkpatrick (1979) argued that authoritarian regimes are friendly pro-American governments and supportive of U.S. security interests. Authoritarian governments were, in Kirkpatrick's opinion, also less repressive and more receptive to democratic transformation and liberalization. Communist totalitarian governments, on the other hand, were inimical, and anti-American. Authoritarian governments can transition to democratic forms of government while totalitarian governments cannot. Thus, the United States ought to support authoritarian regimes by ignoring their human rights violations. This was most pronounced in Central America, the primary focus of the Reagan Administration's anti-communist crusade. The only hope for a totalitarian regime to convert to democracy and human rights protections was if the government was destroyed and rebuilt. Consequently, the United States had to condemn violations in the Soviet Union, Eastern Europe, and their proxies in Central America and the Caribbean. Reagan promised to contain the Soviet Union and reverse its gains in the Third World.

Because Congress and the American public were unlikely to support a foreign policy based exclusively on fighting communism (a lesson learned from the Nixon Administration), the Reagan Administration formulated a foreign policy in terms of promoting democracy. Human rights would be defined very narrowly to include only democracy and individual freedom. Thus, U.S. human rights policy would be used to politically attack the USSR and its proxies by exposing the Soviet bloc's human rights violations to the world. Elliot Abrams, Assistant Secretary of State for Human Rights and Humanitarian Affairs under Reagan, stated: "You could make the argument that there aren't many countries where there are gross and consistent human rights violations except the communist countries because they have the system itself. It is certainly a plausible way of reading the statute" (as quoted in Maechling 1983, 130). The Reagan Administration had too often justified supporting foreign aid to right-wing governments allied with the United States by deceitfully claiming that these countries showed improvement in their human rights standards. Human rights abuse defined as communist regimes was merely a rhetorical device for Reagan to win over Congress and the American public to his foreign policy agenda and to persuade Congress to provide foreign aid.

The second phase of Reagan's human rights policy was the actual promotion of democracy, exhibiting a sense of international cooperation, and the establishment of cordial—or at least tempered—relations with the Soviet Union. Risse and Sikkink (1999) suggest that human rights acceptance and democracy promotion began with an instrumental or strategic motivation. Reagan started using the language of human rights and democracy to condemn the USSR, Nicaragua, and Cuba, but soon the Administration became "obliged to a minimal consistency in its foreign policy, and thus eventually actively encouraged democracy in authoritarian regimes which the Republicans viewed as loyal allies, such as Chile and Uruguay" (Risse and Sikkink 1999: 10). Rhetorical acceptance led to identity transformation and bureaucratic internalization.

Carothers (1991) suggests that the reason for the change was the unrelenting pressure from Democrats to include democracy and human rights concerns in U.S. foreign policy. Even the moderates in Congress expected Reagan's rhetoric to become reality. The media and the American public wanted to know what the government was doing to achieve these declared goals and how well the process was unfolding. Moreover, in an effort to counter critics' accusations that his human rights policy was simply about anti-communism, Reagan began to mildly condemn the human rights abuses in right-wing dictatorships. The shift can also be explained by the retirement of the staunch anti-communist ideologues who were replaced by a more pragmatic team of advisors that counseled Reagan to persuade friendly authoritarian leaders to reduce human rights violations and allow limited democratic participation (Forsythe 1990: 447).[8]

The Reagan Administration viewed human rights and American foreign aid through the Cold War prism. The goal of the Reagan Administration's foreign policy was to overthrow communism. Shultz remarked to the House Committee on Foreign Affairs that "Our security and economic assistance programs are essential instruments of our foreign policy and are directly linked to the national security and economic well-being of the United States" (1983: 93). However, foreign aid also exhibited a two-phased pattern. Foreign aid, both economic and military, was a primary tool of U.S. foreign policy in Reagan's first term. To this end, Reagan would vastly increase security assistance to pro-American Third World countries during both terms in office. Forsythe (1987) reports that security assistance went up by approximately 300 percent from 1980 to 1984. Anti-communist dictators were well received and lavished with generous economic and military aid packages. In an effort to bleed the Soviet Union and its proxies, Reagan armed and funded counterinsurgency rebels or "freedom fighters" throughout the world, regardless of their human rights records. Military regimes tended toward conservative anti-communist ideologies and could more easily be bought off with large grants of technologically advanced military hardware. The price for securing U.S. geopolitical interests was paid by the local population in the restriction of democratic ideals and human rights violations. The Reagan Administration would continue to supply the Middle East with foreign aid and, not surprisingly, Reagan greatly increased the aid going to Latin America and the Caribbean. However, Congress was unsympathetic to Reagan's overreliance on security assistance, and it endeavored to refocus U.S. foreign aid toward development assistance through amendments and earmarks.

Military aid continued to be high during Reagan's second term in office, but development assistance, food aid, and multilateral assistance declined substantially. Even ESFs, Reagan's preferred economic aid budget category, declined after 1985. Relations with the Soviet Union were improving and the U.S. economy was experiencing historically high deficits and consequently could no longer politically or financially support Reagan's massive foreign assistance budgets. The Balanced Budget and Emergency Deficit Control Act (1985), also known as the Gramm-Rudman-Hollings Act, curtailed the lavish spending of Reagan's first term. Reagan, however, would circumvent Congressional restrictions by the use of reprogramming and emergency powers, that is, by moving funds from Congress approved programs to programs he wanted to fund.

Reagan also reversed Carter's policy of arms transfers as an exceptional tool of foreign policy. Reagan signed the Conventional Arms Transfer Policy on July 8, 1981which superseded Carter's 1977 document. Reagan viewed arms transfers as an essential element of U.S. foreign policy. The Reagan Administration believed that Carter's restrictions had undermined the defense of nations that are vital to America's security. Reagan viewed the transfers of conventional arms and other defense articles as an essential element of the U.S. global defense policy and indispensable to the pursuit of foreign policy regardless of the human rights conditions in the recipient country. With this in mind, in 1981, the U.S. government set up the Special Defense Acquisition Fund (SDAF),[9] designed to speed the delivery of arms by allowing the DOD to procure weaponry in anticipation of foreign government's military needs. It would also reduce the need to withdraw equipment from U.S. military service inventories during crisis. During the Reagan Administration, the SDAF had a $900 million ceiling.

In addition, the Reagan Administration was able to circumvent the human rights conditions by interpreting the wording "consistent pattern of gross violations" in such a way that even the worst human rights violators showed some level of improvement. In 1983, due to executive misuse, Congress closed the consistent pattern loophole by removing the word "consistent" from the legislation (Sections 116, 502B, and 701).

Contrary to Reagan's attempt to first abandon and then disingenuously redefine human rights, human rights would actually become institutionalized in U.S. foreign policy under his tenure. Lister (1987) commented that many people thought the human rights bureau would be abolished during the Reagan era. It was not that Reagan did not try to emasculate HA. Reagan nominated Ernest Lefever to the post of Assistant Secretary of State for Human Rights and Humanitarian Affairs. Lefever, a well-known critic of Carter's human rights policy, advocated the repeal of all U.S. legislation linking human rights with foreign assistance because it interfered with the fight against communism. The Senate Foreign Relations Committee overwhelmingly voted down Lefever's nomination. Later, Reagan left the position vacant for months until he settled on Elliot Abrams. Rossiter suggests that the Human Rights Bureau under Abrams operated more as a public relations bureau for anti-communism than as an advocate for human rights (1984: 22–23). Elliot Abrams believed that "To prevent any country from being taken over by a Communist regime is in our view a very real victory for the cause of human rights" (Mower 1987: 26). Cynthia Brown concludes that the Human Rights Bureau, while administered by Abrams, "functioned as a promotional agent and appointments secretary" for anti-communist repressive organizations and regimes (2003).

But, as it turned out, "human rights policy had been institutionalized, it had strong bipartisan support in Congress, human rights legislation passed in previous years was still in force, and our annual human rights reports to Congress were still required by law" (Lister 1987: 1). Furthermore, by the time of Reagan's Presidency, human rights had become sufficiently embedded into bureaucratic decision-making, and HA had established bureaucratic networks and contacts, thus ensuring human rights perpetuation in the foreign policy institutions. By 1984, according to Rossiter (1984), HA became a safe place for career officers since the battles and name-calling had subsided. Therefore, it was able to attract skilled administrators who professionally and efficiently implemented the provisions of the human rights legislation. In fact, Warshawsky (1980) suggests that many young career-minded Foreign Service officers would enthusiastically accept a position in HA since advancement within the new bureau could be much swifter than in top-heavy agencies. Furthermore, human rights were now viewed as essential to foreign policy by many foreign service officers, and HA offered them a unique opportunity to commit to their principles. Hostility by other bureaus also "helped forge a camaraderie" among those individuals dedicated to human rights (Warshawsky 1980: 196).

Conclusion

The United States has institutionalized human rights in foreign policy since the 1970s. Ideas and rhetoric matter greatly impact the evolution of U.S. foreign policy. Human rights constituted a rebuff of the Cold War philosophy that had dominated U.S. foreign policymaking since 1945. However, the development of that policy ebbed and flowed, advanced and retreated, depending on the presidential administration and the power struggle inherent in foreign policymaking. Yet, as human rights gained acceptance as a concern within foreign policy over the course of the Cold War, it was also often relegated to a secondary concern. By the end of the Cold War, national security would remain the primary determinant of foreign policy and foreign aid allocations. Of course, U.S. human rights policy strained relations with some human rights abusing states but, as Lister noted, as a

> result of our [human rights] efforts, there has been less torture in some countries, there have been fewer political murders, fewer 'disappeared,' more names published of political prisoners being held,

more prisoners actually released, states of siege lifted, censorship relaxed, more elections and more honest elections.

(1987: 2)

The advantages of a human rights policy surely outweighed the disadvantages.

During the Cold War's ideological battles, human rights issues were often relegated to a low priority. However, as the next chapter will illustrate, with the passing of the Cold War, many thought that now was the time for U.S. human rights policy to flourish. Throughout the Cold War human rights were slowly being institutionalized in the foreign affairs and military bureaucracy. With the collapse of the Soviet Union, and the U.S. apparent victory over communism, human rights and democracy seemed assured. The end of the Cold War brought a new hope for peace and prosperity. However, the post–Cold War era was riddled with ethnic conflicts, nationalistic civil wars, and genocide. The "New World Order" was very similar to the Cold War era in terms of human rights violations, humanitarian crises, and foreign aid needs. The next chapter will investigate whether this new hope was realized.

Notes

1 Many thanks to Sarah Eliason from the Rapoport Center for Human Rights and Justice, School of Law at the University of Texas at Austin, for hunting down the correct links to the George Lister archives.
2 In 1973, the U.S. Attorney for Maryland opened an investigation into Agnew for conspiracy, bribery, extortion, and tax fraud when he was Governor of Maryland. Confronted with incontrovertible proof of his guilt, Agnew took a plea deal where he would plead *nolo contendere* to one felony income tax evasion charge and step down from the office of Vice President.
3 In order to avoid being impeached and removed from office due to the Watergate scandal (and additionally to charges of tax invasion, improper use of government agencies, accepting personal gifts, and obstruction of justice), Nixon resigned the Presidency in August of 1974.
4 On September 8, 1974, Ford issued a "full, free and absolute pardon" to Nixon for crimes he may or may not have committed while in office. Although Ford testified to the Subcommittee on Criminal Justice of the House Judiciary Committee that there was no previous deal in place, there were reports that, prior to assuming the presidency, Nixon's Chief of Staff Alexander Haig had contacted Ford to discuss the possibility of a presidential pardon, along with several other possible actions to take in the matter of Nixon's resignation.
5 In January 1975, Ford told a group of journalists he was having lunch with that he feared the Rockefeller Commission (examining CIA excesses) would dig up secrets that needed to be kept. The journalists asked "Like what" to which Ford replied "Like assassinations!" (see Olmsted 2016: 114–115). Due to Congressional and public pressure, Ford was compelled to sign "Executive Order 11905, United States Foreign Intelligence Activities," February 18, 1976, banning the use of assassinations as a tool of foreign policy.

6 Ford approved covert CIA military aid to anti-communist factions in the Angolan Civil War. In what can only be seen as a continuation of the Nixon propensity to ignore Congressional will, Ford conducted his own little secret war, ignoring the legal requirements of the War Powers Act. Ford failed to inform Congress about the sending of aid as required by law.
7 Derian explains that one of the reasons she was chosen for the position was that she was a woman. Carter wanted to appoint women to high positions. But, as a woman she also had to fight a misogynistic tradition at the DOS. Derian relates a story that, in the margins of memos, Foreign Service officers would write remarks such as "Who does this babe think she is? What does she know about this?" (Derian 1996: 33).
8 George Shultz replaced Alexander Haig as Secretary of State, Foreign Service officers replaced Jeane Kirkpatrick, and Richard Schifter replaced Elliot Abrams as Assistant Secretary of State for the Bureau of Human Rights and Humanitarian Affairs.
9 The SDAF was authorized under the International Security and Development Cooperation Act of 1981.

References

Cynthia Brown. 2003. *Lost Liberties: Ashcroft and the Assault on Personal Freedom*. New York: New Press.
David Carleton and Michael Stohl. 1985. "The Foreign Policy of Human Rights: Rhetoric and Reality from Jimmy Carter to Ronald Reagan." *Human Rights Quarterly* 7(2): 205–229.
Thomas Carothers. 1991. *In the Name of Democracy: U.S. Policy toward Latin America in the Reagan Years*. Berkeley: University of California Press.
James Carter. 1977. "Statement by President Carter on U.S. Arms Sales Policy, 19 May 1977." http://www.mfa.gov.il/mfa/foreignpolicy/mfadocuments/yearbook2/pages/212%20statement%20by%20president%20carter%20on%20us%20arms%20sales.aspx
Jeffrey Claburn. 1994. "Public Constraints on Assassination as an Instrument of U.S. Foreign Policy." *International Journal of Intelligence and Counterintelligence* 7(1): 97–109.
Kenneth Cmiel. 1999. "The Emergence of Human Rights Politics in the United States." *Journal of American History* 86(3): 1231–1250.
Stephen Cohen. 1982. "Conditioning U.S. Security Assistance on Human Rights Practices." *American Journal of International Law* 76(2): 246–279.
William Colby. 1989. "Public Policy, Secret Action." *Ethics and International Affairs* 3(1): 61–71.
Patricia Derian. 1996. *Interviewed by Charles Stuart Kennedy*. The Association for Diplomatic Studies and Training Foreign Affairs Oral History Project http://adst.org/wp-content/uploads/2013/12/Derian-Patricia.19961.pdf
Jack Donnelly. 1995. "Post–Cold War Reflections on the Study of International Human Rights," in *Ethics and International Affairs: A Reader*. Joel Rosenthal, ed. Washington, DC: Georgetown University Press.
Elizabeth Drew. 1977. *American Journal: The Events of 1976*. New York: Random House.
Daniel Drezner. 2000. "Ideas, Bureaucratic Politics, and the Crafting of Foreign Policy." *American Journal of Political Science* 44(4): 733–749.

David Forsythe. 1987. "Congress and Human Rights in US Foreign Policy: The Fate of General Legislation." *Human Rights Quarterly* 9(3): 382–404.
David Forsythe. 1990. "Human Rights in U.S. Foreign Policy: Retrospect and Prospect." *Political Science Quarterly* 105(3): 435–454.
Thomas Franck and Edward Weisband. 1979. *Foreign Policy by Congress*. New York: Oxford University Press.
Donald Fraser. 1979. "Human Rights and U.S. Foreign Policy." *International Studies Quarterly* 23(2): 174–185.
Bernard Gwertzman. 1975. "U.S. Blocks Human Rights Data, on Nations Getting Arms." *New York Times*, November, 19.
Lawrence Haas. 2012. *Sound the Trumpet: The United States and Human Rights Protection*. Lanham, MD: Rowman & Littlefield Publishers.
Charles Jones. 1994. *The Presidency in a Separated System*. Washington, DC: Brookings.
Victor Kaufman. 1998. "The Bureau of Human Rights during the Carter Administration." *Historian* 61(1): 51–66.
Barbara Keys. 2014. *Reclaiming American Virtue*. Cambridge, MA: Harvard University Press.
Jeane Kirkpatrick. 1979. "Dictatorships and Double Standards." *Commentary* 68(5): 34–45.
Henry Kissinger. 1974. "Minutes of the Secretary's Staff Meeting," October 22, 1974 in Foreign Relations of the United States, 1969–1976, Volume E-3. http://history.state.gov/historicaldocuments/frus1969-76ve03/d244
Henry Kissinger. 1999. *Years of Renewal*. New York: Simon and Schuster.
Michael Lind. 2002. *Vietnam The Necessary War: A Reinterpretation of America's Most Disastrous Military Conflict*. New York: Free Press.
George Lister. 1987. "U.S. Human Rights Policy: Origins and Implementation." *Current Policy* No. 973. https://law.utexas.edu/humanrights/lister/assets/pdf/Human%20Rights%20Bureau/originsandimplementation%20.pdf?id=txu-blac-glp-302
Don Luce. 2009. "The Tiger Cages of Viet Nam." *Historians against the War*. http://www.historiansagainstwar.org/resources/torture/luce.html
Charles Maechling. 1983. "Human Rights Dehumanized." *Foreign Policy* 52: 118–135.
Carlyle Maw. 1976. Testimony. International Security Assistance Act of 1976: Hearing before the House Committee on International Relations, 94th Congress, 1st and 2nd Sessions, 207–208. Washington, DC: U.S. Government Printing Office.
Edwin Maynard. 1989. "The Bureaucracy and Implementation of US Human Rights Policy." *Human Rights Quarterly* 11(2): 175–248.
Mathew McCubbins and Thomas Schwartz. 1984. "Congressional Oversight Overlooked: Police Patrols versus Fire Alarms." *American Journal of Political Science* 28(1): 16–79.
Yanek Mieczkowski. 2005. *Gerald Ford and the Challenges of the 1970s*. Lexington: University of Kentucky Press.
Glenn Mower. 1987. *Human Rights and American Foreign Policy*. New York: Greenwood Press.
Samuel Moyn. 2010. *The Last Utopia – Human Rights in History*. Cambridge: Harvard University Press.

Kathryn Olmsted. 2016. "US Intelligence Agencies during the Ford Years," in *A Companion to Gerald R. Ford and Jimmy Carter.* Scott Kaufman, ed. Malden, MA: John Wiley & Sons, Inc.

John Prados. 2003. *Lost Crusader: The Secret Wars of CIA Director William Colby.* New York: Oxford University Press.

Thomas Risse and Kathryn Sikkink. 1999. "The Socialization of International Human Rights Norms into Domestic Practices: Introduction," in *The Power of Human Rights: International Norms and Domestic Change.* Thomas Risse, Stephan Ropp, and Kathryn Sikkink, eds. Cambridge: Cambridge University Press.

Caleb Rossiter. 1984. *Human Rights: The Carter Record, the Reagan Reaction.* Washington, DC: Center for International Policy.

William Schmidli. 2011. "Institutionalizing Human Rights in U.S. Foreign Policy: U.S.-Argentine Relations, 1976–1980." *Diplomatic History* 35(2): 351–377.

George Shultz. 1983. Testimony, Foreign Assistance Legislation for Fiscal Year 1984–85 House Committee on Foreign Affairs (16 February).

Kathryn Sikkink. 2004. *Mixed Signals: U.S. Human Rights Policy and Latin America.* Ithaca, NY: Cornell University Press.

Brad Simpson. 2005. "'Illegally and Beautifully': The United States, the Indonesian Invasion of East Timor and the International Community, 1974–76." *Cold War History* 5(3): 281–315.

Umberto Tulli. 2012. "'Whose rights are human rights?' The Ambiguous Emergence of Human Rights and the Demise of Kissingerism." *Cold War History* 12(4): 573–593.

United States Senate. 1975. *Senate Resolution 21, Resolved, to Establish a Select Committee of the Senate to Conduct an Investigation and Study of Governmental Operations with Respect to Intelligence Activities.* 94th Congress (1975–1976).

Howard Warshawsky. 1980. "The Department of State and Human Rights Policy: A Case Study of the Human Rights Bureau." *World Affairs* 142(3): 188–215.

David Weissbrodt. 1977. "Human Rights Legislation and United States Foreign Policy." *Georgia Journal of International and Comparative Law* 7: 231–284.

James Wilson. 1977. "Diplomatic Theology – An Early Chronicle of Human Rights at State," unpublished narrative, "Human Rights and Humanitarian Affairs – Wilson Memoir" folder, box 1, James M. Wilson Papers, Gerald Ford Library.

James Wilson. 1999. *Interview by Charles Stuart Kennedy.* The Association for Diplomatic Studies and Training Foreign Affairs Oral History Project. https://cdn.loc.gov/service/mss/mfdip/2004/2004wil14/2004wil14.pdf

Robert Zimmerman. 1993. *Dollars, Diplomacy and Dependency: Dilemmas of U.S. Economic Aid.* Boulder, CO: Lynne Rienner.

3 U.S. Human Rights Policy in the Post-Cold War Era
A Decade of Lost Opportunities

During the Cold War, human rights issues were consigned to a secondary status by the perceived need to contain communism. The end of the Cold War brought a new promise of peace and prosperity. There was a general euphoria in the West that threats to international security were over and peace, democracy, and human rights would define the next period of global order. With the fall of communism, the United States had unmatched military and economic power and no enemy, which provided the Bush, Sr. and Clinton Administrations the unique opportunity to support and expand democracy and human rights in this unipolar moment. Bush, Sr.'s new world order would be "characterized by the rule of law rather than the resort to force, the cooperative settlement of disputes rather than anarchy and bloodshed, and an unstinting belief in human rights" (Bush, Sr. 1991). There was hope that human rights and democracy could now be successfully pursued globally. Many expected that the United States would now be able to apply a universal standard to human rights and would censure human rights abuses wherever and whenever they occurred. On the other hand, those who associated human rights violations with communism thought the job was done. Democracy and capitalism, precursors to human rights attainment, were won. This conclusion led to many missed opportunities.

With the end of the Cold War came a monetary peace dividend: savings from defense spending. Thus, the United States greatly reduced its foreign aid budget. During the Cold War, the allocation of foreign aid was directly related to the bipolar division of the world. After the Cold War, anti-communism no longer became the primary justification for foreign aid allocation, and there was no longer a compelling reason to support right-wing dictatorships either. Unfortunately, in the post-Cold War era, the reduced levels of foreign aid and its distribution would still be influenced by the recipient country's geopolitical and commercial potential.

Since the rise of U.S. human rights policy in the 1970s, the U.S. government had used the carrot and stick method of foreign aid provisions or terminations, along with the publication of the State Department's annual *Country Reports on Human Rights Practices*, to encourage states to adhere to human rights standards. During the post-Cold War era, however, the United States would embrace the more extreme method of humanitarian interventions. The U.S. rhetoric of supporting human rights and stopping abuses resulted in a rise of humanitarian interventions. The Clinton Administration's assertive multilateralism would be used "for humanitarian purposes, such as combating famine and other natural disasters and in cases of over-whelming violations of human rights" (Lake 1994: 768). Interventions in Kuwait, Panama, Somalia, Haiti, Bosnia, Iraq, and Kosovo involved, rhetorically at least, the protection of human rights. Certainly, there were other interests motivating U.S. involvement too: rogue states and regional conflicts were the new threats to U.S. security and U.S. national interests.

The Bush, Sr. Administration (1989–1993)

President George Herbert Walker Bush, Sr. oversaw the dissolution of the Soviet Union and the collapse of communism. With the end of the Cold War and the U.S. victory over the Soviet Union, conditions were finally in place for the implementation of a consistent and coherent U.S. human rights policy. Perhaps now was the time for the application of American ideals of democracy and human rights, so long delayed due to the need to contain communism and Soviet aggression. Indeed, Bush, Sr. had the opportunity and the goodwill of Congress to redefine U.S. foreign policy. However, given Bush, Sr.'s personality as a cautious, moderate, and middle of the road conservative, he was unlikely to be a force for policy change (Kegley 1989). After all, there remained lingering doubts regarding the abrupt end of the Soviet Union. Thus, human rights were of little significance in Bush, Sr.'s primary goal of defending the international status quo of American supremacy and maintaining global stability. Was the end of communism a clever or desperate ploy to weaken the NATO alliance and disrupt the bipolar framework that ordered the international system?

As we saw in previous chapters, the institutionalization of human rights into U.S. foreign policy began during the second Reagan term. It would continue during the Bush, Sr. Administration. Sikkink defines an institutionalized human rights policy as one where "human rights concerns [are] now a regularized part of the policy process. It [did] not mean that human rights concerns would dominate any particular policy decision" (2004: 182). The State Department accepted the responsibility to collect and authenticate human rights conditions in foreign client states as part of its normal standard operating procedures. Standard operating procedures are "routine methods that facilitate coordinated and concerted actions" (Halperin 1974: 252). The development of new standard operating procedures takes time and energy. Therefore, these procedures are unlikely to be abandoned. Becoming entrenched ensures the procedures' permanency in bureaucratic functioning. In addition, the Bureau of Human Rights and Humanitarian Affairs (HA) gained competence, status, and resources. Human rights officers in the regional bureaus and embassies were hired and trained in the human rights procedures and became proficient in their responsibilities toward human rights reporting. Thus, the implementation of human rights policy was able to continue in the immediate post-Cold War era despite Bush, Sr.'s lack of interest in the issue.

Bush, Sr.'s Administration is also associated with reduced rancor in Washington. Bush, Sr. chose inner circle advisors who were temperamentally similar to him and ideologically compatible. Even Bush, Sr.'s relationship with Congress was, superficially at least, compromising and cooperative. However, Bush, Sr. endeavored, and often succeeded, to govern without Congress. The pragmatic president displayed a chilling character trait, one reminiscent of Nixon's suspicion and mistrust. Bush, Sr. believed "secrecy to be a necessary, regular element of presidential decision making" (Barilleaux and Rozell 2004: 90). Bush, Sr. relied on secrecy to bypass Congress and concealed information from the American public (Kegley 1989). Bush, Sr. would prevaricate, relying on a variety of secret devices to supersede Congressional will and mandate. Bush, Sr.'s strategy to govern without the impediment of Congress focused on the use of bureaucratic structures and regulations, secret opinions policy, national security directives that were withheld from Congress, and the use of signing statements whereby the president would announce his interpretation and enforcement of the law (Tiefer 1994). Although all administrations attempt to control the flow of information, "what makes the Bush, Sr. administration unusual is the extent to which it makes policy outside the normal processes of the separation of powers" (Barilleaux and Rozell 2004: 112). For example, the Justice Department refused to show or even acknowledge to Congress legal memorandum opinions. And Bush, Sr.'s restrictions on a free media were used to sanitize the Gulf War. Bush, Sr. implemented a policy of press censorship through the use of press-pool journalists (only chosen journalists were given access to select sites and soldiers) and further established a security review process with all information provided to the press via the military only. The American public would not see the return of flag-draped American coffins or the "collateral damage" from stealth bombers, cruise missiles, and smart bombs on the lives and property of Iraqi citizens. Fiske (1991) stated that the United States fought a war for freedom in Kuwait by abolishing freedom of the press in the United States. The result was that Bush, Sr. "could purposely override the will of Congress or conceal important presidential actions by resorting to secret directives" (Barilleaux and Rozell 2004: 105). The lesson learned here is that the president can control public opinion with manipulation and selective dissimulation of information.

With the end of the Cold War, Congress and the American public thought the peace dividend ought to include monetary savings to the federal budget. As a result, Congress passed the Budget Enforcement Act of 1990 (PL 101-508), which greatly reduced security assistance so that, by 1992, the majority of small recipients of U.S. bilateral security aid no longer received any money. Of course, the Camp David Accords participants, Israel and Egypt, would be protected from the post-Cold War reduction in foreign aid. Congress wanted to refocus the diminished level of U.S. foreign aid toward fostering economic development, advancing human capital, and promoting democracy.

Congress redirected aid toward the transitioning countries of Eastern European by passing the Support for East European Democracy Act (1989) (SEED; PL 101-513) and the Freedom for Russian and Emerging Eurasian Democracies and Open Markets Support Act (1992) (PL 102-511). Given the political importance of ensuring that transitioning countries would not backslide and would remain on the path of liberal capitalism, the United States provided large foreign assistance packages. The new direction in foreign aid focused on Eastern and Central Europe, and an overall reduction of aid, generally, required eliminating or greatly decreasing foreign assistance not only to Latin America, but also to Asia and Africa. Latin America, a major recipient of U.S. foreign aid during the Reagan Administration, was losing the competition for aid, loans, and investment to the transitioning states of Eastern Europe and the geopolitically important Middle East. Since Third World countries were no longer prizes in the now obsolete superpower competition, there was little reason to provide them with economic or military aid. These Third World countries, once heavily armed by the superpowers, were no longer able to apply the same level of ruthless control over their populations, and they experienced a reemergence of ethnic conflicts, civil wars, and genocides.

Bush, Sr. believed that, in order to promote stability in the Gulf region, the United States ought to provide economic and military aid. The carrot of a generous aid package would be an incentive "for Iraq to moderate its behavior and to increase our influence with Iraq" (White House 1989: 2). The stick in this carrot and stick approach to human rights performance was to place sanctions on Iraq if it failed to conform to chemical and biological weapons restrictions. In March 1988, Saddam Hussein used chemical weapons against Iraqi Kurds, killing over 5,000 civilians and injuring an additional 10,000. This was not an isolated incident. Yet, up until the time he invaded Kuwait, Hussein received aid and friendship from the Bush, Sr. Administration. In a 1992 speech before the Center for National Policy, Gore accused Bush, Sr. of "blindly [ignoring] the evidence already at the Administration's disposal of Iraqi behavior in the past regarding human rights, terrorism, the use of chemical weapons, and the pursuit of advanced weapons of mass destruction"

(1992). The United States supplied the weapons that Hussein used against his own people with the knowledge, and indeed collusion, of the Bush, Sr. Administration.

Besides withholding information from Congress and the American public, the Bush, Sr. Administration had little compunction against deceitful and fraudulent acts. Frantz and Waas (1992a) report that a list of export licenses to Iraq was deliberately altered, deleting military designations of materials and arms, before it was submitted to Congress. Their report also notes that former Commerce Secretary Robert A. Mosbacher knew of the changes. This was part of "the Administration [attempted] to keep Congress from learning the extent of U.S. assistance to the regime of Saddam Hussein in the years and months leading up to Iraq's invasion of Kuwait" (Frantz and Waas 1992b). Furthermore, the Bush, Sr. Administration was aware that the food aid given by the United States to Iraq had been redirected to buy arms and technology for nuclear weapons. In order to provide aid to Saddam, Bush, Sr. signed waivers providing Export-Import Bank loan guarantees to Iraq. Iraq was in default on $2 billion to the Export-Import Bank[1] of the United States (Kellner 1992). The Bush, Sr. Administration essentially continued the arms transfer and overall security assistance policies of the Reagan Administration despite Iraq's persistent human rights violations.

Bush, Sr. first used the phrase "New World Order" on September 11, 1990 in a speech to justify the Gulf War following Iraq's invasion of Kuwait. Bush, Sr. stumbled around looking for a justification to launch a war in the Persian Gulf. The initial justification, Iraq's invasion of Kuwait giving Hussein control of 40 percent of the world's oil reserves, prompted the anti-war movement's slogan of "no blood for oil." Going to war for oil did not resonate with the American public. Human rights would thus become an instrument of war. With "Nayirah" (the daughter of the Kuwaiti ambassador to the United States) fabricated testimony before the Congressional Human Rights Caucus,[2] the Bush, Sr. Administration found its rationale to go to war. Ross states that Americans supported the war effort "when the emphasis was mostly on human rights and the need to confront an international evil" (1992: 329). The United States was going to defend human rights, restore democracy, and save Kuwaiti babies from a Hitler-like monster. Once the war ended, though, Bush, Sr. had to moderate the issues of human rights and democracy since the end of the war did not establish respect for human rights or democracy in either Kuwait or Iraq.

Culpably, the Bush, Sr. Administration inadvertently instigated a rebellion by the Kurds in the North and the Shi'ite in the South of Iraq in the aftermath of the Gulf War. However, he would abandon these groups to Hussein's retaliation.

Bush, Sr. feared that a Shi'ite revolt could bring about a power shift in Iraq, thus strengthening Iran. Bush, Sr. also was worried that the Kurdish unrest would spread to Turkey's Kurdish ethnic minority and renew calls for a Kurdish state, thus destabilizing Turkey, a dutiful ally and NATO member. Protecting the human rights of the Kurds and Shi'ites proved to be politically inconvenient. Wolfowitz was serving as Undersecretary of Defense in 1991 and later admitted that the Administration knew the extent of, yet attempted to ignore, the human rights violations resulting from the Bush, Sr. inspired uprisings:

> We had pilots flying overhead watching helicopters slaughter Iraqis. We had our divisions on the south side of the Euphrates watching the Republican Guards go south to slaughter Iraqis.
> (Wolfowitz 2011)

Bush, Sr. belatedly and grudgingly ordered a no-fly zone in both the north and the south of Iraq to protect the insurgents from Hussein's murderous wrath. In Nye's opinion, Bush, Sr.'s new world order had little to do with justice and a lot to do with the distribution of power in the international system. Nye states, "The problem for the Bush, Sr. Administration was that it thought and acted like Nixon, but borrowed the rhetoric of Wilson and Carter" (1992: 84). Bush, Sr.'s conception of the new world order relied heavily on American leadership and military strength. The United States was attempting to establish its hegemonic agenda.

Since the Nixon years, U.S.-China relations had become more cordial, revolving primarily around trade and investment. When the Chinese government ordered its troops to end student protests in Tiananmen Square, it did so with brutal repression. Chinese students were calling for democratic reforms, respect for human rights, the release of political prisoners, and freedom of speech and of the press. On June 4, 1989, Chinese troops attacked the unarmed and peaceful protesters, killing 2,600 (as reported in U.S. House of Representatives Resolution 285, issued on June 5, 1989). President Bush, Sr. condemned China's use of lethal force with distinctly pragmatic and restrained language. Bush, Sr. ordered a suspension of both governmental and commercial arms sales to China, canceled bilateral government official visits, and delayed U.S. approval of international loans. However, these sanctions were temporary measures meant to dissuade Congress from adopting more severe economic sanctions against China. Even with evidence that Chinese exports used forced labor, the Bush, Sr. Administration sought to preserve U.S.-China relations and continued to grant most favored nation (MFN) status in violation of U.S. law. The Smoot-Hawley Tariff Act (1930) makes it illegal to import goods produced "wholly or in part in any foreign country by convict labor or/and forced labor or/and indentured labor under penal sanctions" (U.S. Tariff Act of 1930). Congressional Democrats attempted to withdraw China's MFN trading status unless China improved its human rights practices and refrained from using slave labor.

Bush, Sr. fought legislation that would attach conditions to the renewal of MNF trade status for China, twice vetoing the legislation. The brutal crackdown on pro-democracy protesters would not be allowed to "seriously damage our hard-won gains" with the Chinese government and the Chinese market (Bush, Sr. and Scowcroft 1998: 97).

During Bush, Sr.'s tenure, Congress remained an active player in furthering U.S. human rights policy. The U.S. Senate ratified several international human rights treaties that it had ignored for decades. These include the International Convention on Civil and Political Rights (1992), the Convention on the Abolition of Forced Labor (1991), and the Convention on the Prevention and Punishment of the Crime of Genocide (1988). Congress also passed domestic legislation that affects the international protection of human rights. The International Narcotics Control Act (1989) allows funding only to countries that maintain democratic governments and respect human rights. The act requires the president to submit to Congress a determination that the armed forces and law enforcement agencies of the recipient country are not engaged in human rights violations. Bush, Sr., when signing the legislation into law, complained about the "unreasonable" restrictions and "cumbersome" reporting requirements (Bush, Sr. 1990: 1). In 1991, Congress passed the Torture Victim Protection Act. The act provides victims with the ability to file civil suits in the United States, after exhausting local remedies, against individuals who, while acting in an official capacity for any foreign government, engaged in torture or extrajudicial killing. On March 12, 1992, President George H.W. Bush signed the Torture Victim Protection Act of 1991 with the sentiment that U.S. courts "would become embroiled in difficult and sensitive disputes in other countries and possibly ill-founded or politically motivated suits . . . and would also be a waste of our own limited and already overburdened judicial resources" (Bush, Sr. 1992).

Once again, the Latin American region received lower priority during the Bush, Sr. years than it had experienced during the Reagan era. Bush, Sr.'s foreign policy toward Latin America was primarily an antidrug policy. In 1989, the Bush, Sr. Administration enacted the "Andean Initiative" targeting drug production through U.S. military assistance, although minor levels of economic aid and trade benefits were also included. The $2.2 billion aid package was sent to Colombia, Bolivia, and Peru to combat the production of narcotics. After three years, the program was declared a failure and found to have no effect on reducing the supply of cocaine and heroin to the United States (Crandall 2002). It did greatly increase the level of human rights violations though. The International Narcotics Control Act (1992) restricted the use of counter-narcotics funds to be used against insurgent activity. Bush, Sr.'s antidrug foreign policy is also reflected in the removal of General Manual Noriega of Panama. In 1988, to the surprise and embarrassment of the White House, Noriega was indicted for drug trafficking by two federal grand juries in Miami and Tampa (Florida). The Bush, Sr. Administration decided to use military force to remove Noriega from office and bring him to Miami to face drug charges. With the deployment of over 25,000 troops, Operation Just Cause was the largest military action since the Vietnam War. Although the ouster of General Manuel Noriega, along with the installation of the democratically elected government of President Guillermo Endara, substantially improved human rights, human rights protections were not the primary rationale for the invasion. While the Endara regime can be criticized for many human rights failings, according to Human Rights Watch, the state does:

> not systematically engage in acts of physical violence against its citizens; criminal law no longer is employed routinely to suppress political dissent; freedom of expression, while not absolute, is exercised and respected; and courts and prosecutors, though still subject to political direction and influence, operate far more independently than they did under the Noriega regime.
>
> (1991: 1)

Improvements in human rights conditions were simply a pleasant externality of Bush, Sr.'s attempt to eliminate an embarrassing asset. Noriega was recruited by the CIA while Bush was chief of that intelligence agency (Drumbrell 1997). While campaigning for President, Bush claimed not to have known about Noriega's drug trafficking until the 1988 indictments. Bush, running on an antidrug platform, had to shield himself from the Democrat charges that he was coddling an old friend and drug dealer, by distancing himself from Reagan's approach to Panama. However, it was shown that Bush received a briefing from the U.S. Ambassador to Panama Everett Briggs in 1985 indicating Noriega was heavily involved in drug trafficking.

U.S. human rights policy was legislated over the opposition of the Nixon Administration, suffered from failed implementation during the Carter Administration, was redefined and usurped by the Reagan Administration, and was now, due to historical circumstances (the end of the Cold War and superpower rivalry), primed to succeed. However, even if the Bush, Sr. Administration actively employed human rights language, Bush, Sr. tended toward an agnostic response to human rights violations and international crises. Bush, Sr. simply had little interest in furthering the cause of human rights, and he missed the opportunity to redirect America's foreign policy toward human rights protection.

The Clinton Administration (1993–2001)

With the post-Cold War era firmly established, U.S. aid could be directed to the promotion of democracy and human rights (Lai 2003). There was little fear that the ex-Soviet and Soviet sphere countries would backslide to communism. With this assurance perhaps now human rights could flourish as a foreign policy objective. The election of William "Bill" Jefferson Clinton brought hope among the human rights community that the human rights moment had finally arrived; human rights would finally be a cornerstone of U.S. foreign policy. Clinton appointed human rights advocates to positions of power in his administration. Clinton chose Warren Christopher, who chaired the Inter-Agency Group on Human Rights and Foreign Assistance during the Carter Administration, to be his Secretary of State. Clinton selected John Shattuck, the former director of the American Civil Liberties Union and vice chair of Amnesty International, as the Assistant Secretary of State of the newly renamed Bureau of Democracy, Human Rights, and Labor (DRL). Later, Harold Hongju Koh, a renowned human rights professor and lawyer, served as head of the DRL during Clinton's second term. Madeleine Albright, the U.S. Ambassador to the U.N. during Clinton's first term and Secretary of State during his second term as president, was a fervent advocate for humanitarian interventions on behalf of human rights. Anthony Lake, Clinton's National Security Advisor, is credited as the architect and advocate of the policy of enlargement. Both Albright and Lake also subscribed to the concept of "democratic peace," and they have been referred to as "humanitarian hawks" (Brands 2008). Shattuck also referred to himself as a "human rights hawk" and a "human rights warrior" (2003: 7). The preferences and principles of Clinton's advisors encouraged a foreign policy based on democracy and human rights. In addition, the Clinton Administration also filled many midlevel positions with people knowledgeable about and sympathetic to human rights (Mertus 2004). To the surprise of human rights NGOs, the State Department actually wanted NGOs' advice and participation. Yet, the post-Cold War era presented an unprecedented, but missed, opportunity for the development of a universal acceptance of human rights.

Clinton was, after all, elected with a mandate to fix America's domestic economic troubles. In fact, it was Christopher's job to keep foreign policy off Clinton's desk so that he could fulfill his campaign pledge to focus "like a laser beam" on the economy (Peceny 1999). However, foreign issues, often involving massive human rights violations and humanitarian crises, could not be ignored. Upon entering office, Clinton was faced with U.S. military involvement in Somalia, Haiti, and Iraq, and he had to prepare for an airlift in Bosnia. To tackle the challenges of the post-Cold War era, multilateralism in humanitarian intervention was seen by the Clinton Administration as an effective tool to respond to mass violations of human rights. The use of multilateral operations held several advantages for the Clinton Administration. Multilateralism was believed to be cheaper for the United States since other developed countries would pay part of the international security costs. Furthermore, the turn to multilateral organizations would allow Clinton to pursue his foreign adventures and foreign aid provisions without the support of Congress. Assertive multilateralism would allow the United States to exercise moral leadership, legitimate its adventures, and reduce the costs through burden sharing. Although gross violations of human rights might trigger humanitarian intervention and the use of force, the United States would not become entangled in "reckless crusades" (Clinton 1992: 21).

While the promotion of human rights and democracy would be among the fundamental goals of U.S. foreign policy, Lake clarified that the United States "at times need to befriend and even defend undemocratic states for 'mutually beneficial reasons'" (1993). The mutually beneficial reason was often the economic prosperity of the United States. Clinton's new, overarching grand strategy in foreign policy was democratic enlargement combined with economic prosperity. This point was emphasized by Secretary of Commerce Ron Brown (1994) too when he stated that the Clinton Administration was deeply concerned with human rights and that the improvement of human rights was best accomplished by being commercially engaged with the abusing state. According to Brinkley, the Clinton Administration believed that if emerging democracies "developed consumer-oriented middle classes with the desired appetites for American products, peace and prosperity could become a reality" (1997: 117). American economic prosperity and superiority in trade relations were key to both U.S. and the world's security concerns. Clinton's merging of economic policy with security policy would favor the strong developing economies of Mexico and South Korea, but it would also marginalize Sub-Saharan Africa and other desperately poor regions. Similarly, Oliver (2004) notes that Clinton's primary foreign policy line, the policy of democratic enlargement, first sought to strengthen and consolidate relations among the core capitalist states (the United States, Europe, Japan, Canada, Mexico, and South Korea, primarily) and the regimes and institutions that promote global trade. As Oliver argues, the Clinton Administration believed that "American economic recovery and long-term prosperity were inextricably intertwined with global economic growth and especially that of the democratic capitalist core" (2004: 53). Subsequently, the goal was to encourage greater trade with the larger, newly democratizing economies of Latin America, and, finally, to bring in nondemocratic potential trading partners through trade and diplomatic contacts (China and Russia, in particular). To this end the Clinton Administration would utilize the military and foreign aid. The lack of any credible threat to the U.S. hegemonic position in the 1990s helped to justify the assumption that economic prosperity was the only true national security issue facing the United States.

In the former Soviet republics, including Central Asia, the U.S. primary foreign policy goals included the promotion of human rights and democracy (Nichol 1996). Yet, as Nichol reports, "the majority of Central Asian states appear more authoritarian than during the Gorbachev period, according to many observers, and commit many human rights abuses" (1996). But there was no call for a reduction in foreign aid as a sanction for bad behavior since the U.S. government feared a rise in Islamic fundamentalism. Thus, as long as the abusive, authoritarian Central Asian regimes in Kazakhstan, Kyrgyzstan, Tajikistan, Turkmenistan, and Uzbekistan served U.S. economic and security interests, there was little concern for these countries' denial of democracy and their flagrant abuse of human rights (Rumer 2002). The United States provided ample amounts of security assistance to them in contradiction to the Leahy Laws (see below) and 502B of the FAA.

Although Clinton's early foreign policy actions and rhetoric raised expectations that human rights would have a central place in the new administration's guiding principles, his later foreign policy decisions and his narrow focus on the economy quickly crushed the rising expectations of the human rights community. Clinton, Shattuck believed, did not understand

> what it would take for him to achieve both his human rights and trade priorities. He would have to stand up to a recalcitrant Chinese government and resist the pressure of the American business community—a two-pronged strategy that would require him to be willing to spend a great deal of his own political and diplomatic capital to achieve.
>
> (2003: 229)

The Clinton Administration would not allow human rights violations to interfere with advantageous trade negotiations and pursuits. This is most clearly evident with the delinking of MFN trading status and human rights in the case of China. In 1994, trade privileges to China were renewed despite the lack of any human rights improvements. In fact, Kagan states that the "China policy was taken away from the State Department and the Pentagon and given to the money boys at Commerce, at Treasury, at the U.S. Trade Representative's office" (2001: 26). The delinking of human rights and MFN status can be traced to the concerted lobbying efforts of business groups and multinational corporations who viewed China's cheap labor and potential consumer markets as vital to their own economic interests. Not to extend MFN status to China would have cost U.S. business interests numerous export opportunities. But even impoverished regions were important if they could further Clinton's geo-economic goals. Clinton stated that "for decades we viewed Africa through Cold War prism...We supported leaders on the basis of their anti-Communist or anti-apartheid rhetoric perhaps more than their action... and the United States... simply ignored the realities of Africa" (1994: 14). The United States was one of the major importers of Nigerian crude oil. The United States did not impose sanctions against Nigeria even in the face of brutal human rights conditions in the 1990s. For the Clinton Administration, commercial interests were the primary concern. U.S.-Africa relations, during the Clinton era, were based on trade as opposed to foreign aid.

The Rwandan genocide provides a useful example of how bureaucratic politics and congressional-presidential-bureaucratic conflict affect U.S. human rights policy. The Rwandan genocide left upward of one million Tutsis and moderate Hutus dead. Roughly two million people were made refugees, and another million became internally displaced. The killing officially came to an end on July 16, 1994. Once the situation was no longer dangerous, the U.N., in cooperation with the United States, established Operation Support Hope whereby the U.S. military would aid the Rwandan refugees by protecting and distributing the desperately needed humanitarian relief supplies. Although the Clinton Administration was aware of the government-sponsored ethnic violence in Rwanda (see, for example, the State Department's 1994 *Country Reports on Human Rights*, which detailed the atrocities), it refused to call the mass killing genocide. The Clinton Administration downplayed the humanitarian crisis in Rwanda and actively impeded U.N. peacekeeping operations to stop the genocide. According to Burkhalter (1994/1995), bureaucratic infighting delayed the U.S. response to the Rwanda genocide. The State Department's Africa bureau fervently argued for stronger policy measures including an increase in troop levels and sanctions. The Bureau of International Organization Affairs, the U.S. liaison with the U.N., distrusted the U.N. peacekeeping operation and "undercut the Africa bureau's efforts to promote a larger U.N. presence in Rwanda" (Burkhalter 1994/1995: 48). The Pentagon opposed committing troops to another U.N. African peacekeeping operation. The Somalia disaster still weighed heavily.[3] Thus, when the various agencies met to discuss policy options the Pentagon's wishes prevailed. The Pentagon also used its strategic alliances within Congress to oppose funding allocations. Other Congressional subcommittees, such as the Africa Subcommittee of the House Foreign Affairs Committee and the Africa Subcommittee in the Senate, were active vocal supporters of an enlarged mandate in Rwanda but could not defend it against the more powerful Defense Appropriations Subcommittees and the Pentagon. The result of the bureaucratic infighting was Clinton's Presidential Decision Directive 25 and the refusal to expand the United Nations Assistance Mission for Rwanda (UNAMIR).

Similarly, Clinton's policy of intercepting and returning Haitian refugees, a continuation of Bush, Sr.'s strategy, brought him in conflict with Congressional members and humanitarian groups and was causing a rift in the executive bureaucracy. Clinton's Democratic allies in Congress and liberal constituents were demanding a change in policy. Tom Harkin (D-Iowa) called Clinton's actions "embarrassing and shameful" during the

Senate Foreign Relations subcommittee on Western Hemisphere Affairs (Goshko 1994: A15). In April 1994, six Democratic Congress members[4] staged a sit-in in front of the White House in protest of Clinton's Haitian policy. However, a majority of Congressional members were not supportive of intervention and were willing to continue forcefully repatriating Haitian refugees or holding them in refugee camps outside the United States in Guantanamo Bay, Cuba. The Haitian policy also created divisions within the executive branch. National Security Advisor Tony Lake and his assistant Sandy Berger were strong advocates for military intervention in Haiti. Deputy Secretary of State Strobe Talbott was initially hesitant regarding intervention and the DOS played a peripheral role in the Haitian policy that originated from the National Security Council. Later, the DOS determined that Haiti's proximity to the United States and the refugee producing human rights violations made it a vital national interest.

Thus, Aryeh Neier, the cofounder of Human Rights Watch, argues that the Clinton Administration enacted a new double standard. The Clinton Administration vocally condemned human rights violations by "pariah states or the governments of countries that are not considered politically or economically important," but it refused to condemn repressive governments deemed to be economically important to U.S. interests (Neier 1996–1997: 96). Consequently, the Clinton Administration failed to forcefully denounce Russia's oppression in Chechnya; it ignored China's subjugation of Tibet; and it remained silent in the face of Turkey's repression of the Kurds.

Even Clinton's pet human rights concern, women's rights, confronted a double standard. The Human Rights Watch World Report 2000 reveals that the Clinton Administration's commitment to women's human rights was jeopardized by its desire to further advantageous economic and strategic dealings with oppressive governments. The Clinton Administration only feebly reproached Mexico, an important trading partner for the United States, for the flagrant discrimination experienced by Mexican women, while raucously deriding the Taliban for its abuse of women's rights. The Human Rights Watch report continued by noting that, rather than making women's human rights "mainstream," as promised by President Clinton and Secretary of State Albright, the United States instead allowed women's rights to become the bargaining chip whenever other interests—from trade and investment to national security—came to bear (Human Rights Watch 2000).

A case in point is Clinton's failure to follow through with the ratification of the Convention on the Elimination of All Discrimination Against Women (CEDAW). At the World Conference on Human Rights in Vienna (June 1993), Secretary of State Warren Christopher announced that the Clinton Administration would move forward with CEDAW. In 1980, President Carter signed CEDAW. However, the United States failed to ratify CEDAW in order to preserve several legal gender discriminatory practices surrounding the rights of women in combat, in the workplace, and in terms of reproductive health. Although abortion is not specifically mentioned in CEDAW, it does provide for "access to health care services, including those related to family planning" (Article 12). Opponents of a women's right to control her own body fear that CEDAW will allow women to make the determination of whether or not she bears a child. Clinton did initially advocate for the ratification of CEDAW. However, when the Democrats lost the majority of the U.S. House and Senate during the midterm elections in 1994, the new Senate Foreign Relations Committee Chair, Jesse Helms (R-NC), sent CEDAW back to the Senate Foreign Relations Committee for consideration, tabling it indefinitely. Clinton would not pursue the ratification of CEDAW. Clinton's rocky relationship with Congress intensified with his impeachment hearings, making the ratification process near impossible. Clinton, at this point, was unwilling to expend his dwindling political capital on securing the rights of women.

During Clinton's tenure in office, Congress both propelled and hampered U.S. human rights policy. With the confidence that the Soviet Union was no longer a threat and that there was no serious prospective enemy to take its place, the new majority freshman congressmen of the 104th Congress sought to reduce government spending on foreign affairs, battle Clinton on every issue of foreign policy, and focus on the domestic economy. With the Republicans gaining control of both houses of Congress after the 1994 midterm elections, Congress enacted legislation that would restrict foreign aid. Congress drastically cut the foreign aid budget and reduced funds to the DOS.

The 104th Congress' "Contract with America"[5] included the National Security Restoration Act, which severely restricted the use of DOD funds for U.N. peacekeeping operations unless specifically authorized by Congress, limited the use of U.S. troops for peacekeeping operations unless the president determines it is in the nation's security interest, and called for the United States to actively assist former Soviet bloc countries to gain full membership in NATO. The National Security Restoration Act also limited U.S. assessments for U.N. peacekeeping activities to 25 percent of the total costs (down from the 31 percent previously assessed), and it outlawed the use of U.S. funds unless U.S. manufacturers and suppliers were given equal opportunity to bid for lucrative peacekeeping contracts to provide equipment, services, and materials. In practice, this meant that the United States expected that its weapon manufacturers would receive at least as much in contracts as the United States paid in assessments. Among Clinton's critics, this fact, along with Clinton's economic priorities in foreign policy, gave rise to suspicions that Clinton may have exploited peacekeeping operations to augment the weapons industries.

Furthermore, the Republican majority of the 104th Congress sought to reduce government spending on foreign affairs—including foreign aid. The newly elected Congress members vowed to reduce the deficit and the overall size of government. Since foreign aid is a discretionary program, it was an easy target. In addition, in the opinion of many conservatives, U.S.-funded international family planning organizations performed or promoted abortions. In 1995, Jesse Helms (R-NC) sought to eliminate the foreign aid bureaucracy altogether since, in his opinion, the money was simply going down a "rat hole." The aid to Israel and Egypt, along with those programs that benefit U.S. business, remained virtually intact in Congress' campaign to reduce foreign aid allocations. And new programs such as those that financed the restructuring of the transitional states of the former Soviet empire siphoned funds from the most poverty-stricken regions. In order to continue to provide increasing amounts of U.S. aid to transition countries, those former Soviet Republics and Eastern European countries moving from communism to capitalist economies, Congress reduced funding for Asia, Africa, and Latin America.

On the other hand, Congress passed several pieces of legislation that benefited the cause of human rights. Congress ratified two international treaties protecting human rights in 1994: the Convention on the Elimination of All Forms of Racial Discrimination, and the Convention against Torture and Other Cruel, Inhuman or Degrading Treatment or Punishment. Congress also ratified the Convention Concerning the Prohibition and Immediate Action for the Elimination of the Worst Forms of Child Labor in 1999. In 1998, Congress established the Human Rights and Democracy Fund (HRDF) under the management of the DRL. The HRDF performs as venture capital, funding risky new or innovative programs, to advance democracy and to promote human rights. The funds are directed to countries, "including many insecure and undemocratic country contexts that are critical to U.S. national security interests" (U.S. DOS website www.state.gov/j/drl/p/).

Due to NGO lobbying and Congressional concern about violations of religious freedom abroad, in 1998, Congress passed the International Religious Freedom Act (IRFA). Hertzke and Philpott credit the creation of the IRFA with "the emergence of a formidable network of determined activists who document persecution and press for vigorous U.S. action" (2000: 75). These groups brought their concerns to Congress to take action. The act is a result of the 1993 International Operations and Human Rights Subcommittee of the House of Representatives hearings on religious persecution. The law establishes an Office on International Religious Freedom within the State Department led by an Ambassador at Large. The duties of this office are to monitor religious persecution and compile an annual report on the religious freedom of foreign countries, advising the President and Secretary of State on religious freedom abroad, and representing the United States with foreign governments on issues of religious freedom. The act also requires the Executive to restrict or deny U.S. foreign assistance to any country that violates the religious freedom of its citizens. The act specifies a list of punitive actions the president must choose from, unless he opts to issue a waiver for countries vital to the U.S. national interest.

In 2000, Congress passed the Trafficking Victims Protection Act (TVPA). The TVPA was designed to combat trafficking in human beings. It also required effective punishment for traffickers, and aimed to protect victims. The Trafficking Act requires annual reports on trafficking as part of the State Department's *Country Reports on Human Rights*. The TVPA sets up a three-tiered measure of governmental compliance: governments that fully comply, governments that do not yet fully comply but are making significant efforts, and governments that do not fully comply and are not making significant efforts. The TVPA reduces presidential options by requiring the imposition of sanctions, and it prohibits nonhumanitarian assistance to foreign governments that tolerate or condone severe forms of trafficking, unless the president waives the prohibition. Clinton strongly opposed the bill's mandatory sanctions, arguing that these requirements limited the president's flexibility to work with countries to improve their efforts to thwart human trafficking. Attached as a rider to the TVPA, the Violence Against Women Act (to combat domestic violence, stalking, and sexual assault) was also passed.

Dietrich (2006) notes that, during this time, Congress shifted from broad legislative restrictions toward targeted legislation. Consequently, the United States could limit aid or trade due to human rights violations without having to call the abusing state a human rights violator. The primary legislation restricting aid to countries with poor human rights records was Section 502B of the Foreign Assistance Act, which denies security assistance to "any country the government of which engages in a consistent pattern of gross violations of internationally recognized human rights." Because this law has been ignored or downplayed by every administration, in 1998 Congress passed the Leahy Laws[6] (also known as the Leahy Amendments), named for its author Senator Patrick Leahy (D-VT). The Leahy Laws prohibit the transfer of assistance or training to foreign security forces that perpetrate gross violations of human rights. The Leahy Laws require a vetting process of individual personnel and whole security, military or police units before they can become eligible for U.S. security assistance. As an indication of the importance of the Leahy Amendments, in 2017, the United States provided approximately $25 billion in security assistance (including ESF) (White House 2016) that was scrutinized by Congress.

There are two versions of the Leahy Law. One covers the State Department's foreign assistance budget, and the other covers the Department of Defense funding. There are several differences between the two amendments. In order to restore funding, the State version requires recalcitrant states to take "effective steps" to bring the responsible persons to justice, while the DOD version requires the state to take "all necessary corrective steps." Unlike the DOD version, the State version of the Leahy Law also has a "duty to inform" clause. The State Department must promptly inform the foreign government why assistance was withheld. Moreover, the DOD includes a waiver that allows for extraordinary circumstances and an exception if the recipient country suffered a disaster or humanitarian crisis. The Leahy Law differs from 502B in that it applies to specific individuals and units within a country (and may not affect the level of assistance to a country) while 502B applies to the aid package to a specific country. The vetting process involves the DRL along with the embassies and regional bureaus. Among the sources of information used by vetters is the DOS's *Country Reports on Human Rights*, along with NGO reports (Serafino et al. 2014). Unfortunately, research indicates that U.S. counternarcotic foreign assistance to Latin American countries, even with the vetting required by the Leahy Laws, has led to an increase in human rights violations (Bartilow and Eom 2009, Bartilow 2014). Recipient governments use U.S. funds to finance the expansion of the state's coercive capabilities to use against drug dealers and smugglers. But these repressive institutions are also used against regular law-abiding citizens.

Clinton disingenuously claimed that the Leahy Laws were unnecessary since the U.S. government already withheld military aid to human rights-abusing military forces. The ultimate problem with the Leahy Laws was, in Sikkink's words, that "the United States discovered that [it] is very difficult to find units with no history of human rights violations" in Colombia, and, one would assume, several other U.S. Third World allies (2004: 200). Clarke et al. (1997: 88) report that security assistance, during Clinton's first term, as a percentage of a declining foreign aid budget, actually increased. This can be explained not only by the White House's acknowledged usefulness of arms transfers, but also by the fact that Egypt's and Israel's share of U.S. military aid was untouched in a declining budget.

When commerce was not an issue, Clinton did undertake some policies that were beneficial to human rights. The Clinton White House advocated the establishment of multilateral war crimes tribunals for the former Yugoslavia (1992) and Rwanda (1994). Clinton endorsed the goal of establishing the International Criminal Court in 1995, and the U.S. delegation was active in shaping the Rome Statute. Clinton revised the State Department's investigation of human rights conditions, now requiring each organizational section within U.S. embassies around the world to contribute to and corroborate human rights information. Section 5 of the *Country Reports on Human Rights* detailing the possibility of discrimination based on race, sex, religion, disability, language, or social status must now include subcategories for the "most vulnerable" within these groupings. In addition, the Clinton Administration supported strengthening human rights institutional mechanisms, particularly the creation of a U.N. High Commissioner for Human Rights, in the U.N. during the 1993 World Conference on Human Rights held in Vienna, Austria.

However, if there were political costs, the Clinton Administration could easily neglect human rights concerns. The 1997 Convention on the Prohibition of the Use, Stockpiling, Production and Transfer of Anti-Personnel Mines and on their Destruction, known as the Ottawa Treaty, proves an illustrative example. The Ottawa Treaty prohibits the use, production, or transfer of antipersonnel mines. States are required to destroy their stockpiles and to clear mined areas within 10 years of becoming a party to the treaty. Land mines indiscriminately take the lives and limbs of thousands of civilians, often children, around the world each year. Clinton, at the behest of the DOD, refused to sign the Convention unless it was amended to allow the United States to use over one million land mines it placed along the North-South Korean border for at least another 19 years (9 years beyond the treaty limit). Clinton and the military believed that removing the land mines would place U.S. soldiers at risk (Shenon 1997).

In sum, Clinton "raised the banner of human rights" but he made no serious attempts to initiate a U.S. human rights policy or to elevate human rights as a policy concern (Kane 2003: 790). The editors of *Foreign Policy* concluded that "Clinton was a champion of human rights. When it suited him" (2000:19). Although human rights rhetoric often suited him, his actions were never as assertive. Clinton often spoke out forcefully on behalf of human rights, in order to satisfy domestic constituencies, but he failed to use the U.S. diplomatic or economic position to secure human rights standards.

Conclusion

The promise of new opportunities after the Cold War for reassessing and redirecting international efforts toward establishing and protecting human rights was squandered. Both President Bush, Sr. and President Clinton must assume responsibility for policies that have wasted post-Cold War opportunities. The policy of containment died with the Cold War, but its continued demise was uncertain during the Bush, Sr. years. The Clinton Administration was the first administration since the end of World War II (WWII) not to inherit the grand strategy of containment. The Clinton Administration was free to fully incorporate human rights and liberal democratic principles into U.S. foreign policy. However, there is little to the "New World Order" or to "Democratic Enlargement" that protected, promoted, or propelled an authentic U.S. human rights policy.

With the end of the Cold War, the United States could reduce its global responsibilities, foreign bases, and deployments, thus saving the

U.S. taxpayer billions of dollars annually. The Bush, Sr. and Clinton Administrations argued that, as the sole remaining superpower, the United States had a moral responsibility to lead and protect the New World Order and to expand market-oriented democratic governments. Therefore, a drastic reduction in military expenditures was not possible. Arms manufacturers and their military and government stooges, fearing a loss of profits, lobbied for increases in military spending, modernizing U.S. weapons systems, greater access to foreign markets, and an expanded and better equipped NATO increasingly involved in humanitarian missions. Between Bush, Sr. and Clinton, the United States deployed troops overseas 21 times. Some of the deployments involved only a few military advisors to assist in the evacuation of U.S. citizens, such as in Liberia in 1990 and 1996, or Albania, Congo, Gabon, and Cambodia in 1997. But others deployed thousands of U.S. service members and cost billions of dollars. The 1991–1992 Gulf War engaged over half a million U.S. soldiers and $54 billion in U.S. treasury (Fischer 2012).

The events of 9/11, as examined in the following chapters, changed both the public's and Congress' attitude toward requiring human rights standards when supplying repressive governments with military aid, perhaps appearing to put a negative end to any progress and advancement of U.S. human rights policy. After September 11, anti-terrorism replaced anti-communism as the primary rationale for granting U.S. bilateral foreign aid. Republicans joined Democrats in the support for higher levels of foreign aid.

Notes

1 The Export-Import Bank provides loans for transactions when commercial banks are unable or unwilling to lend the money due to political or commercial risks.
2 In October 1990, the Congressional Human Rights Caucus held hearings on alleged human rights violations in Kuwait. Tom Lantos (D-CA) and John Porter (R-IL) chaired the Caucus. Nayirah tearfully testified that she witnessed Iraqi soldiers taking newborn infants out of incubators at the al-Addan hospital in Hadiya, leaving them to die on the cold floor. The story was later revealed to be a public relations hoax constructed by the public-relations firm Hill and Knowlton and paid for by the Kuwaiti government. The purpose was to drum up American public support for the war. There is no evidence that the Bush Administration knew of the deception.
3 Somalia was experiencing a severe drought and civil warfare that produced a famine killing over 300,000 people and placing two million in immediate danger of death by starvation. In December 1992, just weeks before Clinton assumed office, Bush, Sr. deployed troops into Somalia on a humanitarian mission, known as Operation Restore Hope. U.S. soldiers were sent to protect food supplies and other relief supplies from being stolen by rival warring clans. However, in October 1993, 19 U.S. soldiers were killed in the Battle of Mogadishu. The American public demanded Clinton withdraw U.S. troops as they were not willing to spend American blood on a humanitarian mission in a country of little strategic or economic importance.

4 The members were arrested and quickly released. The protesters were Major Owens of Brooklyn, Donald M. Payne of New Jersey, Barbara-Rose Collins of Michigan, Ronald V. Dellums of California, Joseph P. Kennedy II of Massachusetts, and Kweisi Mfume of Maryland.
5 The *Contract with America* (1994) was a conservative document/promise by the Republican Party, written by Newt Gingrich and Dick Armey, to shrink the government, lower taxes by reducing the federal budget and eliminating money spent on foreign operations, along with welfare reform. As a result, in the 1994 midterm elections the Republicans gained 54 House seats and 9 Senate seats.
6 The 1997 Leahy Amendment was directed toward prohibiting Colombia counternarcotics aid to any military unit that committed gross violations of human rights. In 1998, it would be extended to all security forces that receive U.S. security assistance.

References

Ryan Barilleaux and Mark Rozell. 2004. *Power and Prudence: The Presidency of George H. W. Bush*. College Station: Texas A&M University Press.

Horace Bartilow and Kihong Eom. 2009. "Busting Drugs While Paying with Crime: The Collateral Damage of U.S. Drug Enforcement in Foreign Countries." *Foreign Policy Analysis* 5(2): 93–116.

Horace Bartilow. 2014. "Drug War's Collateral Damage: U.S. Counter-Narcotic Aid and Human Rights in the Americas." *Latin American Research Review* 49(2): 24–46.

Hal Brands. 2008. *From Berlin to Baghdad: America's Search for Purpose in the Post-Cold War World*. Lexington: University Press of Kentucky.

Douglas Brinkley. 1997. "Democratic Enlargement: The Clinton Doctrine." *Foreign Policy* 106 (Spring): 110–127.

Ron Brown. 1994. Press Briefing by Deputy National Security Advisor Sandy Berger, Secretary of Treasury Lloyd Bentsen, Secretary of Commerce Ron Brown, U.S. Trade Representative Mickey Kantor, and Under Secretary of State for Economic Affairs Joan Spero. 7 December. http://www.presidency.ucsb.edu/ws/index.php?pid=59842

Holly Burkhalter. 1994/1995. "The Question of Genocide: The Clinton Administration and Rwanda." *World Policy Journal* 11(4): 44–54.

George Bush, Sr. 1990. "Out of These Times... a New World Order." *Washington Post*, 12 September.

George Bush, Sr. 1991. "Address to the 46th Session of the United Nations General Assembly in New York City." 23 September. www.presidency.ucsb.edu/ws/index.php?pid=20012&st=&st1=#axzz1nlKZtQcP

George Bush, Sr. 1992. Statement on Signing the Torture Victim Protection Act of 1991, 12 March. www.presidency.ucsb.edu/ws/index.php?pid=20715

George Bush, Sr. and Brent Scowcroft. 1998. *A World Transformed*. New York: Vintage Books.

Duncan Clarke, Daniel O'Conner, and Jason Ellis. 1997. *Send Guns and Money: Security Assistance and U.S. Foreign Policy*. Westport, CT: Praeger.

William Clinton. 1992. "President-Elect Clinton's Foreign Policy Statements December 12, 1991–November 4, 1992." *Foreign Policy Bulletin* 3(3): 2–23.

Bill Clinton. 1994. "Developing a New U.S. Policy Towards Africa." The White House Conference on Africa, 26–27 June. Washington, DC: Africa Regional Services, USIS.

Russell Crandall. 2002. *Driven by Drugs: US Policy toward Colombia*. Boulder, CO: Lynne Rienner Publishers.

John Dietrich. 2006. "U.S. Human Rights Policy in the Post-Cold War Era." *Political Science Quarterly* 121(2): 269–294.

Editors, Foreign Policy. 2000. "Think Again: Clinton's Foreign Policy." *Foreign Policy* 121 (November/December): 18–28.

Beth Fischer. 2012. "Military Power and US Foreign Policy," in *US Foreign Policy*. Michael Cox and Doug Stokes, eds. Oxford: Oxford University Press.

Robert Fiske. 1991. "Free to Report What We're Told," in *Gulf War Reader: History, Documents, Opinions*. Micah Sifry and Christopher Cerf, eds. New York: Random House.

Douglas Frantz and Murray Waas. 1992a. "Testimony on Iraq Export List Is Contradicted." 24 June. LA Times. http://articles.latimes.com/1992-06-24/news/mn-857_1_export-licenses

Douglas Frantz and Murray Waas. 1992b. "Attempted Cover-Up of Aid to Iraq to Be Probed: Congress: Panels to Investigate Administration's Efforts to Restrict Access to Data on Assistance to Hussein." 8 March. LA Times. http://articles.latimes.com/1992-03-08/news/mn-6098_1_saddam-hussein

Al Gore. 1992. "Speech by Senator Al Gore" Center for National Policy. 29 September. www.ibiblio.org/pub/academic/political-science/speeches/clinton.dir/c135.txt

John Goshko. 1994. "Haiti Policy at Impasse." *The Washington Post* A15, 9 March.

Morton Halperin. 1974. *Bureaucratic Politics and Foreign Policy*. Washington, DC: Brookings Institution Press.

Allen Hertzke and Daniel Philpott. 2000. "Defending the Faiths." *National Interest* 61(Fall): 74–81.

Human Rights Watch. 1991. *Human Rights in Post-Invasion Panama: Justice Delayed is Justice Denied*. www.hrw.org/legacy/reports/1991/panama/

Human Rights Watch. 2000. *World Report 2000*. New York: Human Rights Watch.

Robert Kagan. 2001. "Clinton Legacy Abroad: His Sins of Omission in Foreign and Defense Policy." *Weekly Standard* January15: 25–28.

John Kane. 2003 "American Values or Human Rights? U.S. Foreign Policy and the Fractured Myth of Virtuous Power." *Presidential Studies Quarterly* 33(4): 772–800.

Charles Kegley. 1989. "The Bush Administration and the Future of American Foreign Policy: Pragmatism, or Procrastination?" *Presidential Studies Quarterly* 19(4): 717–732.

Douglas Kellner. 1992. *The Persian Gulf TV War*. New York: Routledge.

Brian Lai. 2003. "Examining the Goals of US Foreign Assistance in the Post-Cold War Period, 1991–1996." *Journal of Peace Research* 40(1): 103–128.

Anthony Lake. 1993. "From Containment to Enlargement." Speech given at Johns Hopkins University. 21 September. www.mtholyoke.edu/acad/intrel/lakedoc.html

Anthony Lake. 1994. "American Power and American Diplomacy." *U.S. Department of State Dispatch* 5(46): 766–769.

Julie Mertus. 2004. *Bait and Switch: Human Rights and U.S. Foreign Policy.* New York: Routledge.
Aryeh Neier. 1996/97. "The New Double Standard." *Foreign Policy* 105(Winter): 91–101.
Jim Nichol. 1996. "Central Asia's New States: Political Developments and Implications for US Interests." Congressional Research Service #93108. CRS Issue Brief for Congress.
Joseph Nye. 1992. "What New World Order?" *Foreign Affairs* 71(2): 83–96.
James Oliver. 2004. "The Foreign Policy Architecture of the Clinton and Bush Administrations." *White House Studies* 4(1): 47–69.
Mark Peceny. 1999. *Democracy at the Point of Bayonets.* University Park: Penn State University Press.
Jeffery Ross. 1992. "Religion, Human Rights and Foreign Policy: An Interpretive Essay," in *The New World Order: Rethinking America's Global Role.* Carol Rae Hansen, ed. Flagstaff: Arizona Honors Academy Press.
Boris Rumer. 2002. "The Powers in Central Asia." *Survival* 44(3): 57–68.
Nina Serafino, June Beittel, Lauren Ploch Blanchard, and Liana Rosen. 2014. *"'Leahy Law'" Human Rights Provisions and Security Assistance: Issue Overview.* Washington, DC: Congressional Research Service.
John Shattuck. 2003. *Freedom on Fire.* Cambridge: Harvard University Press.
Philip Shenon. 1997. "Clinton Still Firmly Against Land-Mine Treaty." *New York Times*, 11 October. www.nytimes.com/1997/10/11/world/clinton-still-firmly-against-land-mine-treaty.html
Kathryn Sikkink. 2004. *Mixed Signals: U.S. Human Rights Policy and Latin America.* Ithaca, NY: Cornell University Press.
Charles Tiefer. 1994. *The Semi-Sovereign Presidency: The Bush Administration's Strategy for Governing Without Congress.* Boulder, CO: Westview Press.
United States Department of State. *DRL Programs.* www.state.gov/j/drl/p/
The White House. 1989. "U.S. Policy Toward the Persian Gulf." *National Security Directive* 26, 2 October.
The White House. 2016. Congressional Budget Justification. Foreign Assistance Summary Tables, Fiscal Year 2017. www.state.gov/documents/organization/252735.pdf
Paul Wolfowitz. 2011. "The Gulf War: Twenty Years Later." *Council on Foreign Relations.* www.cfr.org/event/gulf-war-twenty-years-later-0

4 The Prevaricator in Chief
George W. Bush (2001–2009)

Anti-terrorism poses an ongoing challenge for U.S. human rights policy. Due to the unprecedented exceptional threat to the nation due to terrorism, President George Walker Bush supporters called for heightened deference to the executive branch. The threat of terrorism, and the need to employ counterterrorism strategies to "disrupt and destroy" terrorist groups, prompted the United States to employ policies that violate domestic and internationally recognized human rights, many policies of which are still in place today. In order to protect the nation during this period of national peril, a temporary deviation from human rights protections was deemed necessary. This was the trade-off between security and liberty. The price of fighting terrorism was paid by a loss of human rights, not only by the loss of rights of suspected terrorists, but also by citizens of foreign lands. Even the human rights of American citizens were made subordinate to national security concerns, as they started to be surveilled or detained. As has been well documented, George W. Bush's global crusade against an amorphous evil often brushed aside the rule of law, restricted human rights protections for the American people, authorized the torture of foreign citizens, allied the United States with undemocratic regimes, and openly ignored U.S. legislation banning the disbursement of foreign aid to human rights abusing regimes (Keating 2014). Since September 11, anti-terrorism has replaced anti-communism as the primary rationale for granting U.S. bilateral foreign aid. Foreign aid, as evidenced by the copious increases in aid to Iraq and Afghanistan, was a major tool in Bush's war on terrorism. Revelations of torture and prisoner abuse in Abu Ghraib and CIA black sites, along with the recognition that grave human rights abusing countries were among the main recipients of U.S. foreign assistance, opened debates about the role that human rights should play in shaping American foreign policy in the war on terror. Unfortunately, "security and human rights have again increasingly come to be seen as competing rather than reinforcing concerns" (Donnelly and Whelan 2018: 223). Defense contractors and other business concerns, on the other hand, found the global war on terror to be both patriotic and profitable with the huge expansion of the defense and foreign aid budgets.

Olmsted believes that the "origins of George W. Bush's imperial presidency" goes back to the Ford administration. During that time, "the president and his aides worked assiduously—and ultimately successfully—to ensure that the executive branch retained its secrecy and power" (Olmsted 2016: 115). Among Ford's key advisors were Donald Rumsfeld, Dick Cheney, and Bush, Sr. As Mayer (2008) reports, Bush's Vice President Cheney, the "doomsday expert," spent years practicing for the opportunity to expand intelligence agency powers to operate in the shadows or on the "dark side." Cheney and his minions wished to work in deep secrecy, where normal rules of law and decency do not apply. Secretary of Defense Donald Rumsfeld was also "in favor of discarding inconvenient notions of military honor and military law" (Forsythe and McMahon 2017: 94). Under the Bush Administration, the United States, once the champion of human rights and fundamental freedoms, decisively and strategically abridged the human rights of American and foreign citizens within the United States and abroad.

Torture (and Other Violations of Human Rights) and Its Justification

Given the extreme and exceptional threat of terrorism, the Bush Administration believed that derogations from existing human rights and humanitarian norms were justified to protect against security threats. In order to prevent future terrorist attacks, the Bush Administration believed that the United States was required to turn to the dark side where a "lot of what needs to be done here will have to be done quietly, without any discussion, using sources and methods that are available to our intelligence agencies" often using any means at necessary (Cheney 2001: 6–7). Thus, shortly after the attacks on the Twin Towers, Bush signed a classified Memorandum of Notification that gave the Director of the CIA the authority to "undertake operations designed to capture and detain persons who pose a continuing, serious threat of violence or death to U.S. persons and interests or who are planning terrorist activities," thus giving the CIA extensive authority to determine who, why, and how long to detain subjects incommunicado (Senate Select Committee on Intelligence 2014: 11). Later, the CIA decided that it should detain individuals who may be able to provide information on high-value targets but were not high value themselves. In reaction to the Memorandum of Notification, the CIA set up extraordinary rendition programs where enhanced interrogation techniques were used to extract information from detainees. Enhanced techniques are those that "incorporate physical or psychological pressure," including

> the attention grasp, walling, the facial hold, the facial slap (also known as an insult slap), the abdominal slap, cramped confinement, wall standing, stress positions, sleep deprivation beyond 72 hours, the

use of diapers for prolonged periods, the use of harmless insects, the water board, and other such techniques.

(Tenet 2003: 2)

The practice of torture was so widespread and commonplace in Iraq that the International Committee for the Red Cross determined that it was "beyond exceptional cases and might be considered as a practice tolerated by the coalition forces" (ICRC 2004: 3). A Human Rights Watch report on the abuse of detainees in the control or custody of the United States concludes that torture had taken place not solely at Abu Ghraib but rather at several other detention centers worldwide (Brody 2005). These U.S.-sanctioned abuses led to the deaths of several individuals. Army and Navy investigators determined that many of the deaths were confirmed or suspected acts of homicide (Jehl and Schmitt 2005).

Human Rights Watch (2005) believes that Rumsfeld and Tenet created an atmosphere that allowed and even encouraged the use of torture to obtain actionable intelligence. After the 9/11 attacks, the United States launched a secret rendition program, what Owens and Pelizo (2009) refer to as organized state kidnapping, whereby suspected terrorists were secretly captured and covertly transferred to countries known to practice torture. At the same time, the CIA built a global spider's web of clandestine renditions, black sites, and third-country prisons (Marty 2006). CIA-controlled black sites in foreign countries were used to interrogate "high-value" detainees. The purpose of secret detention, according to the Human Rights Council of the U.N., "is to facilitate and, ultimately, cover up torture and inhuman and degrading treatment used either to obtain information or to silence people" (2010: 5). Torture was the all-too-probable outcome of holding unknown persons in undisclosed places in the context of the war against terror. Secret detention or enforced disappearance removes the victim from domestic and international legal protections and safeguards, particularly that of *habeas corpus* and the right not to be tortured. The Open Society Foundation's 2013 detail study on CIA black sites documents the foreign complicity of 54 countries[1] in the capturing, transporting, housing, detaining, interrogating, and torturing of suspected terrorists. Evan a Senate Select Committee on Intelligence (2014) study report on the matter further determined that "CIA personnel, aided by two outside contractors,[2] decided to initiate a program of indefinite secret detention and the use of brutal interrogation techniques in violation of U.S. law, treaty obligations, and our values" (Feinstein 2014: 2). The Senate Select Committee on Intelligence concluded in the Findings and Conclusions section that the "interrogations of CIA detainees were brutal and far worse than the CIA represented to policymakers and others" (2014: 3). The report concluded that Bush's torture program did not produce actionable intelligence, but instead led to false confessions, desperate admissions of fictional plots, and other inaccurate information.

However, rendition would become the preferred method during the last years of the Bush Administration. The CIA began to hand over direct control of secret detention sites, relying on foreign governments to capture, detain, and interrogate midlevel terror suspects or those who sympathized with the suspects. Extraordinary rendition is the transfer of a detainee into the custody of a foreign government with the knowledge that the foreign government may use torture or "enhanced techniques" during interrogation.

Bush Administration's acceptance and authorization of the use of torture are not merely an imprudent decision made in the fog of war, but a deliberate and calculated choice. Lawyers and political leaders within the White House, the DOJ, and the DOD focused on prevaricate deliberation, that is, how to redefine and reinterpret the law to allow the use of torture. DOD and DOJ lawyers went to great lengths to legally defend the Bush Administration's use of human rights abuses as official government policy. The Bybee and Yoo memorandums, collectively known as the Torture Memos, attempted to reinterpret positive domestic and international law (indeed, torture is a violation of *jus cogens* peremptory norm of customary international law) to authorize the use of torture, or cruel, inhuman, and degrading treatment as a legal interrogation method. After conducting a scholarly examination of the evidence, Greenberg and Dratel conclude that the memos were a

> systematic attempt of the US government to authorize the way for torture techniques and coercive interrogations procedures, forbidden under international law with the concurrent express intent of evading liability in the aftermath of any discovery of these practices and policies.
>
> (2005: i)

Deputy Assistant Attorney General in the DOJ, Professor Yoo, authored a 2002 memo that endorsed a reinterpretation of the Geneva Conventions regarding the protection of prisoners from torture. Yoo deceptively claimed that federal law and the U.N. Convention Against Torture prohibiting the use of torture did not apply when interrogating foreigners overseas. Members of al-Qaeda and the Taliban, in Yoo's opinion, were thus not protected by the Conventions because of the unique category of armed conflict, a war on terrorism, in which they were involved. The Geneva Conventions did not cover detainees because they were not soldiers in the conventional sense and they were outside the territory of the United States.[3] In addition, Yoo also claimed that the indefinite detention at Guantánamo Bay did not violate the Eighth Amendment of the U.S. Bill of Rights since detainees were not incarcerated as punishment "in the context of the criminal process" (Waldron 2005: 35). Guantánamo was and continues to be a "legal black hole" or a "netherworld" since it lies outside U.S. territorial boarders. U.S. law did not apply, issues of innocence and proof were deemed irrelevant, and, as a military base, it was possible to restrict prying media's and NGO's eyes from seeing what was occurring (Forsythe and McMahon 2017, Donnelly and Whelen 2018).[4]

The Bybee Memo, written by Jay Bybee of the Office of the Legal Counsel (OLC) in the DOJ for Alberto Gonzalez, counsel to the President, so narrowly defined the meaning of torture that it did not cover all cases of the deliberate infliction of pain. Torture, according to Bybee, only included the infliction of excruciating and agonizing pain that could be associated with death or organ failure. The term "torture" should be "reserved for extreme deliberate and unusually cruel practices, for example, sustained systematic beatings, application of electric currents to sensitive parts of the body and tying up or hanging in positions that cause extreme pain" (Bybee 2002: 16–17). Thus, enhanced interrogation techniques were not torture if international treaties against torture and domestic torture statutes (18 U.S. Code § 2340) were properly interpreted. Furthermore, any restriction against the use of torture was an unconstitutional constraint on the President's power as Commander in Chief. Bybee writes, "Congress may no more regulate the President's ability to detain and interrogate enemy combatants than it may regulate his ability to direct troop movements on the battlefield" (2002: 35). As Commander in Chief, Bybee claims, the president's power to control the conduct of operations during a war is expansive and cannot be limited by Congressional mandate.

Secretary of Defense Donald Rumsfeld used both the Yoo and the Bybee memoranda to legally justify the use of enhanced interrogation techniques (Nowak 2006).[5] Sanders (2018) claims that what is new about the methods of the Bush Administration is that they did not deny, but instead rationalized and produced legal justifications for violations of human rights (what she calls "plausible legality"). The Bush Administration has "aimed to redefine, reinterpret, and when possible, reconstruct the law to accommodate human rights violating practices. It casts cruel, inhuman, and degrading interrogation, indefinite detention and unfair trials, and warrantless surveillance as legal and permissible" (Sanders 2018: 14). Torture and inhuman treatment in interrogations was redefined as lawful and permissible enhanced interrogation and did not rise to the level of prohibited acts.

Suspected terrorists are neither domestic citizens nor foreign soldiers; thus, they can be legally denied the protections of the U.S. Constitution and the Geneva Conventions. The Bush Administration denied prisoners the status of "prisoners of war" under the Third Geneva Convention that required prisoners to have protections according to international humanitarian and human rights law, along with provisions for proper legal assistance. Conversely, they were not considered civilians, which denies them protection under the Fourth Geneva Convention. Instead, they were "enemy combatants" and were held incommunicado, denied contact with a lawyer, and were not given access to a court. Secrecy remained an important aspect of torture policy, and these arguments were only exercised when the world learned of the CIA and DOD's excesses.

Unlike previous administrations that may have been involved with torture, Bush (2006) admitted that the CIA employed "alternative set of procedures" when interrogating detainees. However, Bush deceptively claimed that these alternative procedures were tough but "designed to be safe, to comply with our laws, our Constitution, and our treaty obligations," and vetted by the DOJ and CIA lawyers. Thanks to the deliberate misinterpretation of domestic and international law by the DOJ and CIA lawyers, Bush could claim that "the United States does not torture" (Bush 2006). On the basis of the torture memos written by Yoo and Bybee, the Bush Administration employed enhanced interrogation techniques, developed a global network of extraordinary rendition flights, and maintained secret detention facilities.

Bush's Wars on Terror

Bush's platform during the 2000 presidential campaign promised a humble foreign policy focused on free trade and the development of a new missile attack intervention system. On the campaign trail, Bush underscored his skepticism about nation-building missions. Bush criticized Clinton for his "open-ended deployments and unclear military missions," and he promised to be more circumvented in sending U.S. forces abroad (Bush 1999). There would be no Clinton-style interventionist nation building. This all changed with the September 11 terrorist attacks. The neoconservatives[6] within the Administration saw 9/11 as an opportunity for a profound reworking of American foreign policy priorities. Bush's Secretary of Defense, Donald Rumsfeld, in an interview with the *New York Times*, stated that the events of September 11 provided the United States an opportunity to refashion the world (Rumsfeld 2001). The Bush Administration's promotion of democratic reform took the shape of armed conflict designed to entirely rebuild countries after America's image. The primary objective was to remake Afghanistan and Iraq into fully functioning democratic and capitalist states. The support of democracy soon became associated with the use of force, creating democracies at the point of a gun and through massive amounts of foreign aid, as was exemplified by the wars in Iraq and Afghanistan.

The U.S. war on terror gave extensive and often indiscriminate powers to the executive branch, and it increased the power of the intelligence agencies. The United States engaged in extraordinary rendition, opened secret detention centers known as black sites, conducted mass surveillance of citizens' and non-citizens' activities and communications, and limited judicial protections to suspected terrorists while holding detainees indefinitely without adequate access to the American legal system or the Geneva Conventions.

Presidents often "package" their foreign policy decisions to minimize their challengers' opposition and to garner wide public support. Thus, Halperin et al. report that

> President Bush inflated and slanted intelligence to convince the American public that Iraq was a direct threat to the United States by virtue of its possession of weapons of mass destruction and its support for the al Qaeda terrorist group.
>
> (2006: 80)

Pillar contends that the Bush Administration "cherry picked" data and deliberately distorted evidence, "rather than using the intelligence community's own analytic judgments," in order to persuade Congress and the American public to back his decision to go to war (2006: 24). The Bush Administration even created the Policy Counterterrorism Evaluation Group, housed in the Pentagon, to produce intelligence that supported the administration's determination to attack Iraq. Contrary to the prevarications by the Bush Administration, Iraq was not purchasing uranium ore in Africa, nor was there a strategic alliance between Saddam Hussein and al-Qaeda.[7] These self-serving falsehoods were told to prey on the American public's fear of another terrorist attack and to garner Congressional support for an attack on Iraq.

In addition, the American public was told that the war with Iraq would be quick and inexpensive. Andrew Natsios, head of USAID, gave an interview to Ted Koppel on *Nightline* (April 2003) assuring the American public that the cost to the U.S. taxpayer to rebuild Iraq would be a mere $1.7 billion. Even Rumsfeld found this total to be incredulously small (Ricks 2006). Rumsfeld believed that the Iraq War and reconstruction would be between $50 and $60 billion, a large portion to be paid by other countries and by Iraqi oil revenues. Natsios obviously wanted to keep his job and misrepresented the costs. In 2002, Larry Lindsey, Bush's economic adviser and head of the National Economic Council, estimated that the Iraq War would reach $200 billion. Lindsey was dismissed due to the dispute over the projected costs (Stiglitz and Bilmes 2008).

There were, however, serious conflicting opinions and public clashes between Secretary of State Colin Powell and Secretary of Defense Donald Rumsfeld. Drew called the conflict between Powell and Rumsfeld "unprecedented in their intensity and openness" (2003: 22). Colin Powell, Bush's first Secretary of State, was a force of moderation leading up to the invasion of Iraq. Powell was skeptical about the wisdom of invading Iraq. He thought that the best option was for the United States to build a strong coalition and get U.N. support for U.S. actions. Powell worried that a unilateral invasion of Iraq would split the anti-terrorism coalition.

Powell's views often clashed with the neoconservative advisors on the desirability of unilateral action. Paul Wolfowitz, as Deputy Secretary of Defense, was a strong vocal advocate of attacking Iraq and removing Saddam Hussein from power. Rumsfeld believed that a regime change in Iraq was the key to stability in the Middle East. Moreover, the economic benefits of regime change in Iraq would be great due to the increase in the world's oil supply. Powell, the voice of reason and moderation, was soon marginalized from the inner circle of decision-making.

Bush's personality trait of seeing everything in terms of black and white "tolerates no open disagreement among advisers in other matters. He has fired some members of his administration for raising questions about his policies" (Drew 2003: 22). But Powell was "unsackable" because of his popularity with the American public. In order to ensure enthusiasm for the invasion of Iraq, Rumsfeld restricted the planning to a small group of DOD elite and national security officials, thus eliminating the opinions of anyone who questioned the wisdom, legality, or morality of the invasion. CIA Director Tenet described the decision-making process as a "runaway freight train" (2007: 385) because there was "no formal discussion of alternatives and especially of downsides occurred" (Dobel 2010: 65). Understandably, the military was reluctant to enter into injudicious and inadequately resourced interventions that lacked public support. Halperin et al. (2006) explain that military leaders warned the Bush Administration against going to war with Iraq. Military leaders who thought the invasion, occupation, and recreation of Iraq would require a massive number of troops, treasury, and time were ignored since Rumsfeld believed the operation could be done quickly, with few troops, given the technological sophistication of U.S. military forces.

Powell's State Department was denied participation altogether (Halperin et al. 2006). The fact that the State Department was cut out of planning for the war partially explains the difficulties of the postwar reconstruction period. Planning and resources for postwar or peacekeeping operations were neglected since Bush and his advisors thought that they would be greeted as liberators. There simply was no plan on what to do after "mission accomplished." The Bush Administration anticipated a quick victory in Iraq and failed to plan for postwar reconstruction or anticipate the rise of insurgency.

Bush's war of opportunity, the invasion of Iraq, left thousands of innocent Iraqis dead. The numbers of civilian casualties in the invasion and occupation of Iraq vary widely. Iraq's Ministry of Health's statistical department was ordered to stop counting civilian deaths in late 2003 by command of Iraq's Coalition Provisional Authority, so the data are intermittent and spotty (Associated Press 2003). The Iraqi government has recorded 87,215 war deaths between 2005 and 2009, but it also estimates that the actual number is 10–20 percent higher due to the number of missing and of those who were buried without official records (Gamel 2009).

The Iraq Body Count (IBC) (2010) project has placed the number of civilian deaths at between 99,151 and 108,234 from the years 2003 to 2009. The IBC further reports, using data leaked by WikiLeaks, that the U.S. military recorded 109,032 violent deaths between 2004 and 2009 in Iraq. Of this number 66,081 were civilian, 15,196 were host nation non-civilians, 23,984 were enemies, and 3,771 were friendlies. These figures do not capture the thousands more who have been wounded or died due to the devastating effect of the war on Iraq's infrastructure and economy. Nor does it record the deaths as a result of the insurgency, counterinsurgency, and sectarian violence that followed the disbanding of the military and police forces. The rhetoric of the global war on terror led to the wars in Afghanistan and Iraq, to detention centers and CIA black sites, and to surveillance of both American and foreign citizens around the globe. The U.S. moral authority was tarnished by the snubbing of the rules of war providing protections to combatants.

Coalition of the Willing

The U.S.-led invasion of Iraq in 2003 was not backed by a majority of foreign governments or by world public opinion. Instead, the Bush Administration relied on a hodgepodge of generally small poor countries that were economically dependent on the United States to build the coalition of the willing (COTW).[8] Very few countries joined out of a conviction or concern about the threat posed by Hussein.[9] Foreign aid was a particularly important incentive to support Bush's invasion of Iraq. Newnham concluded that "Many other members of the COTW were also dependent on U.S. aid for their very survival. The 2004 USAID budget showed that 70% of the coalition states received development aid, often in very substantial amounts" (2008: 186). As an example, U.S. foreign aid made up 57 percent of Micronesia's budget. Consequently, there was little doubt that Micronesia would devotedly support Bush's war of opportunity.

Proponents of the U.S.-led war in Iraq believe that the United States provided foreign aid to help defer the costs of supporting the United States. Newman writes that "Egypt and Jordan demanded large payoffs for their unpopular support of the United States, as well as for economic losses caused by the war" (2008: 187). The costs included sending troops, fending off local opponents to the government's decision, the transport, maintenance, and specialized equipment for U.S. allied soldiers, and the normal disruption of trade and tourism associated with war. Aid packages were an important means of reimbursement thereby encouraging states to support the U.S. war effort. The 2003 War Supplemental budget called for an additional

> $74.8 billion in the FY2003 Emergency Supplemental for ongoing military operations in Iraq, postwar occupation, reconstruction and relief in Iraq, *international assistance to countries contributing to the*

war in Iraq or the global war on terrorism, the cost of the continued U.S. presence in Afghanistan, and additional homeland security.
(emphasis mine, Belasco and Nowels 2003: 1)

Iraq coalition countries were handsomely compensated by the Bush Administration with increased economic and military aid (Gibler and Miller 2012).

Critics of the war claim that the United States bought foreign troops and political support in a desperate attempt to legitimize the invasion of Iraq. The critics' claims are bolstered by the fact that the foreign troops were contributed at symbolic or token numbers. South Korea provided the greatest number of troops (outside the United States or Great Britain) with only 3,300 troops. Poland was the second largest contributor with 2,500 troops, while Estonia sent only 31 troops, Macedonia provided 37 troops, and Albania 70. Nearly half of the coalition partners were members in name only, providing symbolic diplomatic support. But they did not provide troops on the ground. In any case, the Bush Administration demanded only token diplomatic support from the countries in question, and the United States did not require any substantial military commitment. States that supported the U.S. efforts in the war on terrorism were assured large amounts of U.S. foreign aid, and they could be sure of Washington's silence if they chose to violate the human rights of their citizens. The Bush Administration easily overlooked an abusive country's human rights record[10] since it wanted wide support for the U.S. efforts in the war on terror. Bush routinely provided waivers for states that abused the human rights of their citizens, justified by the abuser's pledge to support the U.S. war on terror. In the war against global terrorism, the United States claimed it had to partner with states with dubious human rights practices and records, and it ended up providing these violators with foreign aid. After all, in this perilous post-9/11 world, many analysts and government officials expressed the belief that the U.S. economic, military, and strategic support should not be hampered by idealistic concerns for human rights. Thus, the Bush Administration played "fast and loose with the international law of human rights" (Forsythe 2011: 776).

Women's Rights as Validation for the Global War on Terror

Women's rights were another tool in Bush's disparaging of the Taliban and the terrorist organization al-Qaeda, led by Osama Bin Laden. Laura Bush, explaining her husband's commitment of force against Afghanistan, stated that "The fight against terrorism is also a fight for the rights and dignity of women" (2001). After the events of 9/11, advancing women's rights and concern about the treatment of women in Afghanistan gained rhetorical support from members of Congress.

Saving women from oppression under the Taliban government served U.S. strategic interests in order to build support for the War on Terror (Tickner 2002, Young 2003). The newfound concern for women's rights was a political campaign to rally domestic and international support for the war on terror. In the 2002 State of the Union Address, George W. Bush declared: "The last time we met in this chamber the mothers and daughters of Afghanistan were captives in their own homes, forbidden from working or going to school. Today women are free, and are part of Afghanistan's new government" (Bush 2002b). Laura Bush reaffirmed her husband's justification during her speech to the U.N. Commission on the Status of Women where she stated:

> Afghanistan under the Taliban gave the world a sobering example of a country where women were denied their rights and their place in society. Today, the world is helping Afghan women return to the lives they once knew.
> (L. Bush 2002)

Advancing women's rights in Afghanistan and Iraq gained support from members of Congress. Regrettably, the call to emancipate and empower women was an opportunistic attempt to strengthen support for the wars. It was not intended to secure rights for women. Feminists warned that

> the Bush Administration appears to have hijacked the issue [of women's human rights] for its own ends, the notion that women's rights could be delivered through the use of stealth bombers and through the funding of high profile initiatives requires extra careful scrutiny.
> (Ware 2007:181)

Afghan women were portrayed as passive victims of the Taliban and al-Qaeda who had to be saved by American soldiers. Hunt (2002) believes that the Bush Administration's use of women's rights as justification for the war was meant to conceal the effects of the war on women. Afghan women faced the all-too-common gender-specific weapon of war, that is, rape, as a form of retaliation when one or the other side took control of a region. The U.S. ally in Afghanistan in the fight against the Taliban, the United Front, formerly known as the Northern Alliance, "have sexually assaulted, abducted, and forcibly married women during the armed conflict, ... and have [placed] severe restrictions placed on their liberty and fundamental freedoms" (Human Rights Watch 2001). Moreover, concern for women's rights did not extend to their right to health. Despite the fact that the DOS's inquiry into the U.N. Population Fund concluded that the organization was not using resources to fund abortions, the Bush Administration continued to withhold Congressionally allocated assistance, thus depriving women of urgently needed reproductive health care

(Schweid 2004). In 2001, the lifetime risk of maternal death for an Afghan woman (at 7.96 percent) was over 8 times the world average (0.92 percent) and nearly 400 times greater than the risk for U.S. women (0.02 percent) (U.N. World Development Indicators). While the maternal mortality rate, in 2001, was 1,050 per 100,000 live births compared to the U.S. ratio of 13 per 100,000 live births (U.N. World Development Indicators). Nor did the Bush Administration's concern for women's rights extend to the women in Saudi Arabia and Kuwait, traditional U.S. allies. Indeed, Smith (2002) notes that the Taliban's religious police force, known as the Department for Promotion of Virtue and Prevention of Vice, was modeled after Saudi Arabia's Committee for the Promotion of Virtue and Prevention of Vice. Over the years, the rights of Afghan women have slowly and marginally improved. However, "there is a looming fear that women's rights will be negotiated away in the quest to end the war" (Lemmon 2011).

Foreign Aid as a Tool in the Global War on Terror

During the Cold War, foreign aid was driven by anti-communist motives. Pro-American dictators could count on substantial U.S. foreign assistance despite widespread human rights abuses. The post–Cold War era, many hoped, would bring a peace dividend in the form of reduced U.S. foreign assistance with a focus on development and basic human needs. Yet, just a decade later, with the 9/11 attacks, aid would reemerge as a primary strategic tool in U.S. foreign policy. Economic aid is meant to win the hearts and minds of the people by improving their lives and livelihoods, and fostering greater levels of public cooperation, thereby discouraging public support of insurgents. Military aid gives the government greater resources to fight terrorist organizations at the behest of the United States. Azam and Thelen show that the allocation of foreign aid is a method of "delegating the fight against terrorism to the recipient governments within their sphere of influence… what matters for aid policy is not its impact on potential terrorists but its effects on the recipient governments" (2010: 254). The U.S. links aid to encourage recipient governments to implement enforcement and prevention efforts against terrorism. Nevertheless, the Foreign Assistance Act is still a legally binding law that instructs the President to formulate military and economic assistance programs to promote human rights. During the Bush Administration, in the words of Callaway and Matthews, foreign aid was "not used as leverage to entice improvement in human rights conditions. In fact, it is given with no strings attached to some of the most egregious violations of human rights worldwide in the name of national security" (2008: 63). Foreign aid was to serve counterterrorism objectives regardless of the human rights consequences.

Upon entering office, Bush was skeptical of foreign assistance. But after the terrorist attacks, he became a strong advocate and consequently increased the U.S. foreign aid budget to histrionic levels. Although the

United States has always used foreign aid strategically, 9/11 shifted the role of foreign aid as a tool of foreign policy. In 2004, the U.S. Office of Management and Budget declared that "the United states will provide extensive assistance to states on the front lines of the anti-terror struggle, both in terms of financial assistance and training and support for allied governments" for "assistance to countries around the world that have joined us in the war on terrorism" (OMB 2004). In particular, the document singles out the frontline states of Afghanistan, Colombia, Jordan, Pakistan, and Turkey as crucial to the global war on terror.

Following the tragedy of September 11, Congressional support for foreign aid increased. Several staunch conservatives, including Senator Jesse Helms, who had previously been foreign aid's biggest and loudest opponents, suddenly became strong supporters of foreign aid and debt relief. Republicans now joined Democrats, many of whom had long supported the granting of foreign assistance, in the support for higher levels of foreign aid. The purpose of foreign aid was twofold: to support governments backing the U.S. government's war on terror, and to reduce the appeal of terrorist ideology. Foreign aid could be used to encourage coalition building while facilitating military operations and coordination between the United States and its allies in the global war on terror. But foreign aid would also be used to reduce poverty and inequality, thought to be the source of terrorist activity (Bush 2002a). Bush (2002a) stated at the U.N. International Conference on Financing for Development summit in Monterrey, Mexico that "We fight against poverty because hope is an answer to terror." And providing people with a positive future would lessen their desire to embrace a radical Islamic ideology.

The Bush Administration initiated a transformation of the foreign aid process. Under Bush, the volume of foreign aid increased dramatically. Bush created two new economic aid programs, the Millennium Challenge Corporation and the President's Emergency Program for AIDS Relief, in addition to greatly increased military aid. Furthermore, the DOD assumed a major role in the allocation of development aid independent of the USAID and the DOS. The State Department considers foreign aid to be a diplomatic tool while the USAID believes that foreign aid is a necessary tool for international development. The DOD, on the other hand, believes that foreign aid is simply another tool for security and power, either to subdue or to subjugate. This often leads to clashing organizational missions within the same country programs undercutting the effectiveness and efficiency of U.S. aid.

Economic Aid

George W. Bush described himself as "compassionate conservative," which he defined as "a conservatism that cares about them [the poor], and makes a concerted effort to help them bring lasting change into their lives" (2000: xi) through government support and encouragement of faith-based and charitable organizations' programs. It is compassionate to increase the levels of U.S. foreign aid, and it is conservative to require the recipient government to implement reforms that reduce corruption, open their markets, observe the rule of law, and respect human rights, as required by FAA legislation (Bush 2002a). Bush also attempted to implement "hope" as an answer to terror. To fulfill this objective, development aid also increased from the 2002 level of $10 billion to $15 billion by 2006 by creating the Millennium Challenge Account (MCA).[11] The MCA was established in 2004 to provide economic aid to countries that fulfill eligibility criteria in three areas: good governance (promoting democracy, fighting corruption, respecting human rights, and adhering to the rule of law), economic freedom (free market economy, fostering enterprise and entrepreneurship, and promoting open markets and sustainable budgets), and social investment (providing adequate health care and education) (Tarnoff 2014). The MCA has been said to represent a significant change in the allocation of U.S. economic assistance. Indeed, the MCA funds are not tied to procuring goods and services from U.S. vendors.

President Bush's Emergency Plan for AIDS Relief (PEPFAR) was also created in 2003 and renewed in 2008. PEPFAR was designed to support an array of HIV/AIDS prevention, treatment, and care activities. PEPFAR "elevated HIV/AIDS into the mainstream discourse on evolving US global security interests in the post-September 11 era" (Morrison 2007: 68). This program, "the largest commitment by any nation to combat a single disease" (Salaam-Blyther 2014: 1), has been credited with historic declines in AIDS-related deaths and new HIV infections (Oxfam America 2014: 13). The PEPFAR called for $15 billion to be spent over five years to combat the HIV/AIDS epidemic. The 2008 renewal called for a doubling of funding, that is, an additional $30 billion over the next five years.

It should come as no surprise that aid to Africa was incorporated into the counterterrorism agenda of the Bush Administration as the weak and failing states of Africa were a haven for al-Qaeda operatives and other violent extremists. Using the words of Miles, "With respect to Africa, poor nations with high percentages of Muslim populations have been reconceptualized as potentially dangerous breeding grounds or oases for Islamist extremism" (2012: 30). The African focus of PEPFAR "would serve the duel purposes of meeting global moral obligations and stemming new transnational security threats....[while] counterbalancing the ongoing US military intervention in Afghanistan and the coming intervention in Iraq" (Morrison 2007: 71). The AIDS epidemic was undermining both development and stability in Africa. Africa would soon see a rise of extremism. The DOD implemented PEPFAR programs because doing so supported national security and regional stability, and it "provides goodwill humanitarian aid capable of countering terrorist recruiting efforts" (Ingram 2011: 669). The virus can also erode the combat readiness of African troops, thereby lowering their potential value as a partner in the global war against terror (Heinecken 2003). The U.S. Africa Command (Africom), founded in 2007, was in need of regional partners. An integral part of Africom's mission was to protect U.S. national security by securing political influence, training allies in fighting terror, and protecting access to the growing oil production in Sub-Saharan Africa. Thus, Africa would be a major recipient of Bush's newly created foreign aid initiatives in an effort not only to fulfill the President's commitment to "compassionate conservatism," but also to secure access to African oil and other national resources (Owusu 2007) and to prevent Africa from becoming a safe haven for terrorists. Foreign aid is often the main source of external finance in many African countries. Thus, the United States could greatly influence the policies and behaviors of the recipient country.

Critics believe that the Bush Administration's sudden and unparalleled commitment of resources to improve the life conditions of the poor and ill was an attempt to offset growing criticism of his Iraq policy and to improve America's image as a result of the revelations of his use of enhanced interrogation techniques, black sites, and extraordinary renditions. Certainly, saving innocent victims from the consequences of the AIDS epidemic would further his claim to be a compassionate conservative.

Since 9/11, ESFs (see Chapter 2) funding's primary purpose has been to support U.S. strategically important countries in the war on terror. The president can use economic aid to support or influence strategically important states in lieu of military aid when military aid is politically infeasible, thus avoiding a congressional debate on the ethical, moral, or political consequences of providing military aid to recalcitrant countries. Furthermore, the new direction of U.S. foreign aid "will divert aid away from the poorest countries and communities, and weaken donors' commitment to poverty reduction" (Oxfam 2005: 49). Woods (2005) believes that the global war on terror was funded in part by diverting funds away from developmental purposes. Not only would the share of military aid to total aid increase, but also would a larger share of economic aid be directed toward ESF programs to recipients such as Iraq, Afghanistan, Pakistan, and other strategically important countries. Statistical studies confirm this fear. The initiation of the war on terror redirected and refocused U.S. foreign aid policy. Poor geopolitically irrelevant countries received a declining share of economic aid in an increasing foreign aid budget (Fleck and Kilby 2010, Lai 2003).

Military Aid

Military aid was expanded to include what was once considered strategically irrelevant countries. In order to provide aid to coalition partners and "frontline" allies in the global war against terror, the Bush

Administration made extensive use of the "extraordinary circumstances" exception found in Section 502B of the Foreign Assistance Act. Section 502B of the Foreign Assistance Act states that no security assistance will be provided to any country that engages in a consistent pattern of gross violations of internationally recognized human rights, unless the president submits to Congress a detailed explanation of what the extraordinary circumstances entail. The majority of U.S. foreign aid, during the Bush Administration, was directed to support military operations in Iraq and Afghanistan, and for the global war on terror.

The Bush Administration's use of military aid as a tool for fighting terrorism is clearly seen in the increase of foreign aid to Iraq and Afghanistan. Foreign aid, traditionally an instrument of national security, was to become the cornerstone of the war on terror. After the terrorist attacks of September 11, foreign aid was also closely linked to the U.S. military operations in Afghanistan and Iraq. The largest assistance program since the Marshall Plan, which helped rebuild Western Europe after World War II, was to reconstruct Iraq. The majority of the funds allocated to the reconstruction of Iraq were held in the Iraq Relief and Reconstruction Fund, which was directly controlled by the President and managed by the newly created Coalition Provisional Authority. The Iraq Reconstruction costs were budgeted to over $20 billion in fiscal year 2004 alone, thus doubling the amount of U.S. bilateral foreign aid given to the rest of the world (Tarnoff and Nowels 2004). The Congressional Research Service reports that, from 2002 to 2010, reconstruction aid to Afghanistan and Iraq was approximately $104 billion (Tarnoff and Lawson 2018). The reconstruction costs of Iraq alone, from 2002 to 2013, were over $60 billion (CBS News 2013). Lubold (2017), of the *Wall Street Journal*, reports that the cost for the global war on terror, fought in Afghanistan, Iraq, Syria, and Pakistan, was $5.6 trillion from 2001 to 2017, and these costs continue to rise today.

Political stability is seen as a prerequisite for U.S. security interests, so the provision of arms to a government that may use force against its citizens to remain in power can be justified. The Bush Administration believed that those developing states that are home to or targets of terrorist groups should not have to fight terrorism without the support of the United States. By militarily supporting a pro-American foreign government, the United States could prevent the recipient state from falling prey to terrorist activity. The provision of military aid, the advocates of Bush's foreign policy objectives believed, simply compensated coalition partners for the costs expended in eliminating the global scourge of terrorism. Developing countries that were coalition members in the global war on terrorism averaged over $130 million in military aid, while countries that were not members of the U.S.-led coalition received a mere $18 million in U.S. bilateral military aid. Equally revealing is the fact that countries identified by the State Department as being targets of or home to terrorist organizations received an average of $190 million in U.S. bilateral military aid. Developing states confronted with terrorism organizations should not have to choose between providing their citizens social services and protecting them from terrorists. U.S. military aid is necessary for foreign governments to counter terrorist insurgents. As the oft-repeated popular refrain clearly states, "it is better to fight terrorists over there than over here." Unsurprisingly, military aid distribution was greatly influenced by the recipient country's strategic potential in the war on terror.

Of particular importance was Pakistan's geostrategic position. Despite being ruled by a military dictatorship reliant on the abuse of human rights to maintain control, Musharraf's regime received substantial economic and military assistance from the United States. Pakistan was, after all, a frontline ally in the fight against terrorism, and its geographic location was extraordinarily advantageous. Other accommodating countries received similar strategic benefits. Rumer (2002) argues that the poor human rights conditions in Kazakhstan, Kyrgyzstan, Tajikistan, Turkmenistan, and Uzbekistan became even less of a concern after 9/11. These countries' records of repression and their dismal human rights conditions did not present a barrier to the Bush Administration's continued military and economic relations. In fact, the war on terror made Central Asia even more important in U.S. geo-security policy, thus guaranteeing these brutal regimes an abundant source of economic and military assistance.

Many of the transition countries, most notably Romania and Poland, have been recently accused of being involved in a "'spider's web' of human rights abuses" resulting from the CIA rendition scandal (Silva 2006). In the opinion of Bush's critics, these countries were being paid off for their questionable and illegal practices. The transition states were eager to provide support for the U.S. wars on terrorism and the occupation of Iraq, and they were rewarded for their cooperation with military aid. Ten of the transition countries, dubbed the "New Europe," were signatories of the Vilnius letter that diplomatically supported the invasion of Iraq.[12] Large military aid packages were a reward for these countries' political, diplomatic and military support.

Military aid is a political instrument of U.S. foreign policy allowing the U.S. access and influence in the domestic and foreign affairs of other states. One of the most effective tools in U.S. human rights policy is the threat or actual denial or reduction of foreign aid. Burgermann concludes that a military regime's dependence on U.S. foreign aid and the threat of the loss of that aid can be major factors in the reduction of human rights abuses and, often, can provoke a return to democracy (2004). Incidentally, this was also a proclaimed foreign policy goal of the Bush Administration. Unsurprisingly, military aid distribution was greatly influenced by the recipient country's support for the U.S. war on terror.

However, and in blatant opposition to the Bush Administration's global campaign for democracy, the United States squandered its opportunities to advance human rights by failing to implement U.S. legislation tying the distribution of military aid to the country's human rights records.

Critics believe that the Bush Administration's provision of military aid was a carrot or bribe to buy a coalition to support U.S. efforts in fighting the war on terrorism focused on the regime change in Iraq (Gilfeather 2003). The U.S. invasion of Iraq was profoundly unpopular in many countries. Large aid packages guaranteed that foreign governmental leaders would defy public opposition and support the war. The White House justified military aid as "providing vitally needed equipment, supplies, and training" for "our partners and allies in operations in Iraq and the ongoing war against terrorism" (Federation of American Scientists 2004). Proponents claim that the increase in military aid was necessary to offset the costs for willing coalition members who may face high domestic political and economic backlash because of their support of the U.S. foreign policy.

Providing the means for a government to brutally control its population is likely to result in blowback. The Bush Administration's reliance on military aid to fight the global war on terrorism would backfire, generating anti-American sentiments that could actually aid further terrorist recruitment (Johnson 2003). The United States cannot win the war on terrorism if it loses the hearts and minds of the common citizen at home and abroad. The abuse of U.S. foreign aid, providing the tools for a despot's repression of his citizens, was a political blunder, one that ultimately would be contrary to the security interests of the United States. As Human Rights Watch concludes, "when the United States disregards human rights, it undermines that human rights culture and thus sabotages one of the most important tools for dissuading potential terrorists" (January 2005). The events of 9/11 and the subsequent global war on terror led to a reduction or elimination of human rights protections, for both foreign and U.S. citizens, in the name of national security.

DOD's Increasing Role in Foreign Aid

Inexplicably, the DOD became a donor and administrator of development and humanitarian aid. The DOD established its authority in the provision of development aid via Defense Department Directive 3000.05, *Military Support to Stability, Security, Transformation, and Reconstruction (2005)*, which declared that stability and development operations were core missions on a par with combat operations. Thus, along with its traditional control over military assistance, the DOD under the Bush Administration administered and dispensed billions of dollars in U.S. economic and development aid (Spear 2016). Prior to September 11, the DOD controlled 3.5 percent of U.S. economic and development aid. In 2005, the

DOD disbursed 22 percent of U.S. economic aid (Lancaster 2008).[13] The DOD's incursion into traditional development activities had many worried that short-term security concerns would dominate U.S. development policies and long-term diplomatic goals. The DOD's reconstruction and stability programs faced severe bureaucratic resistance from the DOS and USAID because the increased role of DOD came at the expense of the State Department and USAID in administering and implementing foreign aid. The State Department and USAID claimed that DOD's programs were redundant of their own well-established programs. The newly created and controlled DOD security programs allowed the DOD to expand its jurisdiction over foreign assistance justified once again by the need to fight the war on terror. However, "defense-funded programs are *not* governed by the Foreign Assistance Act and therefore *not subject to the human rights and democracy restrictions* therein (with the exception of the Leahy Law)" (emphasis mine, Withers 2005: 6). These programs duplicated the existing security and development assistance programs governed by the Foreign Assistance Act.

Control over the billions of dollars of U.S. aid to Iraq caused strife between the DOS and the DOD, leading to several heated exchange between Powell and Rumsfeld (Perlez 2003). Spear (2016) believes that the DOD appropriation and control over U.S. economic and development aid was due to the bureaucratic weakness of the USAID and its inability to respond quickly to the post-9/11 security needs of the United States. The USAID's lack of capacity can also be attributed to the lack of funding commensurate with the demands made upon it.[14] A reduction in staff led to a loss of expertise, thereby limiting the agency's technical competency and making it dependent on the better staffed and funded DOD (Atwood et al. 2008). The DOD simply had a greater organizational capacity than either the USAID or the DOS. In addition, security in Iraq and Afghanistan was often too dangerous for USAID or State Department personnel to operate. Provincial Reconstruction Teams (PRTs) were civilian-military units designed to aid in the reconstruction of Afghanistan and Iraq. PRTs were set up and staffed by the DOD, along with development experts and State Department diplomats, to fund projects related to development (Lancaster 2008). However, many of the PRTs could not recruit civilian personnel to staff the units. In the turf battle for control over foreign aid, the DOD was the winner, the DOS a far second, and the USAID the clear loser (Spear 2016).

According to Lancaster (2008), the 2006 National Defense Authorization Act (NDAA) in effect allowed the DOD to set up its own military assistance program. Section 1206 of the NDAA permits the Pentagon to use up to $300 million of its own funds to train and equip foreign military forces in counterterrorism and stability operations. Section 1206, unlike existing military aid programs such as FMF and the IMET program (see Chapter 1), does not require the DOD to work with the DOS in determining recipients or levels of funding. The DOD has a freehand in determining the type, amount, and recipient of its aid. DOD's aid programs are often not subject to Congressional earmarks, thus providing the DOD with a freehand to determine which projects get funded. In addition, oversight and reporting requirements are minimal, with the DOD determining if the funds are spent successfully.

Congressional Actions and Inactions

Congress rarely enacts significant constraints on a president's use of military force if his party controls Congress (Bradley and Morrison 2012). And it is even less likely when the Congress and the American public are intimidated by fears of future terrorist attacks. The partisan composition of Congress can increase the independence and power of the president. For the first six years of Bush's two terms in office, the Republican Party controlled both the House and the Senate. "With this control," write Howell and Pevehouse, "they [Republicans] managed to limit legislative hearings about the Iraq War, squelch initiatives to establish fixed timetables for the return of troops, and temper legislative efforts to amend or overturn various aspects of the president's military and diplomatic agenda" (2007: 229).

Congress passed several pieces of legislation relating to terrorism and counterterrorism, the most notable being the USA Patriot Act, at the behest of the President. Explaining the relationship between human rights, security, and foreign policy, Donnelly and Whelan write: "human rights are about protecting the citizen from the state. National security is about protecting the state from its (perceived) enemies...the rights of citizens may need to be sacrificed" (2018: 222). Legislation was drafted by the DOJ that dangerously encroached on the civil liberties guaranteed by the Bill of Rights. The Patriot Act amended the 1978 Foreign Intelligence Security Act, thus expanding the U.S. government's surveillance powers. The Patriot Act granted federal agencies broad powers to conduct searches, to use electronic surveillance, and to detain suspected terrorists. The introduction to the act states that its purpose is to "To deter and punish terrorist acts in the United States and around the world, to enhance law enforcement investigatory tools, and for other purposes" (Public Law 107–56).

The Patriot Act gave the federal government the authority to initiate covert searches known as "sneak-and-peak searches" in a person's home, office, or vehicle without the person's knowledge. The Patriot Act also allowed for "roving wiretaps" whereby the surveillance order attaches to the target rather than to the communication device. In the past, if a target changed phones, the government agency would have to seek a new surveillance order. The government can now conduct searches and wiretaps without having to show probable cause of criminal activity. In addition, the Patriot Act permitted the government to freeze the assets of any person under investigation, providing secret evidence to a closed session court (Cole 2004). Thus the government has unfettered access to personal, business, and other records under the Patriot Act. The government can collect an individual's financial, phone, travel, medical, and even library records. This provision is not restricted to those believed to be an "agent of a foreign power," but rather applies to ordinary Americans. Furthermore, it is a crime for the entity ordered to produce the records to inform the individual that his/her records were requested.

In the rush and hysteria to pass the Patriot Act, Congress spent less than one day debating provisions of the 343-page document that significantly changed more than 15 existing laws (O'Connor and Rumann 2003). Attorney General John Ashcroft described the new sweeping law enforcement powers that excessively curtail civil liberties as a "careful, balanced, and long overdue improvements to our capacity to combat terrorism, it is not a wish list: It is a modest set of essentials" (2001: 1). The Act passed the House on October 24, 2001, by a vote of 357 to 66, and it passed the Senate the next day, by a vote of 98 to 1. The Patriot Act was signed into law by President George W. Bush on October 26, 2001. The bill was renewed with few substantive amendments on March 2, 2006.

According to O'Connor and Rumann (2003), opponents suggest that the Patriot Act is a wish list of new law enforcement powers, not narrowly focused on combating terrorism, that Congress had rejected in the past as too invasive. Senator Russ Feingold, the lone dissenting vote in the Senate over passage of the Patriot Act, warned that "the Administration's proposed bill contained vast new powers for law enforcement, some seemingly drafted in haste and others that came from the FBI's wish list that Congress has rejected in the past" (as quoted in O'Connor and Rumann 2003: 1706n233). Representative Robert L. Barr Jr. also remarked on the speed of passage and desire of law enforcement to take advantage of the circumstances to expand their law enforcement powers. In fact, the Patriot Act allowed federal authorities to go on fishing expeditions against U.S. citizens with no ties to terrorism. The Patriot Act is still being used against those suspected of garden-variety crimes (Isikoff 2003).

As a result of 9/11, congressional oversight declined dramatically. The rally-around-the-flag phenomenon united political parties, the media, governmental institutions, the general public, interest groups, and even the international community. Unfortunately, it also muted congressional criticism and prevented a thoughtful challenge to Bush's foreign policy initiatives. Congress feared being held responsible for any subsequent terrorist attacks and permitted the expansion of presidential powers forfeiting their right to challenge and scrutinize presidential actions. Congressional members were forced to either support the president or be labeled unpatriotic. But, "the making of sound U.S. foreign policy," write Ornstein and Mann, "depends on a vigorous, deliberative, and often combative process that involves both the executive and the legislative branches" (2006: 82). Congress failed to fulfill its constitutional responsibilities as partner and co-collaborator in the making of foreign policy. Consequently, "Bush triumphed over a cowed Democratic leadership" (Kane 2003: 795).

Ohaegbulam (2007) believes that Congress abdicated one of its primary responsibilities, that is, its oversight of the Bush Administration's waging of the global war on terror. Ignoring the evidence, Congress allowed itself "to be persuaded by unsubstantiated claims by a hawkish Bush administration about threats from a nuclear-armed Iraq to grant the administration the authority to make a decision that was constitutionally and traditionally theirs" (Ohaegbulam 2007: 5). The American public was split on whether or not to go to war with Iraq, with 40 percent in favor of war, another 40 percent approving of the war if it was legitimized by the U.N., and the final 20 percent against the war (Ohaegbulam 2007). Yet, U.S. Congressmen and women, as representatives of the people, ignored the will of the people and acquiesced to the wishes of the President. Congress gave to the President absolute discretion to wage a preventive war against Iraq. Because of Congressional acquiescence and deference to the president, Congress was reduced to the role of bystander with little authority to do anything but pay the bills accompanying the invasion and occupation of Iraq. The Bush Administration forcefully pushed for unilateral presidential powers and the Congress acquiesced.

At the same time, Congress also took steps to secure human rights protections. For example, Congress ratified the Optional Protocol to the Convention on the Rights of the Child on the Involvement of Children in Armed Conflicts (in 2002) and Optional Protocol to the Convention on the Rights of the Child on the Sale of Children, Child Prostitution and Child Pornography (in 2002). However, due to conservative resistance, it did not ratify the Convention on the Rights of the Child. Congress also passed the 2005 Detainee Treatment Act (DTA) as an amendment to the DOD Appropriations bill for 2006. The DTA of 2005, sponsored by Senator John McCain, establishes a uniform standard for the treatment of detainees and prohibits interrogation practices not authorized in the Army's intelligence interrogation field. However, this does not apply to those detainees housed in non-DOD facilities or who are in the custody of the CIA (Suleman 2006). In addition, the U.S. *Army Field Manual on Intelligence Interrogation* does not cover those who are detained under criminal or immigration law. Eggen and Tate (2005) of the *Washington Post* report that many of the suspected terrorists are convicted of criminal violations, such as making false statements or impeding an investigation, therefore making this protection inapplicable to the majority of detainees. The DTA also expands the geographical scope of protection. Suleman (2006) claims that the DTA can easily be circumvented by the use of extraordinary rendition whereby the detainee is no longer in the custody or effective control of the U.S. government. The DOD resisted being limited to the interrogation techniques found in its own field manual. Di Rita, a Pentagon spokesperson, wrote that "restricting techniques to those published in the manual would make it still easier for captured terrorists to anticipate and resist interrogations" (2005: 12a).

Bureaucratic Policymaking and the Presidential Agenda

Katyal (2006) believes that during the Bush Administration the political model of governance was legislative abdication whereby the executive branch rather than the legislative branch was making the law. The separation of powers was no longer between the executive and the legislative branches but between the different executive agencies. Civil servants and issue experts who are beholden to no administration populate the bureaucracy. Political appointees, on the other hand, are generally less experienced but are loyal to the president, often seeking to advance his agenda. Katyal (2006) explains the virtues of internal divisions among the agencies within the executive bureaucracy. These agencies have differing missions and goals and must negotiate in order to fulfill a vague and abstract presidential objective. Katyal writes: "because each department serves a different core constituency, the overlap should produce internal checks" and, in theory, produce the best policy option (2006: 2326). The entrenched bureaucracy is viewed as a benevolent constraining force to an otherwise imperial presidency providing an internal separation of powers when the Congress falls short. However, this assumption only works if the differing agencies hold similar power and prestige. In the realm of foreign policy, and in particular in foreign aid policy, the DOD certainly holds greater power and resources than does the USAID or even the DOS. General David Barno, Commander of the Combined U.S. Forces 2003–2005, was reported as saying "The war seemed to be between Defense and State and not the US and the Taliban. The bureaucratic turf battles back in Washington were tangible, they were extraordinary" (as quoted in Keane and Wood 2016). As history has shown, the negotiations over aid projects and programs are one-sided, favoring the DOD.

The growth in the use of political appointments and the mistrust of the bureaucracy stems from the perception that the bureaucracy seeks to implement its own agenda, often at the expense of presidential goals. Thus, in order to achieve its objectives and to control the bureaucracy, the president would appoint loyalists rather than experts to key positions. Bureaucrats whose loyalty to the president was uncertain would be transferred, pressured to resign, or excluded from the decision-making process. Moynihan and Roberts write that "Efforts to assert tighter political control of the federal bureaucracy, revived during the Ronald Reagan Administration, were pursued to an extreme under Bush. Loyalty triumphed over competence in selection, and political goals displaced rationality in decision making" (2010: 572). Although the politicization of bureaucratic management has a long history in the United States, in the opinion of Moynihan and Roberts, "the Bush administration pushed the doctrine of politicization more aggressively than its predecessors" (2010: 573). For example, Schedule C appointment, a type of political appointments exempt from competitive or merit hiring requirements, was extended for positions that "involve making or approving substantive policy recommendations" or when the

> work of the position can be performed successfully only by someone with a thorough knowledge of and sympathy with the goals, priorities, and preferences of an official who has a confidential or policy determining relationship with the President or agency head,

including confidential assistants, policy experts, and special counsels (Indiana University 2018), increased by 33 percent during Bush's first term in office (U.S. House of Representatives 2006). This created a climate where federal employees were dependent on the goodwill of the president for continued employment rather than knowing and understanding their jobs. The appointment of ideological loyalists into positions of leadership allowed the president to redefine and reprioritize a bureaucracy's goals.

The Bush Administration sought political loyalty and ideological constancy even in the DOJ. Hiring and firing decisions were predicated on placing "Loyal Bushies"[15] in positions of power. Eisenstein concludes:

> The Bush Administration, especially under Alberto Gonzales, undertook an unprecedented, determined, and multi-faceted effort to appoint U.S. Attorneys who identified with Main Justice's goals, accepted its authority, and actively sought to implement its policies and directives. Support for President Bush appears to have been salient both in determining who should be fired and who hired.
>
> (2007–2008: 242)

Attorney General Alberto Gonzales gave Kyle Sampson and Monica Goodling, two political appointees who lacked prosecutorial experience, far-reaching authority to hire and fire DOJ attorneys based on political and ideological affiliations. Daniel Metcalfe, a 35-year veteran of the DOJ, stated that under Gonzales the new political appointees "whose inexperience in the processes of government was surpassed only by their evident disdain for it" abandoned the traditional DOJ values of integrity and independence (Mauro 2007). Two separate DOJ investigations (DOJ 2008, 2009) into the improper, possibly illegal, hiring practices of the DOJ Honors Program and the Civil Rights Division found that highly qualified potential candidates with liberal leanings were screened out to favor conservative applicants with Republican ideological affiliations. Applicants with civil rights or human rights experience were disqualified as being too liberal. The DOJ investigation of the Honors Program concluded that "many of the deselected candidates had had internships with organizations such as Human Rights Watch or the American Civil Liberties Union (ACLU), or had assisted in defending someone held at Guantánamo Bay" (DOJ 2008). Interning with a Democratic Congress member, working on a human rights journal, or voicing criticism of Bush's foreign policy was enough to disqualify potential candidates. When political appointees rather than career experts command the agency or direct a policy, the competence of the agency and effectiveness of the policy are reduced, along with a decline in morale among career bureaucrats.[16]

The Bush Administration faced very little bureaucratic resistance in implementing his security policies. There were bureaucratic conflicts over control of resources but the bureaucracy, as was Congress and the American public, cowed into compliance (Risen 2006).

Conclusion

The Bush Administration believed that the call to adhere to international human rights and humanitarian law was an attempt by opponents to protect the enemies of the United States and undermine U.S. security (Forsythe 2011). The Bush Administration even questioned the motives of the International Committee of the Red Cross, a highly respected organization known for its neutrality in the service of helping people affected by conflict, ensuring humanitarian protection, and promoting humanitarian laws. Abuses associated with the global war on terror, the Bush Administration believed, were exceptional and justified derogations from accepted human rights standards. Many human rights scholars and activists feared that the U.S. economic strength and its copious foreign aid budget could be used to influence other states' acceptance of U.S. preferences to use torture in the name of anti-terrorism. Indeed, Dunne cautioned that the American practice of torture could lead to a norm cascade "in which torture in the name of anti-terrorism became acceptable" (2007: 284). Similarly, the human rights violations in many foreign countries were no longer viewed as abhorrent by Washington, but were rather accepted as countries' legitimate attempts to curb terrorist activity on their territories. For example, Russia, China, and Colombia were now believed to be countering terrorist insurgents and not simply attempting to eradicate ethnic or political opposition.

Many of the policies enacted during Bush's war on terror violated internationally recognized human rights norms, which, rather than protecting U.S. security, have made the United States less secure by creating wrath and resentment from the victims, their families, and their communities. Bush's human rights violations also alienated U.S. allies. Only by reestablishing human rights as a central tenet of U.S. foreign policy and by upholding democratic values could the United States regain its moral leadership in the world community. The United States gained a false sense of security under Bush. The often-recalled quote by Benjamin Franklin sums up the Bush presidency well: "Those who would give up essential liberty to purchase a little temporary safety deserve neither liberty nor safety."

The human rights violations associated with the Bush Administration, specifically denial of habeas corpus and the use of torture and rendition, as well as the expansive use of surveillance, were significant and systemic. As we will see in the next chapter, Obama continued and expanded many of the Bush-era programs and policies that led to the violations of human rights of American citizens, detainees, and innocent foreign citizens.

Notes

1 These countries include both brutal autocracies and fully functioning liberal democracies: Afghanistan, Albania, Algeria, Australia, Austria, Azerbaijan, Belgium, Bosnia-Herzegovina, Canada, Croatia, Cyprus, the Czech Republic, Denmark, Djibouti, Egypt, Ethiopia, Finland, Gambia, Georgia, Germany, Greece, Hong Kong, Iceland, Indonesia, Iran, Ireland, Italy, Jordan, Kenya, Libya, Lithuania, Macedonia, Malawi, Malaysia, Mauritania, Morocco, Pakistan, Poland, Portugal, Romania, Saudi Arabia, Somalia, South Africa, Spain, Sri Lanka, Sweden, Syria, Thailand, Turkey, United Arab Emirates, United Kingdom, Uzbekistan, Yemen, and Zimbabwe (Open Society Foundations 2013).

2 The two private contractors were former Air Force psychologists John "Bruce" Jessen and James Mitchell (Chwastiak 2015). Chwastiak writes that

> While Mitchell and Jessen had no experience in interrogation and no evidence that harsh tactics would elicit truthful confessions, they did provide the CIA with what it needed, the facade of scientific, psychological, and professional authorization that torture would work.
>
> (2015: 495)

3 Yet, the United States is fighting a war in Afghanistan and Iraq with the conventional tools of warfare, guns, and soldiers (White and Ethan 2018). As Kenneth Roth, Executive Director of Human Rights Watch, states, "The U.S. government cannot choose to wage war in Afghanistan with guns, bombs and soldiers and then assert the laws of war do not apply" (Human Rights Watch 2002). Although there is debate as to whether the terrorist attacks on September 11, 2001 constitute an act of war since wars are traditionally conducted between sovereign nation states, not with non-state actors, the Bush Administration declared it a war and responded to it with military force. The use of military force, in the opinion of legal scholars and even DOD lawyers, mandates the application of *jus in bello* rules (Jinks 2003, DOD 2005). *Jus in bello* rules extend to armed conflicts involving non-state actors (Bradley and Goldsmith 2005).

4 After being subjected to isolation, detention, and torture, the majority of detainees were eventually released to their home countries. Only between 15 and 20 percent were "high-value detainees" (Forsythe and McMahon 2017).

These detainees, their family and friends, and compassionate others became more sympathetic to the call of terrorist recruiters.

5. In 2004, after the public learned of the treatment of detainees at Abu Ghraib, the Yoo Memorandum and the Bybee Memorandum were officially withdrawn.
6. Neoconservatives believe that U.S. security lay not in the balancing of power, but rather in the extension of America's power by military means abroad by making the world a reflection of the United States.
7. Pillar (2006), the National Intelligence Officer for the Middle East of the CIA, believed that Iraq was several years away from developing a viable nuclear weapon and was unlikely to use it unless the regime was in extreme jeopardy.
8. The fact that the majority of the members of the coalition were economically dependent on the United States led Paul Gilfeather (2003) of the *Daily Mirror* to dub the coalition: the "Coalition of the Bribed, Bullied, and the Blind." While Anderson et al. (2003), writing for the Institute of Policy Studies, referred to the coalition as the "Coalition of the Coerced."
9. Great Britain's Tony Blair, Italy's Prime Minister Silvio Berlusconi, and Spain's Prime Minister Jose Maria Aznar were ardent supporters of Bush's invasion of Iraq, believing that Iraqi held weapons of mass destruction and supported terrorist networks. Australia, Denmark, Portugal, and Japan also supported Washington's decision to invade. Soon, however, many of the supporters would withdraw from the coalition when faced with significant political opposition and domestic unrest.
10. Overlooking the human rights records of repressive governments was all the more necessary since, in the words of Forsythe, the Bush-Cheney Administration itself "adopted a policy of torturing and otherwise cruelly treating presumed high-value enemy prisoners after 9/11" (2011: 772).
11. The MCA is managed by the Millennium Challenge Corporation.
12. The Vilnius letter is a declaration of support for the U.S. invasion of Iraq. The February 6, 2003 letter was signed by Albania, Bulgaria, Croatia, Estonia, Latvia, Lithuania, Macedonia, Romania, Slovakia, and Slovenia.
13. By 2009, the Iraqi Relief and Reconstruction Fund was nearly exhausted, thereby reducing DOD's share of foreign aid.
14. It has been said that the DOD employs more military band members than the State Department does Foreign Service Officers (Glain 2009), and it has a budget almost 15 times larger than State.
15. The label "loyal Bushie" refers to political appointees and faithful supporters of Bush and his policies.
16. The use of political appointees undermined the competence of the bureaucracy since agency leaders were selected on the basis of partisan loyalty without consideration of professional qualifications, thus reducing the government's ability to deliver sound policies and public goods. One need only look at Bush's Federal Emergency Management Agency appointee Michael Brown. Brown, a long-time friend of Joe Allbaugh (who ran Bush's 2000 election campaign), had no emergency preparation and management experience as was evident following Hurricane Katrina in August 2005.

References

Sarah Anderson, Phyllis Bennis, and John Cavanagh. 2003. *Coalition of the Willing or Coalition of the Coerced? How the Bush Administration Influences Allies in Its War on Iraq*. Institute for Policy Studies, Washington, DC. www.tni.org/sites/www.tni.org/archives/mil-docs/coalition.pdf

John Ashcroft. 2001. Attorney General John Ashcroft, Testimony Before the Senate Committee on the Judiciary (25 September 2001). www.justice.gov/archive/ag/testimony/2001/0925AttorneyGeneralJohnAshcroftTestimonybeforetheSenateCommitteeontheJudiciary.htm

Associated Press. 2003. "Iraq's Health Ministry Ordered to Stop Counting Civilian Dead From War," *USA Today*, 12 October 2003.

Brian Atwood, M. Peter McPherson, and Andrew Natsios. 2008. "Arrested Development: Making Aid a More Effective Tool." *Foreign Affairs* 87(6): 123–132.

Jean-Paul Azam and Véronique Thelen. 2010. "Foreign Aid versus Military Intervention in the War on Terror." *The Journal of Conflict Resolution* 54(2): 237–261.

Amy Belasco and Larry Nowels. 2003. *Supplemental Appropriations FY2003: Iraq Conflict, Afghanistan, Global War on Terrorism, and Homeland Security Updated April 18, 2003.* https://fas.org/asmp/resources/govern/crs-rl31829.pdf

Curtis Bradley and Jack Goldsmith. 2005. "Congressional Authorization and the War on Terrorism." *Harvard Law Review* 118(7): 2048–2133.

Curtis Bradley and Trevor Morrison. 2012. "Historical Gloss and the Separation of Powers." *Harvard Law Review* 126(2): 411–485.

Reed Brody. 2005. *Getting Away with Torture?Command Responsibility for the U.S. Abuse of Detainees.* New York: Human Rights Watch.

Susan Burgermann. 2004. "First Do No Harm: U.S. Foreign Policy and Respect for Human Rights in El Salvador and Guatemala, 1980–96," in *Implementing U.S. Human Rights Policy.* Debra Liang-Fenton, ed. Washington, DC: United States Institute of Peace Press.

George W. Bush. 1999. "A Period of Consequences, The Citadel, Charleston, South Carolina." 23 September. www3.citadel.edu/pao/addresses/pres_bush.html

George W. Bush. 2000. "Forward," in *Compassionate Conservatism: What It Is, What It Does, and How It Can Transform America.* Marvin Olasky, ed. New York: The Free Press.

George W. Bush. 2002a. President Outlines U.S. Plan to Help World's Poor. Remarks to United Nations Financing for Development Center. Monterrey Mexico, 22 March. https://2001-2009.state.gov/g/oes/rls/rm/2002/10514.htm

George W. Bush. 2002b. "The State of the Union: President Bush's State of the Union Address to Congress and the Nation." 29 January. *New York Times*, 30 January, sec. A, 22, col. 1.

George Bush. 2006. "Trying Detainees: Address on the Creation of Military Commissions." www.presidentialrhetoric.com/speeches/09.06.06.html

Laura Bush. 2001. "Radio Address by Mrs. Bush." Laura Bush on Taliban Oppression of Women, 17 November. www.whitehouse.gov/news/releases/2001/11/20011117.html

Laura Bush. 2002. "Mrs. Bush Discusses Status of Afghan Women at U.N.: Remarks by Mrs. Laura Bush." Commission on the Status of Women. 8 March. www.whitehouse.gov/news/releases/2002/03/20020308-2.html

Jay Bybee. 2002. Memo: "Re: Standards of Conduct for Interrogation under 18 U.S.C. § 2340-2340A," from the Department of Justice's Office of Legal Counsel for Alberto R. Gonzales, Counsel to President Bush. 1 August.

Rhonda Callaway and Elizabeth Matthews. 2008. *Strategic US Foreign Assistance: The Battle Between Human Rights and National Security*. Burlington, VT: Ashgate Publishing Company.

CBS News. 2013. "Much of the $60 Billion to Rebuild Iraq Wasted, Special Auditor's Final Report to Congress Shows." www.cbsnews.com/news/much-of-60b-from-us-to-rebuild-iraqi-wasted-special-auditors-final-report-to-congress-shows/

Dick Cheney. 2001. "Transcript for Sept. 16." NBC News Meet the Press. www.emperors-clothes.com/9-11backups/nbcmp.htm

Michele Chwastiak. 2015. "Torture as Normal Work: The Bush Administration, the Central Intelligence Agency and 'Enhanced Interrogation Techniques'." *Organization* 22(4): 493–511.

David Cole. 2004. "Uncle Sam Is Watching You." *The New York Review of Books*. http://scholarship.law.georgetown.edu/facpub/1

Department of Defense. 2005. Defense Department Directive 3000.05 *Military Support to Stability, Security, Transformation, and Reconstruction (2005)*. https://fas.org/irp/doddir/dod/d3000_05.pdf

Lawrence Di Rita. 2005. "Don't Tie Our Hands: Congress Shouldn't Set Limits on Interrogating Captured Terrorists." *USA TODAY*, A12.

Jack Donnelly and Daniel Whelan. 2018. *International Human Rights: Dilemmas in World Politics*. New York: Westview Press.

Elizabeth Drew. June 12, 2003. "The Neocons in Power." *The New York Review of Books* 50(10): 20–22.

J. Patrick Dobel. 2010. "Prudence and Presidential Ethics: The Decisions on Iraq of the Two Presidents Bush." *Presidential Studies Quarterly* 40(1): 57–75.

Tim Dunne. 2007. "'The Rules of the Game Are Changing': Fundamental Human Rights in Crisis after 9/11." *International Politics* 44(2–3): 269–286.

Dan Eggen and Julie Tate. 2005. "U.S. Campaign Produces Few Convictions on Terrorism Charges." *Washington Post*, A1.

James Eisenstein. 2007–2008. "The U.S. Attorney Firings of 2006: Main Justice's Centralization Efforts in Historical Context." *Seattle University Law Review* 31: 219–263.

Federation of American Scientists. 2004. *Arms, Aid and the War in Iraq*. www.fas.org/gulfwar2/at

Dianne Feinstein. 2014. "Forward by the Committee Chairperson." *Committee Study of the Central Intelligence Agency's Detention and Interrogation Program*. Declassified 3 December. https://fas.org/irp/congress/2014_rpt/ssci-rdi.pdf

Robert Fleck and Christopher Kilby. 2010. "Changing Aid Regimes? U.S. Foreign Aid from the Cold War to the War on Terror." *Journal of Development Economics* 91(2): 185–197.

David Forsythe. 2011. "US Foreign Policy and Human Rights: Situating Obama." *Human Rights Quarterly* 33(3): 767–789.

David Forsythe and Patrice McMahon. 2017. *American Exceptionalism Reconsidered*. New York: Routledge.

Kim Gamel. 2009. "AP IMPACT: Secret Tally has 87,215 Dead." Associated Press (via Fox News).

Douglas Gibler and Steven Miller. 2012. "Comparing the Foreign Aid Policies of Presidents Bush and Obama." *Social Science Quarterly* 93(5): 1202–1217.

Gilfeather, Paul. 2003. "Coalition of the Bribed, Bullied, and Blind." *Daily Mirror*, 22 March.

Stephen Glain. 2009. "The American Leviathan: The Pentagon Has All but Eclipsed the State Department in Setting US Foreign Policy." *The Nation* 289(9): 18–23.

Karen Greenberg and Joshua Dratel. 2005. *The Torture Papers: The Road to Abu Ghraib*. Cambridge: Cambridge University Press.

Morton Halperin, Priscilla Clapp with Arnold Kanter. 2006. *Bureaucratic Politics and Foreign Policy*. Washington, DC: Brookings Institution Press.

Lindy Heinecken. 2003. "Facing a Merciless Enemy: HIV/AIDS and the South African Armed Force." *Armed Forces and Society* 29(2): 281–300.

William Howell and Jon Pevehouse. 2007. *While Dangers Gather: Congressional Checks on Presidential War Powers*. Princeton, NJ: Princeton University Press.

Human Rights Council. 2010. *United Nations. Joint Study on Global Practices in Relation to Secret Detention in the Context of Countering Terrorism*, 13th Session, A/HRC/13/42. http://hrlibrary.umn.edu/instree/A-HRC-13-42.pdf

Human Rights Watch. 2001. *Afghanistan: New War Puts Women's Rights in Peril*. www.hrw.org/report/2001/10/29/humanity-denied/systematic-violations-womens-rights-afghanistan

Human Rights Watch. 2002. *U.S. Officials Misstate Geneva Convention Requirements*, 28 January. www.hrw.org/news/2002/01/28/us-officials-misstate-geneva-convention-requirements

Human Rights Watch. April 2005. "Still at Risk: Diplomatic Assurances No Safeguard Against Torture." *Human Rights Watch Report* 17(4): 1–92.

Krista Hunt. 2002. "The Strategic Co-optation of Women's Rights: Discourse in the 'War on Terrorism'." *International Feminist Journal of Politics* 4(1): 116–121.

Indiana University. 2018. *Government Regulations*. https://gov.iu.edu/policies/lobbying/schedule-c.html

Alan Ingram. 2011. "The Pentagon's HIV/AIDS Programmes: Governmentality, Political Economy, Security." *Geopolitics* 16(3): 655–674.

International Committee of the Red Cross (ICRC). 2004. *Report on the Treatment by Coalition Forces of Prisoners of War and Other Protected Persons by the Geneva Conventions in Iraq During Arrest, Internment and Interrogation*. http://hrlibrary.umn.edu/OathBetrayed/ICRC%20Report.pdf

Iraq Body Count. 2010. "Iraq War Logs: What the Numbers Reveal." www.iraqbodycount.org/analysis/numbers/warlogs/

Michael Isikoff. 2003. "Show Me the Money." *Newsweek*, 1 December, 36.

Douglas Jehl and Eric Schmitt. 2005. "The Conflict in Iraq: Detainees; U.S. Military Says 26 Inmate Deaths May Be Homicide." *The New York Times*, 16 March, A1.

Derek Jinks. 2003. "September 11 and the Laws of War." *Yale Journal of International Law* 28: 1–48.

Chalmers Johnson. 2003. *Blowback: The Cost and Consequences of American Empire*. New York: Henry Holt and Company.

John Kane. 2003 "American Values or Human Rights? U.S. Foreign Policy and the Fractured Myth of Virtuous Power." *Presidential Studies Quarterly* 33(4): 772–800.

Neal Katyal. 2006. "Internal Separation of Powers: Checking Today's Most Dangerous Branch from Within." *Yale Law Journal* 115(9): 2314–2349.

Conor Keane and Steve Wood. 2016. "Bureaucratic Politics, Role Conflict, and the Internal Dynamic of Provincial Reconstruction Teams in Afghanistan." *Armed Forces and Society* 42(1): 99–118.

Vincent Keating. 2014. "Contesting the International Illegitimacy of Torture: The Bush Administration's Failure to Legitimate its Preferences within International Society." *The British Journal of Politics and International Relations* 16(1): 1–27.

Brian Lai. 2003. "Examining the Goals of US Foreign Assistance in the Post-Cold War Period, 1991–96." *Journal of Peace Research* 40(1): 103–128.

Carol Lancaster. 2008. *George Bush's Foreign Aid: Transformation or Chaos?* Center for Global Development. Washington, DC: Brookings Institution Press.

Gayle Tzemach Lemmon. 2011. "Looming Threat to Afghan Women's Rights." Council on Foreign Relations. www.cfr.org/expert-brief/looming-threat-afghan-womens-rights

Gordon Lubold. 2017. "U.S. Spent $5.6 trillion on Wars in the Middle East and Asia: Study." *The Wall Street Journal*, 8 November.

Dick Marty. 2006. "Alleged Secret Detentions and Unlawful Inter-state Transfers of Detainees involving Council of Europe Member States." Parliamentary Assembly. Committee on Legal Affairs and Human Rights Doc. 10957. 12 June. https://chrgj.org/wp-content/uploads/2016/11/Factual-SummaryA-T.pdf

Tony Mauro. 2007. Justice Department's Independence 'Shattered,' Says Former DOJ Attorney. *Legal Times*, 16 April.

Jane Mayer. 2008. *The Dark Side: The Inside Story of How the War on Terror Turned into a War on American Ideals.* New York: Doubleday.

William Miles. 2012. "Deploying Development to Counter Terrorism: Post-9/11 Transformation of U.S. Foreign Aid to Africa." *African Studies Review* 55(3): 27–60.

J. Stephen Morrison. 2007. "What Role for US Assistance in the Fight against Global HIV/AIDS," in *Security by Other Means: Foreign Assistance, Global Poverty, and American Leadership.* Lael Brainard, ed. Washington, DC: Brookings Institution.

Donald Moynihan and Alasdair Roberts. 2010. "The Triumph of Loyalty Over Competence: The Bush Administration and the Exhaustion of the Politicized Presidency." *Public Administrative Review* 70(4): 572–581.

Randall Newnham. 2008. "'Coalition of the Bribed and Bullied?' U.S. Economic Linkage and the Iraq War Coalition." *International Studies Perspectives* 9: 183–200.

Manfred Nowak. 2006. "What Practices Constitute Torture?: US and UN Standards." *Human Rights Quarterly* 28(4): 809–841.

Michael O'Connor and Celia Rumann. 2003. "Into the Fire: How to Avoid Getting Burned by the Same Mistakes Made Fighting Terrorism in Northern Ireland." *Cardozo Law Review* 24: 1657–1751.

Festus Ugboaja Ohaegbulam. 2007. *A Culture of Deference: Congress, the President, and the Course of the U.S.-led Invasion and Occupation of Iraq.* New York: Peter Lang.

Kathryn Olmsted. 2016. "US Intelligence Agencies during the Ford Years," in *A Companion to Gerald R. Ford and Jimmy Carter.* Scott Kaufman, ed. Oxford: Wiley Blackwell.

Open Society Foundations. 2013. *Globalizing Torture: CIA Secret Detention and Extraordinary Rendition.* www.opensocietyfoundations.org/reports/globalizing-torture-cia-secret-detention-and-extraordinary-rendition

Norman Ornstein and Thomas Mann. 2006. "When Congress Checks Out." *Foreign Affairs* 85(6): 67–82.

John Owens and Riccardo Pelizzo. 2009. "Introduction: The Impact of the 'War on Terror' on Executive–Legislative Relations: A Global Perspective." *The Journal of Legislative Studies* 15(2–3): 119–146.
Francis Owusu. 2007. "Post-9/11 U.S. Foreign Aid, the Millennium Challenge Account, and Africa: How Many Birds Can One Stone Kill?" *Africa Today* 54(1): 3–26.
Oxfam. 2005. *Paying the Price: Why Rich Countries Must Invest Now in a War on Poverty*. Oxford: Oxfam International.
Oxfam America. 2014. *Foreign Aid 101: A Quick and Easy Guide to Understanding US Foreign Aid*. www.oxfamamerica.org/static/media/files/Foreign-Aid-101-Mar2014-single-Oxfam-America.pdf
Jane Perlez. 2003. "Pentagon and State Department in Tug-of-War Over Aid Disbursal." *New York Times*, 1 April, B7.
Paul Pillar. 2006. "Intelligence, Policy, and the War in Iraq." *Foreign Affairs* 85(2): 17–25.
Thomas Ricks. 2006. *Fiasco: The American Military Adventure in Iraq*. New York: The Penguin Press.
James Risen. 2006. *State of War: The Secret History of the CIA and the Bush Administration*. New York: Free Press.
Boris Rumer. 2002. "The Powers in Central Asia." *Survival* 44(3): 57–68.
Donald Rumsfeld. 2001. "Secretary Rumsfeld Interview." *New York Times*, 12 October, A1.
Tiaji Salaam-Blyther. 2014. "U.S. and International Health Responses to the Ebola Outbreak in West Africa." CRS Report R43697. Washington, DC: Congressional Research Service.
Rebecca Sanders. September 2018. *Plausible Legality: Legal Culture and Political Imperative in the Global War on Terror*. Oxford: Oxford University Press.
Barry Schweid. 2004. "U.S. Blocks Aid to U.N. Population Fund." *Washington Post*, 17 July, A16.
Senate Select Committee on Intelligence. 2014. *Committee Study of the Central Intelligence Agency's Detention and Interrogation Program*. Declassified 3 December. https://fas.org/irp/congress/2014_rpt/ssci-rdi.pdf
Jan Silva. 2006. "Probe of CIA Prisons Implicates EU Nations." *ABC News* http://abcnews.go.com/International/print?id=2048514
Sharon Smith. 2002. "Using Women's Rights to Sell Washington's War." *International Socialist Review* 21: 39–43.
Joanna Spear. 2016. "The Militarization of United States Foreign Aid," in *The Securitization of Foreign Aid*. Steven Brown and Jörn Grävingholt, eds. Rethinking International Development Series. London: Palgrave Macmillan.
Joseph Stiglitz and Linda Bilmes. 2008. *The Three Trillion Dollar War: The True Cost of the Iraq Conflict*. New York: W.W. Norton and Company.
Arsalan Suleman. 2006. "Detainee Treatment Act of 2005." *Harvard Human Rights Journal* 19: 257–265.
Curt Tarnoff. 2014. *Millennium Challenge Corporation*. CRS Report RL32427. Washington, DC: Congressional Research Service.
Curt Tarnoff and Larry Nowels. 2004. *Foreign Aid: An Introductory Overview of US Programs and Policy*. CRS Report RL98-916. Washington, DC: Congressional Research Service.

Curt Tarnoff and Marion Lawson. 2018. *Foreign Aid: An Introduction to U.S. Programs and Policy*. CRS Report R40213. Washington, DC: Congressional Research Service.

George Tenet. 2003. *Guidelines on Interrogations Conducted Pursuant to the [Redacted]*. www.aclu.org/files/torturefoia/released/082409/olcremand/2004olc12.pdf

Ann Tickner. 2002. "Feminist Perspectives on 9/11." *International Studies Perspectives* 3(4): 333–350.

United Nations. *World Development Indicators*. http://databank.worldbank.org/data/source/world-development-indicators

United States Department of Justice. 2008. *An Investigation of Allegations of Politicized Hiring in the Department of Justice Honors Program and Summer Law Intern Program*. Washington, DC: Government Printing Office.

United States Department of Justice. 2009. *An Investigation of Allegations of Politicized Hiring and Other Improper Personnel Actions in the Civil Rights Division*. Washington, DC: Government Printing Office.

United States House of Representatives. 2006. *The Growth of Political Appointees in the Bush Administration*. Committee on Oversight and Government Reform—Minority Staff Special Investigations Division. Washington, DC: Government Printing Office.

United States Office of Management and Budget. 2004. U.S. Budget for Fiscal Year 2004 Budget, *Department of State and International Assistance Programs*. Washington, DC: Government Printing Office.

Jeremy Waldron. 2005. "Torture and Positive Law: Jurisprudence for the White House." *Columbia Law Review* 105(6): 1681–1750.

Vron Ware. 2007. "The Future of Feminism: What Other Way to Speak," in *Women and Others: Perspectives on Race, Gender, and Empire*. Celia Daileader, Rhoda Johnson, Amilcar Shabazz, eds. New York: Palgrave Macmillan.

George Withers. 2005. "Who's in Charge? Foreign Assistance Responsibilities Shift from State to Defense." Memorandum from the Washington Office on Latin America (November). www.wola.org/sites/default/files/downloadable/Regional%20Security/past/Whos_in_charge.pdf

Jeremy White and Elizabeth Ethan. 2018. "Unintended Victims of Bush's War of Opportunity." Unpublished manuscript on file with the author.

Ngaire Woods. 2005. "The Shifting Politics of Foreign Aid." *International Affairs* 81(2): 393–409.

Iris Young. 2003. "The Logic of Masculinist Protection: Reflections on the Current Security State." *Signs* 29(1): 1–25.

5 The Prevaricator of Change
Barack Obama (2009–2017)

By 2006, the majority of Americans tired of the George W. Bush Administration's fear-mongering, deception, and incompetence as evidenced by a drastic drop in his job approval rating[1] and his party's loss of control of both the House of Representatives and the Senate. In addition, the bipartisan Congressional support for Bush's foreign policy broke down. By 2008, the American public was ready to elect a candidate that personified an "anti-Bush" image (Haas 2012). Barack Obama was that anti-Bush candidate in words if not in deeds. Obama gave grand speeches on the need to improve America's reputation, to foster democracy, and to protect human rights. However, Haas argues that although Obama issued an oratorical call to advance human rights, "he mostly sacrificed the cause [of human rights] to the exigencies of power politics and the dictates of realism" (2012: 145). President Barack Hussein Obama's inaugural speech (2009a) stated that it was a false choice to put America's safety and ideals in opposition. Yet, this was also to be, in the words of Clinton (2009), a policy of "principled pragmatism," requiring flexibility and a case-by-case approach when engaging with foreign countries on their democracy and human rights practices. Bouchet (2013) reports that there is little evidence that principled pragmatism produced many positive results. The Obama Administration was based on prevaricating misdirection.

Amid a general discontent with the policies of the George W. Bush Administration, Obama campaigned on a theme of "change." Obama promised to reverse Bush's foreign policies, by winding down the wars in Iraq and Afghanistan, ending U.S. dependence on foreign oil, and fixing America's economic woes. The election of Obama brought enormous optimism that the unsavory aspects of U.S. foreign policy would come to an end. Many in the human rights community celebrated the incoming president and expected a reversal of the George W. Bush policies regarding human rights. As Mendelson reports, "the expectations could not be higher. At a minimum, observers are looking for the placement of key individuals who will champion human rights or, alternatively, those in key positions to uphold human rights" (2009: 110–111). And Obama did fill key positions with big names known to support human rights.

Hillary Clinton became Secretary of State; Michael Posner was selected for the position of Assistant Secretary for Democracy, Human Rights, and Labor; Harold Hongju Koh was appointed as Legal Advisor for the State Department; Anne-Marie Slaughter became Director of Policy Planning; and Samantha Power became the Special Assistant to the President and Senior Director for Multilateral Affairs. Obama calculatingly placed civil liberty advocates in administrative positions in charge of detainee policy (Alexander 2013). For example, Dawn Johnsen, once staff council for the American Civil Liberties Union (ACLU), became head of the OLC, and Phillip Carter, an army officer and journalist opposed to the use of torture as an interrogation technique, would become Deputy Assistant Attorney General for Detainee Affairs for a short time.

However, Obama also retained many of the George W. Bush Administration's personnel, which highlighted his intentions to continue his predecessor's policies on the war on terror, now renamed overseas contingency operations (OCO), and foreign policy in general. For example, Secretary of Defense Robert Gates (2006–2011) was appointed by George W. Bush and retained by Obama. In addition, Admiral Michael Mullen remained the Chairman of the Joint Chiefs of Staff under Obama; John Brennan, who served under George W. Bush as deputy executive director of the CIA and director of the Terrorist Threat Integration Center, became the National Security Advisor of Homeland Security and counterterrorism advisor to Obama and later was nominated to be director of the CIA.

Similarities and Continuities with George W. Bush's Human Rights Policies in the War on Terror/ Overseas Contingency Operations

Expectations that the Obama Administration would mark a sharp break with the human rights policies and practices of the George W. Bush presidency largely went unfulfilled. Candidate Obama made grand promises to reverse President Bush's human rights policies. Yet, according to Stephan, "at a glance, it appears that President Obama has become the person that candidate Obama ran against" (Stephan 2012: 489). With the election of Obama, Democrats controlled the government. Democrats had considerable strength in the 111th Congress (2009–2011). With control of the government and backed by public support for "change," the Obama Administration should have been able to quickly and easily reform or reverse Bush-era policies. Yet, John Brennan was reported to have said that Obama's counterterrorism policies made Obama's Administration Bush's third term.[2]

Jackson (2011) is not surprised that there was little difference between the George W. Bush and Obama counterterrorism policies. The war on terror was institutionalized and normalized in U.S. foreign policy practices, institutions, and culture. Barring a major crisis, established foreign policy practice is relatively static, stable, and consistent. Thus, the war on terror policies and practices initiated by George W. Bush continued with only minor changes under the Obama Administration. Dietrich and Witkowski (2012) recognized the importance of institutional and structural constraints, such as congressional resistance and the bureaucratic procedures put in place by the war on terror that may have restricted Obama's human rights policy. Jackson (2011) suggests that the all-encompassing principle of counterterrorism contains two mutually constitutive elements. First, the war on terror is socially constructed primarily through the use of language. George W. Bush and his administration used the narrative of war to provide the "explanation, rationale, justification and necessary social consensus" for developing and implementing counterterrorism measures (Jackson 2011: 392). Second, a new principle requires material resources and actions in order to become institutionalized. George W. Bush created a vast bureaucracy with the Department of Homeland Security (DHS), shaped new legislation with the patriot act, and gave unfettered authority to intelligence agencies to surveil citizens and noncitizens alike. These actions also received very high approval from the American public. Furthermore, the bureaucracies, such as the military, the CIA, and the DHS, depend on counterterrorism for their prestige, power, and large budgets. Universities have developed programs and degrees in the areas of security studies and counterterrorism. Military contractors, construction businesses, and weapons manufacturers are all powerful interests that are economically vested in the continuation of the war on terror. Millions of people are employed in the counterterrorism field as analysts, contractors, soldiers, or spies. But, according to Jackson, the primary reason why political opposition to counterterrorism is not successful was because counterterrorism:

> expresses and reaffirms American values by negation: terrorists are the opposite of Americans in that they hate everything that Americans love, such as liberty, democracy, peace, unity and so on. Using the term 'terrorism' or 'terrorist', whether in daily conversation or public debate, therefore, becomes an implicit act of reaffirming American identity and values.
>
> (2011: 398)

Thus, the United States must take up the call to battle in this good versus evil, right against wrong, global challenge. Moreover, counterterrorism provides a good cover for U.S. hegemonic actions. Owing to counterterrorism, the United States has expanded its web of military bases, provided more regimes with economic and military aid, extended its control over oil-rich regions, spied on allies and adversaries, and used its dominance in international organizations to promote its interests. Consequently,

112   The Prevaricator of Change

Obama could not transform U.S. foreign policy regarding the war on terror (or overseas contingency operations as it is now known), even if he wanted. And there is little evidence that he wanted to. Jackson further argues that the war on terror has "become a powerful social structure (a hegemonic discourse) that both expresses and simultaneously co-constructs US interests and identity" (2011: 392). The institutionalization and normalization of Bush's and later Obama's counterterrorism strategies were viewed as simply common sense and good judgment.

Obama's theme of change, given the intensification of public discontent over Bush's violation of human rights both abroad and at home, was simply a rhetorical ploy so long as combating terrorism remained the U.S. primary foreign policy goal. In short, there was little substantive change in U.S. human rights policy by the Obama Administration particularly with respect to his counterterrorism policies and his allocation of U.S. foreign aid.

Permanence of Terror Policy: Guantánamo, Military Commissions, and Rendition

By January 20, 2009, the population of detainees at Guantánamo had been reduced to 242, but it remained symbolic in the continuing war on terror. Guantánamo is a symbol of misguided vengeance and injustice to those who want it closed. For its proponents, Guantánamo serves as a symbol of the need to protect the United States from the ongoing threat to American values from "people who hate us."[3] Within days of his inauguration, Obama attempted to close Guantánamo Bay, or "Gitmo" as it was commonly called. With Executive Order 13492 "Review and Disposition of Individuals Detained at the Guantánamo Bay Naval Base and Closure of Detention Facilities" of January 22, 2009, Obama determined that "prompt and appropriate disposition of the individuals currently detained at Guantánamo and closure of the facilities in which they are detained would further the national security and foreign policy interests of the United States and the interests of justice" (Obama 2009b). Executive Order 13492 required the immediate review of all detainees by an interagency review team led by the U.S. Attorney General. Obama appointed a Task Force to review and report on the appropriate courses of action with regard to the remaining detainees in Guantánamo. Moreover, with Executive Order 13493, "Review of Detention Policy Options," Obama created a Special Interagency Task Force tasked with identifying lawful options for the disposition of Bush's enemy noncombatants housed at Guantánamo (Obama 2009c). The task force was to be co-chaired by the U.S. Attorney General and the Secretary of Defense. Pending the outcome of the review, all military commission courts were shut down.

In January 2009, several Republicans, including John McCain (R-AZ), Lindsey Graham (R-SC), General Colin Powell, and even George W. Bush, favored closing Guantánamo (Mayer 2010). Public opinion supported the closing of Gitmo but when concrete questions about what to do with the detainees, where they would be held after trial, and what rights were to be extended to them were asked, opinion waivered. Just after Obama signed the Executive Orders pertaining to the closure of Guantánamo the *New York Times* reported that a released Guantánamo detainee, Said Ali al-Shiri, had become a deputy leader of al-Qaeda's Yemeni branch and was involved in a terrorist bombing outside the American Embassy in Sana, Yemen. The *New York Times* quotes the Pentagon as claiming that dozens of released detainees "returned to the fight" (Worth 2009: A1). By May 2009, Congress and public opinion had turned. Congress, controlled by the Democrats, voted to prohibit the use of federal funds to "transfer, release, or incarcerate detainees detained at Guantánamo Bay, Cuba, to or within the United States" (U.S. Senate 2010). Soon after, the Fort Hood, Texas massacre (November 2009)[4] and the Christmas Day underwear bomber incident (December 2009)[5] occurred further increasing the American public's fear of releasing or housing detainees within the U.S. homeland. Corcoran (2011) reports that, by June 3, 2009, 65 percent of Americans now opposed closing Guantánamo. With the issue of Executive Order 13567, "Periodic Review of Individuals Detained at Guantánamo Bay Naval Station Pursuant to the Authorization for Use of Military Force," the Center for Constitutional Rights (2011) believes that, by requiring a periodic review of detainees every four years, the Obama Administration actually signaled its intention to keep Guantánamo open as a permanent detention center.

And then there was the issue of where the detainees would be tried. One of the options identified by the Special Interagency Task Force was the use of a military commission system for trying detainees. Obama, as a Senator, voted against Bush-era Military Commissions Act (MCA) of 2006. But as President, Obama sponsored the MCA of 2009. Obama supported the use of military commissions, which he defended as having "a history in the United States dating back to George Washington and the Revolutionary War. They are an appropriate venue for trying detainees for violations of the laws of war" (Obama 2009d). Not only did the MCA of 2009 provide less protection than criminal prosecutions, but it also institutionalized military commissions as an option for prosecution of detainees. The government can now choose between criminal prosecution, a trial by military commission, or no trial depending upon the level of admissible evidence. Thus, against his pledges to bring detainees before U.S. federal courts, on March 7, 2011, Obama reinstated the military commission at Guantánamo Bay in order to bring terrorists to justice.

In 2010, Obama's Special Interagency Task Force determined that at least 48 Guantánamo detainees could not be released due to the extreme threat they posed to the United States and its interests. Yet, they could not be tried either in federal court or by the military commission system because of the highly classified information pertaining to them and their capture. Many detainees were captured in active combat zones where the focus was on intelligence not evidence collection. Therefore, evidence was not collected or properly preserved. Some of the detainees could not be tried due to the mistreatment they received at the hands of interrogators, thereby tainting the evidence and making it inadmissible. These detainees were candidates for indefinite detention under authority of the Authorization for Use of Military Force Act. Preventive detention is indefinite detention based on the possibility that the detainee could engage in hostile action against the United States and its citizens. Thus, Obama acquiesced to the idea that there are individuals who can be deprived of their liberty indefinitely, not because of what they did, but because of what they possibly could do if freed.

In a conventional war, it is permissible under international law to hold enemy soldiers until the end of active hostilities so that they may not return to the battlefield. Champions of preventive detention believe that holding terror suspects is analogous to detaining enemy combatants as prisoners of war. Although the hostilities in Iraq and Afghanistan have wound down, the United States is still today in the midst of a global war on terror. Yet, in a speech at the National Defense University on May 23, 2013, Obama declared the global war on terror to be over. The United States would no longer "define our effort ... a boundless 'Global War on Terror,' but rather a series of persistent, targeted efforts to dismantle specific networks of violent extremists that threaten America" (Obama 2013). With hostilities in Iraq and Afghanistan allegedly ended and the Global War on Terror declared to be over, the debate on the status of the Gitmo detainees under international law has nevertheless remained.

McCrisken (2011) criticizes the failure to close Gitmo as Obama's lack of commitment to use his political capital. The failure to exert his political capital on Capitol Hill in order to fulfill his pledge to reverse Bush's counterterrorism strategy resulted in disappointment among human rights advocates. Despite his pledge to close Guantánamo, there is evidence that Obama even planned to use the facility if needed. Leon Panetta, then director of the CIA, testified to a Senate Intelligence Committee (February 2011) hearing that "We would probably move them [Bin Laden and Ayman Al-Zawahiri] quickly into military jurisdiction at Bagram [an air base in Afghanistan] for questioning and then, eventually, move them probably to Guantánamo" (as reported by Yager 2011).

More troubling is the fact that Obama maintained the controversial policy of rendition, albeit with "more oversight" (Forsythe 2011a, 2011b). Extraordinary rendition is the kidnapping and detention of an individual who is then transported to a third state outside of established judicial processes for interrogation. The practice of rendition takes advantage of the fact that a foreign government in foreign country conducts the actual interrogation, often with the use of torture. Thus, the United States can claim that it is not responsible for the harm done. Obama continued the use of Bush's rendition program, but with stronger "diplomatic assurance" that the detainees would not be mistreated. Whitlock (2013) believes that since Congress prevented the closure of Guantánamo, the transfer of detainees to U.S. soil, and the use of civilian courts to try suspected terrorists, there were only two options available to the Obama Administration. One option was to continue the rendition program to kill suspected terrorists and the second was to increase the use of drones (see below).

Foreign Aid Remains a Tool of Counterterrorism

Foreign aid allocations exhibited remarkable continuity between the George W. Bush and Obama Administrations. The Obama Administration neither reshaped nor refocused U.S. foreign aid allocations. During both presidents' tenure, political and security concerns overrode rhetorical commitments to human rights and legislative intent in the decision of whether or not to grant U.S. aid. For the most part, Obama's "foreign aid policy does not deviate substantially from the goals pursued by the preceding Bush Administration" (Gibler and Miller 2012: 1207). Roth, the executive director of Human Rights Watch, concludes that "Obama followed in the footsteps of successive U.S. presidents by downplaying the importance of human rights" in favor of traditional foreign policy concerns, such as the promotion of economic ties, geopolitical and security interests, or diplomatic cooperation (Roth 2010: 13). However, given the importance of economic and security concerns, it would be unreasonable to expect any president to make the promotion and protection of human rights the sole, or even the primary, objective of U.S. foreign policy. And Obama was no exception.

Change in foreign aid, during the Obama Administration, was not a redirection or realignment of aid motivation, but a matter of scope. The Obama Administration called for a doubling of foreign aid from the George W. Bush Administration, with the majority of the increase going to African nations.

As a general rule, states that experience domestic terrorism receive significantly higher levels of U.S. aid than those with no domestic terrorism. Lis states that "assisting other countries in curbing homegrown terrorism is compatible with American strategic objectives" (2018: 291) because the United States wants to prevent foreign domestic terrorists from becoming international terrorists targeting the homeland. Heinrich et al. (2017) find that when terrorist organizations initiate or expand operations in a country, the importance of this country increases in U.S. foreign policy. As a result, the amount of foreign aid this country receives also increases. Foreign aid, as a tool of counterterrorism, can either "bolster the capabilities of a state that is fighting terrorists or to buy counterterrorism cooperation from states that are located in key regions" (Heinrich et al. 2017: 529).

The surge in terrorist activities in Africa explained in large part the Obama Administration's increase in aid to the continent. Foreign aid, particularly military assistance, can help a state fight insurgents and terrorists, but it can also lead to collateral damage (civilian deaths), or it can be misappropriated by the state to oppress minorities. A study by Gupta et al. (2018) published in the *Journal of Global Health* examined the relationship between a subcategory of U.S. foreign aid, health aid, and the recipient country's geopolitical relevance to U.S. national security interests during the Obama Administration. Two important findings were cited. First, the number of health aid recipients dropped from 74 in 2009 to 56 in 2016, with the reductions coming from the Americas, the Eastern Mediterranean, and Europe, but increases observed in Africa, Southeast Asia, and the Western Pacific. Second, states that presented higher threat levels received less health funding. This is a troubling given the findings of Lis (2018) and Heinrich et al. (2017). Taken together, these findings indicate that states that pose a threat to the United States received higher levels of aid, but not health aid. Rather they received military or economic, perhaps ESF, aid. Bilmes and Intriligator report that "some of the State Department aid budget to the governments of Iraq, Afghanistan, Pakistan, Yemen, and others is actually military or paramilitary assistance to those countries in support of their counterterrorism efforts" (2013: 12). Yet, Savun and Tirone (2018) determined that foreign aid given to promote good governance and strengthen civil society reduced the need for disgruntled citizens to join or support terrorist groups. Thus, U.S. military aid is unlikely to prevent the growth of terrorism, while development aid, which fosters political and social institutions as well as economic growth, can be an effective tool in counterterrorism.

In February 2014, Obama announced U.S. participation in the Global Health Security Agenda (GHSA) with the donation of more than $1 billion. The GHSA was intended to prevent, detect, and mitigate infectious diseases whether naturally occurring, intentional, or accidental.

However, human rights scholars feared that framing global health as a security issue would come at the expense of health as a human right (Amon 2014, DeLaet 2014). Securitizing health has raised public awareness and increased resources, but it also tends to privilege health concerns of developed nations over less developed nations. Thus, infectious diseases that may migrate to rich countries are prioritized over the more common health issues (related to poverty and malnutrition) experienced in poorer countries. Funding for health security threats diverts money from general health care. The origins of many infectious diseases are poverty, social inequalities (due to racism, sexism, etc.), and environmental degradation, factors that the securitization framework does not address (Quinn and Kumar 2014).

Prompted by the global economic recession and food price crisis in 2007–2008, the Obama Administration initiated the Feed the Future

Initiative (FtF) (2010). By 2009, there were over one billion food-insecure people around the world (FAO 2010). FtF was the Obama Administration's global hunger and food security program whose primary goals were about "accelerating inclusive agriculture sector growth" and about "improving nutritional status in developing countries, particularly of women and children" (Ho and Hanrahan 2011: ii). FtF initially focused on 20 countries in sub-Saharan Africa, Asia, and Latin America and the Caribbean, based on the level of chronic hunger in rural communities, potential for rapid and sustainable agricultural growth, and commitment and resources in the recipient government. FtF sought to increase staple grain production through the use of technologies and enhanced inputs (such as improved seeds, fertilizers, irrigation systems, and modern farming methods), expanded markets, and free trade in the least developed countries. To this end, Obama pledged $3.5 billion over three years with additional funding in following fiscal years with the USAID as the lead agency in the implementation of the program and the DOS assisting with diplomatic efforts. The USAID created a Bureau for Food Security to "lead a whole-of-government effort to implement President Obama's Feed the Future initiative" (Shah 2010). The new bureau would be responsible for coordinating the activities of the 11 government agencies, including the major actors, the State Department, the Millennium Challenge Corporation, the Department Agriculture, the Department of the Treasury, the U.S. African Development Foundation, and USAID, in the global fight against hunger. The prime measures of success were child stunting and wasting rates, and the number of underweight women. The empowerment of women is a major theme of FtF. Countries included in FtF had greater agricultural production than other developing countries. According to the USAID, this additional production was worth $2.6 billion in new agricultural sales, with the goal of increasing the incomes of farmers, expanding farm labor opportunities, and providing the non-land owning poor greater access to food (2017). FtF programs also resulted in a 19 percent drop in poverty and a 26 percent drop in child stunting in the focus countries from 2011 to 2017.

The growth of Foreign Military Sales (FMS) is a particularly notable aspect of the three Ds of security (defense, diplomacy, and development are outlined as pillars of U.S. national security strategy) during the George W. Bush Administration and has remained high during the Obama Administration. Once a comparatively small yet important foreign assistance program, FMS had grown to a nearly $70 billion industry by 2012. At one time exports of arms, dual-use technologies, and advanced weapons were directed to NATO, Asian partners, and a couple of Middle Eastern allies. However, the growth of FMS witnessed the expansion of sales to less stable and nondemocratic countries (Irwin et al. 2014). As a consequence, the Obama Administration issued Presidential Policy Directive (PPD)-27 "United States Conventional Arms Transfer Policy (2014)." PDD-27 lists

13 criteria that must be taken into account. Most are similar to President Bill Clinton's 1995 PPD-34 Conventional Arms Transfer Policy. The one new criterion government officials had to consider was:

> The likelihood that the recipient would use the arms to commit human rights abuses or serious violations of international humanitarian law, retransfer the arms to those who would commit human rights abuses or serious violations of international humanitarian law, or identify the United States with human rights abuses or serious violations of international humanitarian law.

Furthermore, PDD-27 specifically requires the United States to restrain from providing FMS if:

> it has actual knowledge at the time of authorization that the transferred arms will be used to commit: genocide; crimes against humanity; grave breaches of the Geneva Conventions of 1949; serious violations of Common Article 3 of the Geneva Conventions of 1949; attacks directed against civilian objects or civilians who are legally protected from attack or other war crimes as defined in 18 U.S.C. 2441.

The United States was already required to take human rights into consideration in arms transfers, but these new criteria and prohibition, in the words of Rachel Stohl, "elevate human rights and humanitarian law concerns to a position of prominence not seen in U.S. policy before" (2014: 17).

Military aid has been given as a counterterrorism tool. It can enable the recipient government to thwart terrorist attacks or decrease the number of groups that are operational through capture, detention, or destruction. However, there is a moral hazard in the allocation of military aid. States that receive large amounts of military aid in order to fight terrorism within their territories have little incentive to destroy terrorist groups; if they do the aid will stop. However, recipient states do have the incentive to exaggerate the threats and overstate their successes in order to assure the continuation of aid. Fighting terrorism can be profitable and can maintain the regime's authority over a well-funded and equipped military apparatus. In addition, the recipient state can use the weaponry given to fight terrorism against run-of-the-mill opposition groups. Because many recipient states are dependent on U.S. military aid to remain in power, the United States is willing to supply aid to countries of interest to prevent regime collapse, even to autocratic but friendly regimes.

The Obama Administration instituted an accounting trick to expand the foreign aid budget. Foreign aid designated OCO allowed Congress to appropriate greater amounts of aid without violating the Budget Control Act, which established caps on discretionary funding. Any funds designated as OCO would not count against the budget limit set by the Budget Control Act. Originally the OCO or "emergency funding" was used for war-related funding. But since 2011, OCO has been used to fund regular operations. With the enormous amounts of resources directed to Iraq and Afghanistan, OCO "makes it possible to keep war-related funding from crowding out core international affairs activities within the budget allocation" (Tarnoff and Lawson 2016: 18). In this way, the President can spend additional U.S. taxpayer provided money while complying with statutory spending limits intended to limit government spending and reduce the deficit.

"Things Are Going to Get Worse"

On December 7, 2008, Obama warned that "things are going to get worse before they get better" (Kornblut 2008). Obama was talking about the economy, but it could also have been a warning to whistleblowers and human rights advocates about the expansion of prosecutions, signature drone strikes, the cover-up of Bush-era atrocities, and detention and torture in the detention facilities at the Bagram Airbase in Afghanistan. The Obama Administration pursued a war strategy that allowed the targeting of "war-sustaining" capabilities. Under this approach, the United States could target economic objects important for the war effort, such as factories or oil refineries, but also dual-use industries that serve the civilian population, in a way that "radically expands the scope of targets a state may legally use force against, with potentially serious consequences for civilians" (Chertoff and Manfredi, forthcoming). However, this was clearly in violation of Article 52 of Additional Protocol I to the Geneva Conventions. Article 52(2) states:

> Attacks shall be limited strictly to military objectives. In so far as objects are concerned, military objectives are limited to those objects which by their nature, location, purpose or use make an effective contribution to military action and whose total or partial destruction, capture or neutralization, in the circumstances ruling at the time, offers a definite military advantage.[6]

If there is any doubt as to whether an object is for military or civilian use, the Geneva Conventions advocate for the presumption of civilian use and therefore prohibited from attack.

Traitors or Whistleblowers: The Government's Desire for Secrecy versus the Public's Right to Know

Despite Obama's pledge of transparency, the Justice Department responded aggressively to prevent disclosure of information of misconduct.

Political challengers, those who questioned the government's policies and programs, had been silenced with threats of prosecution and jail time. The secrecy system, as described by Schlesinger, was "controlled by those on whom it bestowed prestige and protection, it had long since overridden its legitimate objectives" (2004: 344). Secrecy would become the "all purpose means" for the president to "dissemble its purposes, bury its mistakes, manipulate its citizens and maximize its power" (2004: 345). Against this backdrop, Schlesinger notes a "recurrent pattern" of a proud history of leaking government secrets, otherwise known as whistleblowing, since the founding of the United States. As Schlesinger put it:

> When the Republic faced a hard decision in foreign policy and the executive branch had not revealed facts that would enable the people to reach their own judgment, aggrieved citizens felt themselves morally warranted in violating a system of secrecy exploited (as they earnestly believed) by government against the national interest.
> (Schlesinger 2004: 333)

Whistleblowing, in American popular culture, is often associated with heroes, or those who are brave enough to expose hidden misdeeds by the powerful, thereby upholding American values and protecting democracy.

Someone is a leaker if they disclose information (state secrets) that threatens the national security of the United States. Norris describes the distinction between a whistleblower and a leaker as follows: "bad leaks actually harm the nation's defense capabilities or assist its enemies, while good whistleblowing reveals government fraud and abuse" (2013: 696). It is obvious that the government, the entity accused of wrongdoing but also that determines whether the individual is a whistleblower or a leaker, has a vested interest in the outcome. For example, WikiLeaks released documents on the war in Afghanistan, "including information on civilian casualties, the strength of the Taliban, friendly fire episodes" (Knickerbocker 2010). Later, WikiLeaks published information regarding the war in Iraq, "included details of torture and abuse of Iraqi prisoners, secret civilian death counts" (Knickerbocker 2010). This information was not a threat to national capabilities, but it did make the U.S. government look bad and could perhaps make the American public question the morality of governmental actions. Those in power use the label of leaker to describe someone who discloses information that is unfavorable to them. By 2017, there have been only 11 prosecutions under the Espionage Act of government officials or employees, eight of which occurred under the Obama Administration. The Obama transition website, Change.gov, declared that whistleblowing referred to "acts of courage and patriotism, which can sometimes save lives and often save taxpayer dollars, should be encouraged rather than stifled" (Obama 2008). Yet, the Obama Administration aggressively targeted whistleblowers for prosecution.

Papandrea argues that "all leaks expose government secrets and undermine the executive's ability to control the dissemination of information to the public" (2014: 449). Given the low level of national defense capability information that the eight Espionage Act prosecutions under Obama represented, the real reason why the Obama Administration went after these whistleblowers was to control the dissemination of information to the public. It was simply retaliation for those who had embarrassed the Administration by exposing corruption, illegality, incompetence, or inanity. Although the Obama Administration had sought to identify and punish whistleblowers who released information about illegal or legally questionable government activity, it remained apathetic in identifying and prosecuting those involved in the illegal conduct in the first place.

Indeed, a quote attributed to George Orwell sums it all up, "In a time of universal deceit – telling the truth is a revolutionary act."[7] Excessive secrecy and the threat of prosecution for whistleblowing undermine democratic debate and safeguards. Given the encompassing nature of counterterrorism policies and practices, the persecution of truth tellers is unlikely to change in the foreseeable future.

Bagram: Obama's Gitmo

In 2011, Deputy National Security Adviser John Brennan (2011) declared: "We will not send more individuals to the prison at Guantánamo." This pledge was easy to observe since the Obama Administration was sending suspected terrorists to the Parwan Detention Center instead of Guantánamo. The Parwan Detention Center is situated outside of the Bagram military facility and is officially under the control of the Afghan National Army. However, Tutt (2013) determines that the United States functionally controlled the detainees at Bagram until they were transferred to the Afghan government, a long and contentious process. In addition, the detention center is surrounded by U.S. checkpoints and was staffed by U.S. guards.

Bagram Detention Facility initially served as a primary screening facility where detainees would be pipelined to Guantánamo or rendered to foreign countries (Hajjar 2011). Human Rights First (2011) reports that the detained population tripled to 1,700 between Obama's inauguration and Brennan's declaration. Bagram detainees were afforded even fewer rights than those at Guantánamo. The Obama Administration sought to prevent the extension of *habeas corpus* rights, granted in *Boumediene v. Bush*, to the black holes of the Bagram Detention Facilities (Parwan and Tor Jain), claiming that detainees were non-Americans in a theater of war and in a foreign territory, unlike the *de facto* sovereignty the United States has over Guantánamo. Detainees could thus be held without charge until the end of the armed conflict with al-Qaeda and its associated organizations. The Geneva Conventions authorize the parties in an international war to imprison the other side's soldiers until the end of the conflict. Otherwise the soldiers could return to the battlefield. But it also means that detainees are freed when the hostilities end. For a war without end, and a war with an amorphous evil, this was the equivalent to life imprisonment.

When naming Dennis Blair as National Intelligence Director and Leon Panetta as head of the CIA, Obama claimed to order the directors to restore the U.S. record on human rights. Obama stated: "I was clear throughout this campaign and was clear throughout this transition that under my administration the United States does not torture... We will abide by the Geneva Conventions. We will uphold our highest ideals" (2009e). However, there is evidence that there was torture under Obama's leadership. Open Society Foundations reported allegations of abuse in a small detention facility, the notorious Tor Jail or Black Jail, located inside the Bagram Air Base in Afghanistan and run by the U.S. Defense Intelligence Agency and the U.S. Special Operations Forces. "These reports," Open Society Foundations interviews revealed, "included accusations of sleep deprivation, holding detainees in cold cells, forced nudity, physical abuse, detaining individuals in isolation cells for longer than 30 days, and restricting the access of the International Committee of the Red Cross (ICRC)," actions inconsistent with the Army Field Manual and the Geneva Conventions (Open Society Foundations 2010: 2). The Obama Administration called the facility an interrogation facility rather than a detention facility. Therefore, the ICRC did not have the right to visit the site. Furthermore, Obama's Executive Order to close foreign detention facilities excluded those sites used to hold people "on a short-term, transitory basis." Thus, it allowed the CIA to legally hold suspects for a short period of time before they were rendered. Many detainees detained by U.S. forces were thus transferred to the Afghan National Directorate of Security (NDS) with the knowledge that they would be tortured.

Drones and Targeted Killing

In the category of "things are going to get worse" is Obama's expansion of the drone war and assassinations. The contemporary norm against the targeted killing or assassination of a leader remains a formidable restraint on state action. Thomas notes that "[e]ven the lawful targeting of leaders during wartime, which is not properly considered assassination at all, has been rare because of the strength of the norm against assassination itself" (2000: 114).[8] The infrequency of political assassination is due to the stigma associated with the act. This is not to say that states have not violated the norm and have not killed or attempted to kill foreign leaders. But the violating state endeavors to conceal its actions (Senn and Troy 2017). The United States initially denied the use of targeted killings, but eventually acknowledged the policy. Thus, in the words of Senn and Troy, targeted killing "moved from the fringes of undercover activity to the very core of policy-making in national security" (2017: 176). In justifying the use of targeted killings, the United States argued that its use complied with international humanitarian law obligations, in particular, *jus ad bellum* and *jus in bello* principles, military necessary, proportionality, and distinguishing between civilians and belligerents (Jose 2017). However, like his predecessor, Obama prevaricated that long-established and time-honored principles of international humanitarian law "needed to be reinterpreted to reflect the new kind of war it was waging against Al-Qaeda" allowing the use of targeted killings (Jose 2017: 248).[9] Furthermore, since the scope of the war on terror was global, targeted killings in countries the United States was not in conflict with, such as Yemen or Pakistan, were also permissible.

Obama's claim to combat terrorism more morally than his predecessor was contradicted by his use of drone warfare. Harold Koh, legal adviser to the DOS, stated that the United States has the legal right "to use force, including lethal force, to defend itself, including by targeting persons such as high-level al-Qaeda leaders who are planning attacks" (2010). Koh claimed that "using such advanced technologies can ensure both that the best intelligence is available for planning operations, and that civilian casualties are minimized in carrying out such operations" (2010). Yet, as studies by Cronin (2013), Entous (2010), and Stanford Law School and NYU School of Law (2012) have shown, drone attacks were not free of collateral damage or civilian deaths, as the Obama Administration would have had us believe. Collateral damage, to be absolutely clear about what the term means, refers to the injury and death of civilians and the destruction of their homes and businesses. In a speech before the National Defense University in 2013, Obama justified the use of drone warfare: "remember that the terrorists we are after target civilians, and the death toll from their acts of terrorism against Muslims dwarfs any estimate of civilian casualties from." Terrorists' targeting of civilians excused and justified the collateral damage and possible misidentified victims by U.S. drones.

Obama's use of drones was, according to Byman, "the centerpiece of U.S. counterterrorism strategy" because of its success in killing targets, its low cost, and its ability to reduce the risk for U.S. soldiers (2013: 32). Byman further claims that drones are less destructive than actually using soldiers or large-scale air campaigns. Lewis and Holewinsk (2013) question the assumption that drones are surgical in nature and, therefore, less likely to cause civilian injuries and death. In fact, drones "were statistically more likely to cause civilian casualties than were operations conducted by manned air platforms. One reason was limited training for UAS operators and analysts in how to minimize civilian harm" (Lewis and Holewinsk 2013: 60). Furthermore, the lack of transparency in the use of drones "raises significant concerns that civilian casualties will not be properly monitored or investigated" (Lewis and Holewinsk 2013: 60).

Multiple sources report that the majority of drone strikes killed low-level militants without the means to pose a serious threat to the United States (Entous 2010, Bergen and Braun 2012). A New America report (online) found that drone attacks no longer targeted high-value terrorists but rather marked lower-level militants with unsubstantiated links to Al-Qaeda in locales where the United States was not at war.

More worrisome is the fact that, given the accounting method employed by the Obama Administration whereby all military aged males were assumed insurgent combatants, these dead low-level militants were actually civilians. Byman acknowledges that the "U.S. government assumes that all military-age males in the blast area of a drone strike are combatants—unless it can determine after the fact that they were innocent (and such intelligence gathering is not a priority)" (2013: 36). The Obama Administration counted every military-age male killed by their drones as a terrorist, thus blurring important legal, military, political, and moral distinctions between combatants and civilians. It also made it difficult to determine the number of innocent civilians killed. The Obama Administration's accounting practice was so unsavory that the CIA worried that it was "'guilt by association' that has led to 'deceptive' estimates of civilian casualties ...They count the corpses and they're not really sure who they are" (Becker and Shane 2012: A1). A drone victim was thus guilty (and dead or maimed) until proven innocent. This counting method allowed the Administration to report extraordinarily low collateral deaths.

To make matters worse, the Obama Administration signed off on "signature strikes" that targeted groups involved in suspicious activities (whatever these were) rather than identifying specific individuals. When the behavior of a group of men fit a certain pattern, or they had the misfortune to live in an area of known terrorist activity, it was assumed they were terrorists and could be eliminated on mere speculation, without evidence and without a trial. Becker and Shanemay's story in the *New York Times* relays the joke that "when the C.I.A. sees 'three guys doing jumping jacks,' the agency thinks it is a terrorist training camp... Men loading a truck with fertilizer could be bombmakers — but they might also be farmers" (2012). The Obama Administration's use of signature strike drone attacks was a clear violation of human rights law (and of Ford's 1976 executive order banning the practice of assassinations).

Drone target strikes violate international human rights law since civilians are killed in countries that have not declared war on the United States. Legal problems arise "when drones are used in targeted killings outside of traditional or 'hot' battlefields that their use challenges existing legal frameworks" (Brooks 2013: 8). In the absence of an armed conflict, human rights law applies. Under international human rights law, the right to use lethal force is circumscribed. The use of lethal force is only allowed to protect a life (self-defense or the defense of another) when there are no other means and the threat is imminent (Stanford-NYU Law 2012). The Obama Administration used drone strikes in Pakistan, Somalia, Yemen, Mali, and the Philippines. Obama relied on the George W. Bush Administration's conceptualization of the global—any place at any time—war on terror. Thus, anyone could be labeled an enemy combatant and, in the opinion of the Obama Administration, a legitimate drone target.

The determination of who was a legitimate target was based on classified intelligence reporting. The drone attack itself was a covert action, executed without public acknowledgment of what the threat was in the first place (Brooks 2013). When faced with criticism, the Obama Administration argued that

> if a person located in a foreign state poses an 'imminent threat of violent attack' against the United States, the U.S. can lawfully use force in self-defense, provided that the defensive force used is otherwise consistent with law of war principles.
>
> (Brooks 2013: 12)

However, this argument relied on a broad interpretation of the term "imminent." Imminent, according to a 2011 Justice Department opinion, "does not require the United States to have clear evidence that a specific attack on U.S. persons and interests will take place in the immediate future" (DOJ 2011: 7). Attorney General Eric Holder argued that the targeted killings of American citizens via drone strikes were constitutionally permissible if government officials considered that the individual posed "an imminent threat of violent attack" (MSN 2013). In fact, terrorists, both domestic and foreign, were "continually planning attacks against U.S. persons and interest" and "would engage in such attacks regularly" if they could. Thus, a broad concept of imminence meant a perpetual possibility of a future attack. Holder (2012) outlined three criteria for using lethal force in a foreign country. First, the targeted individual had to pose an imminent threat of violent attack against the United States. Second, capture was not feasible. And third, the operation would be conducted in a manner consistent with the laws of war.

Obama's intention to strengthen counterterrorism while respecting international law represented either a contradictory and inconstant policy or was simply hypocritical, depending on one's ideological leanings or moral standards. This is particularly evident in the legality of drone targeting and the international law principle of imminence. Drone attacks are targeted killings "without sufficient clarity about the legal framework" since the targets rarely pose an "imminent lethal threat" to anyone (Roth 2017). The use of drones, or remotely piloted aerial systems, allowed the "US to 'expand the battlefield,' striking targets in places where it would be too dangerous or too politically controversial to send troops" (Brooks 2013: 8).

Cronin points to one beneficial aspect of carefully planned and executed drone attacks[10]: the fear of drone attacks that is "keeping [terrorists] preoccupied with survival and hindering their ability to move, plan operations, and carry them out" (2013: 45). Thus, drone attacks could lower the overall level of violence within a community. Terrorists would also have a more difficult time recruiting if potential insurgents believed there was a real possibility of being killed (on the other hand, the indiscriminate killing of innocent Muslims could become a recruiting tool by alienating local populations). Drones are also cheaper to use and they reduce the political cost associated with American casualties. The unfortunate consequence would be reducing the threshold for determining when to use deadly force, thereby increasing the frequency of drone-targeted killings.

Cronin believes that the capture, rather than killing, of a terrorist leader can effectively disrupt a terrorist network and, at the same time, avoid creating a martyr. But this leaves the question of where the terrorist would be held. McCrisken concluded that "Obama prefers a kill-not-capture policy" (2011: 794). Obama could not repopulate Guantánamo after his campaign pledge to close it down. Thus,

> under Obama, the CIA has killed more people than it has captured, mainly through drone missile strikes in Pakistan's tribal areas. At the same time, it has stopped trying to detain or interrogate suspects caught abroad, except those captured in Iraq and Afghanistan.
> (Dilanian 2011)[11]

The use of targeted killing did solve Obama's political problem of capturing, incarcerating, and interrogating enemy soldiers/civilians/terrorists. Obama had chosen a more direct and concealed solution to terrorists—unmanned Predator drone attacks in Afghanistan, Pakistan, Yemen, Somalia, Iraq, and Syria. Obama's critics believed that taking no prisoner was his practical and politically wily choice behind drone attacks. Senator Saxby Chambliss (R-GA), the top Republican on the Intelligence Committee, commented that the Obama Administration's "policy is to take out high-value targets, versus capturing high-value targets" (as quoted in McCrisken 2011: 35). The political problem associated with detention was thus resolved in a take-no-prisoners drone attack. Consequently, drone strikes "have replaced Guantánamo as the recruiting tool of choice for militants" (Becker and Shane 2012: A1).

The drone program became a rallying cry for recruitment and radicalization. Errant or mistargeted drone strikes increased resentment against the United States and assisted terrorists in recruiting angry tormented civilians. Civilians as collateral damage "may be creating sworn enemies out of a sea of local insurgents" (Cronin 2013: 44) while driving "new recruits to the very terrorist and insurgent groups the United States was trying to eliminate" (Jaffar 2016: 15–16).

The war in Afghanistan, code name Operation Enduring Freedom, officially ended on December 28, 2014 when the United States and NATO transferred full security responsibility to the Afghan government and withdrew their troops. From December 29, 2014 to the present, U.S. involvement in Afghanistan has been called Operation Freedom's Sentinel. The new training and advising mission has involved approximately 10,000 troops.[12] The key to Operation Freedom's Sentinel has been "using unmanned aerial vehicles to conduct intelligence, surveillance, record assistance, and strike mission" (Cutler 2017: 22). Drones have the politically beneficial feature of limiting the number of U.S. soldiers "with boots on the ground" while responding to terrorist threats. Given the benefits of drone warfare, the use of drones would continue into the Trump Administration.

Failure to Prosecute

In 2005, with the continuing controversy over and looming Congressional investigation into allegations of torture and rendition, the CIA destroyed 92 interrogation videotapes taken at a CIA black site in Thailand at the order of Jose Rodriguez, Director of the National Clandestine Service of the CIA. The destruction was a response to the 2005 Detainee Treatment Act. Rodriguez feared that CIA operatives could be held accountable and prosecuted for their cruelty and criminality during interrogations. He admits that he was "getting rid of some ugly visuals" (2012: 193). In January 2008, after the destruction of the tapes became public knowledge, Assistant U.S. Attorney John Durham was charged with conducting a criminal investigation.

In August 2009, Attorney General Holder decided to expand Durham's mandate to include "a preliminary review into whether federal laws were violated in connection with the interrogation of specific detainees at oversees locations." Holder promised that the DOJ would not prosecute anyone who acted in good faith and within the scope of the legal guidance given by the OLC (2009). Durham concluded his investigation in 2010 and did not file criminal charges in the destruction of the tapes. Upon Durham's recommendation, Holder concluded that a further investigation of CIA interrogation techniques was not warranted (Holder 2011) and that no charges would be brought against anyone regarding the deaths of two detainees in CIA custody (Holder 2012). So, despite evidence and admissions by intelligence agency officials and others that they witnessed or participated in the use of torture against detainees, the Obama Administration refused to prosecute offenders. Goldsmith, U.S. Assistant Attorney General leading the OLC, stated that one consequence of OLC's authority to interpret the law is the power to bestow on government officials what is effectively an advance pardon for actions taken at the edges of vague criminal laws...It is one of the most momentous and dangerous power in the government: the power to dispense get-out-of-jail-free cards.

(2007: 96–97)

Obama made it clear that the George W. Bush Administration and its members would not face charges for their potentially criminal conduct relating to the war on terror. In fact, Comar (2013) reports that Obama's DOJ filed papers in a civil suit requesting that "George W. Bush, Richard Cheney, Donald Rumsfeld, Colin Powell, Condoleezza Rice and Paul Wolfowitz be granted procedural immunity" for planning and waging of the Iraq War. The suit, *Saleh v. Bush* (No. 15-15098 (9th Cir. 2017), was dismissed with prejudice. Given the continuity and extension of the Bush-era war on terror tactics, the Obama Administration may have been calculating that prosecution of human rights violators in the government may set a precedent that could be used against them. After all, Obama had continued to pursue the war on terror in noncombat zones in Yemen, Somalia, and Pakistan against unidentified suspects (three men doing jumping jacks, as we saw above).

In addition, an attempt to prosecute George W. Bush Administration officials for their illegal activities in the early interrogation program would have been extremely controversial. There are still many, both within the government and in the American public at large, who believe that torture is a necessary and efficient tool in the war on terror. Prosecution, or even the establishment of a truth commission, was a politically, perhaps legally, risky move that the Obama Administration would not or could not take.

Improvements in Human Rights Policies

The Obama Administration tackled a number of human rights issues favorably. The Obama Administration rhetorically supported many human rights treaties: the Convention on the Elimination of All Forms of Discrimination Against Women, the Convention on the Rights of the Child, and the Convention on the Rights of Persons with Disabilities (CRPD). But Obama also failed to submit any of them to the Senate for ratification.

Interrogation Methods

Within days of his inauguration, Obama issued Executive Order 13491 "Ensuring Lawful Interrogations" that rescinded all "executive directives, orders, and regulations" issued during the Bush era that contravened the U.S. obligations under the Geneva Conventions. Executive Order 13491 stated:

> From this day forward, unless the Attorney General with appropriate consultation provides further guidance, officers, employees, and other agents of the United States Government ... may not, in conducting interrogations, rely upon any interpretation of the law governing interrogation ... issued by the Department of Justice between September 11, 2001, and January 20, 2009.
>
> (Obama 2009f)

Executive Order 13491 also set Common Article 3 of the Geneva Conventions as the "minimum baseline" for treatment, adhering to the Convention against Torture. The order established the Army Field Manual 2-22.3 Human Intelligence Collector Operations (34-52) as the standard for interrogation techniques used by the CIA and DOD.[13] The 2006 revised version of the 1963 Manual specifically prohibits interrogation methods that were associated with the Bush-Cheney-Rumsfield Administration:

> Forcing the detainee to be naked, perform sexual acts, or pose in a sexual manner; Placing hoods or sacks over the head of a detainee; using duct tape over the eyes; Applying beatings, electric shock, burns, or other forms of physical pain; "Waterboarding"; Using military working dogs; Inducing hypothermia or heat injury; Conducting mock executions; Depriving the detainee of necessary food, water, or medical care.
>
> (2006: at 5–21)

Human Rights First (2010) notes that two methods of intimidation, the use of stress positions and sleep deprivation, were not included in the 2006 manual. The new manual included Appendix M, which specifies a new restricted interrogation technique called "separation." Separation is the physical seclusion of the prisoner away from other prisoners, and it can be used on an enemy prisoner of war but only after proper authority is secured. It is a technique that can easily be abused. If, however, physical separation is not feasible, Appendix M allows for the use of goggles, blindfolds, and earmuffs, for up to 12 hours, to "generate a perception of separation." The manual believes that separation will lead to a feeling of futility and surrender, thus making the prisoner more compliant. Human Rights First (2010), relaying the opinion of U.S. Army Colonel Stuart Herrington, stated that separation, correctly used, may allow a willing informant to provide valuable information in a discrete environment away from the eyes of fellow prisoners. President Obama and Attorney General Holder reformed the MCA in 2009 to increase procedural safeguards for the unpriviliged enemy belligerents. For example, it contained a prohibition on statements obtained through cruel, inhuman, and degrading treatment.

Furthermore, to minimize the risk of torture, Obama closed the secret CIA prisons known as black sites, prohibited the CIA from holding detainees except on a "short-term, transitory basis," and granted the International Committee of the Red Cross access to detainees. Moreover, interrogations would no longer be contracted out to non-CIA officers.

LGBTQ Rights[14]

Human Rights First (2017) praised Obama's record on the human rights of the LGBTQ community as unparalleled as a result of his support for by domestic legislation and his promotion of LGBTQ issues in foreign policy. In an address to the U.N. General Assembly, Obama stated that "no country should deny people their rights because of who they love, which is why we must stand up for the rights of gays and lesbians everywhere" (2011a). This speech signaled Obama's attempt to make the United States a leader in securing LGBTQ rights as a universal human rights norm. But the Obama Administration's support for LGBTQ rights had begun earlier.

In the introduction to the State Department's 2009 *Country Reports on Human Rights Practices*, the section on "Discrimination and Harassment of Vulnerable Groups" included for the first time a statement on LGBTQ violations:

> Members of vulnerable groups – racial, ethnic and religious minorities; the disabled; women and children; migrant workers; and lesbian, gay, bisexual, and transgender individuals – often were marginalized and targets of societal and/or government-sanctioned abuse.
> (Department of State 2009)

The LGBTQ community was specifically named as a vulnerable group, with Uganda singled out as an egregious abuser. By 2014, the report listed Cameroon, Zambia, Nigeria, and Russia, along with Uganda, as extreme examples of state abuse against LGBTQ individuals. These countries had placed "restrictions on freedoms of association and assembly" and LGBTQ individuals were "subject to societal harassment, intimidation, threats to their well-being, and were denied access to health services" and life-threatening acts of violence. Countries with less severe violations were also reported.

Uganda, a large recipient of U.S. and international aid, passed an Anti-Homosexuality Bill in October 2009 that criminalized homosexuality and penalizing offenders with execution. After international outcry, the Ugandan Parliament abandoned its attempts to pass the bill. In 2011, the Parliament reopened consideration of the bill that was amended to recommend life imprisonment rather than execution as the sentence for homosexual acts. In response, Obama issued Presidential Memorandum "International Initiatives to Advance the Human Rights of Lesbian, Gay, Bisexual, and Transgender Persons." The memorandum specified that all government agencies had to consider the treatment of sexual minorities in the potential aid recipient country before distributing U.S. foreign assistance. The memorandum directed "all agencies engaged abroad to ensure that U.S. diplomacy and foreign assistance promote and protect the human rights of LGBT persons" (Obama 2011b: 1).

The State Department announced the creation of the Global Equality Fund in December 2011 to promote the human rights of LGBTQ individuals by providing logistical and financial support to civil society organizations and human rights defenders through small grants. In addition, the Fund, according to the State Department website, "provides human rights defenders with legal representation, security, and, when necessary, relocation support" (2013). The fund was modestly funded with $3 million, and managed by the DRL. But it attracted funding from foreign governments, corporations, and foundations, too.

In 2013, the USAID created the LGBTQ Global Development Partnership along with the Swedish International Development Cooperation Agency and several private organizations. The LGBTQ Global Development Partnership provided funding for training, research, and participation of LGBTQ leaders in effective participation in government policymaking. It also advanced economic empowerment by supporting LGBTQ entrepreneurship and business development. In 2014, the White House hosted the Global Lesbian, Gay, Bisexual and Transgender Human Rights Forum to raise awareness of the political, legal, and cultural restrictions that impinge on the rights of sexual minorities. In 2015, Obama created a Special Envoy for the Human Rights of LGBTQ Persons within the State Department to promote and protect the human rights of the LGBTQ community. The State Department's annual *Country Reports on Human Rights Practices* now includes a determination of the human rights conditions of the LGBTQ community.

The use of foreign aid is an important tool for the DOS and the USAID to take action to protect against discrimination and abuse of LGBTQ individuals. However, Comstock (2016) found that U.S. foreign aid to Nigeria and Uganda, countries that penalized homosexuality with death sentences, remained at previous levels or actually increased. Not unlike other human rights concerns, LGBTQ human rights issues played a secondary role in foreign aid allocations under Obama. U.S. human rights policy has always been subordinate to strategic, commercial, and political objectives.

Obama extended LGBTQ rights domestically too. In hard fought battles, Congress, with the support of the President, passed legislation protecting the rights of gay, lesbian, and transgendered citizens. In 2009, Congress passed and Obama signed the Matthew Shepard and James Byrd Jr. Hate Crimes Prevention Act. The act expanded the hate-crime laws to protect victims against crimes motivated by their sexual orientation. In 2010, the Don't Ask, Don't Tell Repeal Act was passed by Congress and signed into law by Obama, thereby allowing gays, lesbians, and bisexuals to serve openly in the U.S. Armed Forces.

Obama also instructed the Department of Justice to stop defending the Defense of Marriage Act of 1996, the law that prohibited the federal government from recognizing same-sex marriages. The Supreme Court found the Defense of Marriage Act unconstitutional in 2013. Obama's Department of Justice filed an amicus brief in support of legalizing same-sex marriage in *Obergefell v. Hodges* (2015), the Supreme Court case that declared same-sex marriage a constitutionally guaranteed right.

The Employment Non-Discrimination Act (ENDA) is legislation proposed to prohibit discrimination in hiring and employment due to individual's sexual orientation or gender identity. ENDA has been introduced to Congress every year since 1994 (with the exception of 2005–2007). Congress has yet to pass the legislation. As a result, in 2014, President Barack Obama issued Executive Order 13672 "Further Amendments to Executive Order 11478, Equal Employment Opportunity in the Federal Government, and Executive Order 11246, Equal Employment Opportunity" protecting LBGTI employees working for government contractors by providing "a uniform policy for the Federal Government to prohibit discrimination… based on sexual orientation and gender identity" (Obama 2014b). At signing, the President avowed: "we're going to prohibit all companies that receive a contract from the federal government from discriminating against their LGBTQ employees. America's federal contracts should not subsidize discrimination against the American people" (Obama 2014c).

Although there are many reasons for the acceptance, however limited it yet remains, for LGBTQ rights, Human Rights First declared: "there is also no doubt that his [Obama's] leadership has been a remarkable catalyst for moving this larger conversation forward" (2017: 3).

Congressional Actions and Inactions

Cohen et al. (2013) outline the two theoretical lines of thought regarding presidential success with Congress. The first is skill. The importance of personal skill in leadership, that is the ability to persuade and to bargain, is paramount. A President cannot simply command since Congress has overlapping powers and the bureaucracy has the ability to obstruct Presidential directives. In fact, Neustadt (1980) believes that the Presidential has an easier time persuading and bargaining with Congress than with his own executive branch because Congress needs the President's cooperation on issues important to it. The second concerns political context. When the President's party controls Congress, party polarization is low, and/or the president's approval rating is high, the President will be more successful in enacting his/her political agenda. Although all Presidents face a less than favorable political context, some Presidents confront an extremely adverse environment. Obama's success relied on a cohesive Democratic majority that passed his policies despite unified opposition from the Republican minority. When the Democrats controlled the House in the 111th Congress (2009–2010), Obama won 94 percent and 87 percent of the roll call votes in respective years. However, when the Republican took control of the House for the 112th Congress (2011–2012), he only won 31 percent and 11 percent in respective years (Cohen et al. 2014). The Republicans picked up 63 seats in the House of Representatives in the 2010 mid-term elections, erasing the gains Democrats had made in the 2006 and 2008 elections. Tea Party-endorsed candidates accounted for more than two-thirds of the Republican wins, thus further mounting political opposition to Obama's liberal agenda.

When a president cannot enact his policy choices by influencing Congressional legislation, he will attempt to accomplish his goals administratively. When Congress delays the president's agenda, he often turns to the use of executive orders bypassing Congress altogether. Presidents have often turned to an administrative presidency strategy, through the use of executive orders and the appointment of loyalists, when faced with a Congress that is not supportive of the president's policy preferences. Obama signed 277 executive orders, but this was still fewer than the 364 signed by Bill Clinton and George W. Bush's 291 (American Presidency Project 2018). By appointing loyalists to positions of power within the bureaucracy, the president is better able to affect policy outcomes. However, at the end of the day, Congress still maintains the power of the purse and the power to legislate presidential behavior.

In order to fund the implementation of the Executive Orders regarding Guantánamo, Obama requested $80 million in supplemental funding. Obama had failed to consult with Congressional members regarding his plans to close Guantánamo and had no plan on where to house the detainees, particularly those who were a severe threat to the security of the United States. Congress steadfastly refused to fund Guantánamo's closure schemes. Without funding, Executive Orders were rendered inoperable. Congress further negated Obama's executive order by using its powers of legislation. The Skelton National Defense Authorization Act 2011 prohibited the use of federal funds to transfer or release detainees from Guantánamo or to use any funds to construct or modify any facility in the United States to house detainees. No elected official wanted to be seen as putting her constituents' safety at risk.

When the Democrats lost the House of Representatives to Republican control in the 2010 midterm elections, Congress also used its power of the purse to prevent the closure of Guantánamo or the transfer of detainees to U.S. prisons for either criminal prosecution or detention. To emphasize its opposition to the closure of Guantánamo and the transfer of detainees into the United States, Congress added a clause in the National Defense Authorization Act, banning the use of DOD funds to construct or modify any facility within the United States to house detainees or to transfer, or assist in the transfer of detainees to or within the United States. Obama strongly objected to the provision but felt compelled to sign the act that funded the U.S. military.

The breakdown of foreign policy consensus led to greater Congressional activism. Congressional support for the President's foreign policy priorities, not surprisingly, was split along partisan lines. Republicans challenged Obama's foreign policy actions, stressing the danger to the American public if counterterrorism strategies were moderated and civil liberties restored to foreigners. Many Democrats, although they supported Obama, were dismayed that he did not shift away from his predecessor's lawless and incompetent policies.

Oftentimes, the shift from presidential to Congressional power is predicated on international crises. When the country experiences a crisis, the president gains greater levels of power with congressional acquiescence and deference. If a presidential action could result in loss of American lives, Congress does not want the responsibility associated with voting to approve the action. Congress is often happy to be circumvented by presidential unilateral action. And if the hostilities become unpopular, Congressional members do not want to be linked with them. But when the pendulum shifts to Congress during times of peace (normalcy or relative stability), we see greater levels of congressional activism and assertiveness. However, the pendulum rarely swings back completely given that war and national emergencies tend to be all-encompassing and penetrating. Overtime, presidents have accumulated greater powers (Rosati and Scott 2007).

The events of 9/11 strengthened the authority of the president. However, by the Obama era Congress and the American public had accepted the changes and limitations wrought by the terrorist attacks. The new normal included a governmental secrecy system, the presidential prerogative to target suspected terrorists, without evidence, worldwide, massive data collection of private information, and continuous and ubiquitous spying, all approved by the Congress and consented to by the American public. Politics reverted back to a more relative calm, a new normal, punctuated periodically by lone wolf attacks or a demented mass shooter.

Congress was able to enact several notable pieces of legislation that benefited human rights under Obama. Congress amended the Leahy Laws during the Obama years (see Chapter 4). In 2011, the wording of gross violations of human rights changed from the plural to the singular. Individuals or units only had to be implicated in a single act of severe human rights abuse. In addition, the standard of proof was lowered from "credible evidence" to "credible information." An exception was made for humanitarian or disaster assistance. To balance the reduction in violations and evidence required to invoke the Leahy Laws, Congress also reduced the burden on the state to remedy the violations. Early Leahy Laws required the state to enact "effective measures" to bring individual or unit violators to justice. Now the state needed only to take "effective steps." In 2013, Congress also included police in its understanding of security forces (Serafino et al. 2014).

Senators John McCain (R-AZ) and Dianne Feinstein (D-CA) presented an amendment to strengthen the prohibition on torture and to assure the International Committee of the Red Cross access to all persons detained by the United States, regardless of location. The McCain-Feinstein amendment to the National Defense Authorization Act (2016) required all government personnel and contractors in every agency and department to abide by the rules and regulations in the Army Field Manual. Section 1889 of the National Defense Authorization Act codified Obama's Executive Order 13491, making the Army Field Manual the standard for interrogation practices.

Yet, Congress failed to ratify two international human rights treaties. In July 2009, Obama signed the Convention on the Rights of Persons with Disabilities (CRPD), but he waited nearly two years to send it to the Senate for consideration. In 2012, the Senate failed to ratify the treaty due to fears that the convention would erode U.S. sovereignty and limit parents' ability to care for special needs children. In addition, given the continued use of extraordinary rendition, Obama could not sign nor could the Senate ratify the International Convention for the Protection of All Persons from Enforced Disappearance.

Bureaucratic Resistance

U.S. policy is often the outcome of bureaucratic implementation and resistance. When a President

> signs off on one proposal over another, how and to what extent this decision is interpreted and then implemented depends once again on multiple layers of bureaucratic players who may or may not share the exact vision of the President or understanding of his intent.
> (Ingber 2013: 377)

A self-regarding, self-aggrandizing, executive bureaucracy often thwarts presidential prerogatives.

The entrenched national security bureaucracy, described as prominent, powerful, unaccountable, and overly secretive during the Bush era, carried over to the Obama Administration. Although Obama blamed

Congress for hindering his ability to close Guantánamo, scholars recognized the bureaucratic forces at work (Huq 2017). Obama retained several of Bush's executive branch personnel in powerful positions within the bureaucracy. Moreover, the most powerful and best resourced bureaucracy, the DOD, opposed the closing of Guantánamo (Bruck 2016). Resistance from the military bureaucracy proved to be the catalyst precipitating legislative limits on detainee transfer. The military bureaucracy obstructed transfers that had already been approved because, in the words of Bruck, Guantánamo was "an asset too important to lose" (2016: 36). The military bureaucracy formed a "bureaucratic-legislative alliance" (Huq 2017) that blocked Obama's aspiration to close the detention center. On the other side, however, the DOS worked to affect the closures since Guantánamo was an impediment to cordial relations with foreign countries whose citizens populated the center or were outraged by its existence.

Huq (2017) suggests that elites in the military and the legislative branch strategically leaked selective information to raise the public's fears that, if released, the detainees would return to terrorist activities. Huq identifies "leaks as a key tool employed by bureaucrats to undermine the President" (2017: 574). It should be noted that the individuals who leaked this information were not subject to whistleblower prosecution. The Obama Administration reserved whistleblower charges for those lower-level officials and bureaucrats who reported public government malfeasance and corruption.

Ingber (2018) points to Obama's political appointees and holdovers from the previous administration as sources of bureaucratic resistance in closing Guantánamo. The continuity of personnel virtually guaranteed upholding the status quo and closing off alternative courses of action. Ingber makes the case that Obama could have pushed the issue but did not want to spend the political capital needed to secure the closure of Guantánamo since he prioritized passing Obamacare.

Conclusion

George W. Bush justified restrictions of civil liberties, the abandonment of the rule of law, and abuses of human rights as temporary aberrations necessitated by the need to secure the safety of the country. The George W. Bush Administration claimed the war on terror was a new type of war requiring a new type of self-justifying defense. Congress and the American public apparently agreed. After eight years, what was once an aberration (unconstitutional policies) became institutionalized and was made durable by the Obama Administration. Surveillance, military commissions, indefinite detention, secrets, and lies are now well-established practices in American politics.

Margulies and Metcalf (2011) argue that Obama's rhetoric of restoring America's reputation, reforming the Bush-era lawless policies, and returning to the rule of law produced quiescence on the Left. With the election of Obama, liberal politicians, advocates, and voting Americans believed "mission accomplished." On the other hand, Obama's speeches generated alarm on the Right as Right leaning politicians believed the work completed by the George W. Bush Administration would be undone, thus leaving the country vulnerable to future terrorist attacks. Yet, in the end, Obama maintained and continued many of the George W. Bush Administration policies. Although Obama shut down secret CIA detention facilities and enhanced interrogation techniques, he declined to investigate the misdeeds. The Obama Administration also failed to prosecute or even establish a truth commission in charge of investigating those who carried out the use of enhanced interrogation techniques. In addition, the President continued the George W. Bush policies of administrative detention by holding suspected terrorists and their supporters indefinitely without charges, and by employing military commissions (Roth 2010). Furthermore, Obama increased the reliance on drone attacks in the ongoing war on terror, and he continued the highly controversial surveillance programs by the National Security Agency.

It is evident that Obama was willing to use "all elements of our power" to fight terrorism (Obama 2014a). But it is also apparent that Obama was reluctant to use many of these tools to support human rights. Obama's failure to advance human rights in OCO by continuing the use of renditions and the Bagram detention center, through excessive secrecy, and by escalating the use of drones set the stage for America, under Trump, to more easily return to a policy of torture and cruelty.

Notes

1 The Gallup Poll numbers indicate that Bush's job approval rating fell to 31 percent in 2006 but would later fall to a low of 25 percent in 2008.
    https://news.gallup.com/poll/116500/presidential-approval-ratings-george-bush.aspx
2 It should be noted that this statement has been reported in news outlets and academic literature, but I could not locate the quote myself.
3 Bush's September 20, 2001 speech to a joint session of Congress asked and answered why terrorists, al-Qaeda and the Taliban, hate us:

> Americans are asking, why do they hate us? They hate what they see right here in this Chamber, a democratically elected government. Their leaders are self-appointed. They hate our freedoms—our freedom of religion, our freedom of speech, our freedom to vote and assemble and disagree with each other.
>
> (Bush 2001)

4 Major Nidal Malik Hasan, an Army psychiatrist and radical Islamic extremist, shot and killed 13 and wounded over 30 others.
5 Umar Farouk Abdulmutallab, a Nigerian national, hid plastic explosives in his underwear in an attempt to take down Northwest Airlines flight 253.

138   *The Prevaricator of Change*

6 Protocol Additional to the Geneva Conventions of August 12, 1949, and relating to the Protection of Victims of International Armed Conflicts (Protocol I), June 8, 1977.
7 The quote is attributed to Orwell but a Google search indicates that there is a contentious debate as to whether he actually said or wrote the statement and if so in which book, talk, or letter.
8 The norm against the targeted killing of political leaders is due to the aversion to treacherous killings (poisoning, being killed in bed, etc.) and the domestic disorder and instability that would result in the loss of the leader.
9 It should be noted that other theorists, notably Altman and Wellman (2008) and Statman (2012), believe that once the principles of *jus ad bellum* are met allowing war, targeted killings are also permissible. Altman and Wellman contend that the targeted killing of a leader may be acceptable if "(1a) the target had rendered himself morally liable to being killed and (2) the risk to human rights is not disproportionate to the rights violations that one can reasonably expect to avert" (2008: 253). While Statmen (2012), making the distinction between law enforcement and war, argues that killing the enemy is the condition of war and targeted killing is simply another tactic in warfare.
10 Cronin (2013) does note that the Obama drone strikes avoided civilian causalities 86 percent of the time but due to the secrecy and concealment of the drone program, critics believe that the noncombatant fatalities are much more common.
11 The heavily redacted Presidential Policy Guidance (PPG) was made public in 2016 after the ACLU secured a federal court order. The PPG formalizes procedures for using lethal force outside areas of active hostilities. Human Rights First (2017), a human rights NGO, criticized Obama's failure to fully transfer the drone program from the CIA to the DOD. Human Rights First believed that the DOD, with its institutional culture of compliance with the Geneva Convention and humanitarian laws and a clear chain of command, would be a better guardian for a lethal weapon of war.
12 Cutler (2017) reports that the United States was doing more than providing training and advice. U.S. soldiers were taking the lead in counterterrorism raids due to the deficiencies of the Afghan forces.
13 Available at https://fas.org/irp/doddir/army/fm2-22-3.pdf.
14 There is a proliferation of inclusionary acronyms: LGBT, stands for lesbian, gay, bisexual, and transsexual; LGBTQ adds queer to the basic term; LGBTI includes intersex individuals; LGBTQIA incorporates asexual; LGBTTQQIAAP includes lesbian, gay, bisexual, transgender, transsexual, queer, questioning, intersex, asexual, ally, pansexual. I will simply use LGBTQ.

References

Janet Cooper Alexander. 2013. "The Law-Free Zone and Back Again." *University of Illinois Law Review* 2013(2): 551–624.
Andrew Altman and Christopher Wellman. 2008. "From Humanitarian Intervention to Assassination: Human Rights and Political Violence." *Ethics* 118(2): 228–257.
American Presidency Project. 2018. *Executive Orders*. www.presidency.ucsb.edu/data/orders.php
Joseph Amon. 2014. "Health Security and/or Human Rights," in *Routledge Handbook of Global Health Security*. Simon Rushton and Jeremy Youde, eds. New York: Routledge.

Jo Becker and Scott Shane. 2012. "Secret 'Kill List' Proves a Tests of Obama's Principles and Will." *New York Times*, 29 May, A1.
Peter Bergen and Megan Braun. 2012. "Drone is Obama's Weapon of Choice." *CNN*, 6 September.
Nicolas Bouchet. 2013. "The Democracy Tradition in US Foreign Policy and the Obama Presidency." *International Affairs* 89(1): 31–51.
John Brennan. 2011. "Strengthening Our Security by Adhering to Our Values and Laws." Speech at Harvard Law School, 16 September, 2011
Rosa Brooks. 2013. The Constitutional and Counterterrorism Implications of Targeted Killing. Hearing Before the Senate Judiciary Subcommittee on the Constitution, Civil Rights, and Human Rights, 113th Cong., April 23, 2013.
Connie Bruck. 2016. "Why Obama Has Failed to Close Guantánamo." *New Yorker*, 1 August.
George W. Bush. 2001. "President George W. Bush's Address to a Joint Session of Congress Concerning the Sept. 11, 2001 Attacks on the US on September 20, 2001." www.washingtonpost.com/wp-srv/nation/specials/attacked/transcripts/bushaddress_092001.html
Daniel Byman. 2013. "Why Drones Work: The Case for Washington's Weapon of Choice." *Foreign Affairs* 92(4): 32–43.
Center for Constitutional Rights. 7 March, 2011. CCR Condemns President Obama's Lifting of Stay in Military Tribunals." https://ccrjustice.org/home/press-center/press-releases/ccr-condemns-president-obama-s-lifting-stay-military-tribunals
Emily Chertoff and Zachary Manfredi. Forthcoming. "Deadly Ambiguity: IHL's Prohibition on Targeting Civilian Objects and the Risks of Decentered Interpretation." *Texas International Law Journal*. doi: 10.2139/ssrn.2997274
Hillary Clinton. 2009. "The Human Rights Agenda for the 21st Century." Speech given at Georgetown University, Washington, DC.
Jeffrey Cohen, Jon Bond, and Richard Fleisher. 2013. "Placing Presidential-Congressional Relations in Context: A Comparison of Barack Obama and His Predecessors." *Polity* 45(1): 105–126.
Jeffrey Cohen, Jon Bond, and Richard Fleisher 2014. "The Implications of the 2012 Presidential Election for Presidential-Congressional Relations: Change or More of the Same," in *The 2012 Presidential Election: Forecasts, Outcomes, and Consequences*. Amnon Cavari, Richard Powell, and Kenneth Mayer, eds. New York: Rowman and Littlefield.
Inder Comar. 2013. "Obama DOJ Asks Court to Grant Immunity to George W. Bush for Iraq War." *Global Research*. www.globalresearch.ca/obama-doj-asks-court-to-grant-immunity-to-george-w-bush-for-iraq-war/5346637
Audrey Comstock. 2016. "Gay Rights and US Foreign Aid: A Look at Nigeria and Uganda." *The Journal of International Relations, Peace Studies, and Development* 2(1), Article 2: 1–16.
Erin Corcoran. 2011. "Obama's Failed Attempt to Close Gitmo: Why Executive Orders Can't Bring about Systemic Change." *University of New Hampshire Law Review* 9(2): 207–235.
Audrey Cronin. 2013. "Why Drones Fail: When Tactics Drive Strategy." *Foreign Affairs* 92(4): 44–54.
Leonard Cutler. 2017. *President Obama's Counterterrorism Strategy in the War on Terror: An Assessment*. New York: Palgrave.

Debra DeLaet. 2014. "Whose Interests is the Securitisation of Health Serving?" in *Routledge Handbook of Global Health Security*, Simon Rushton and Jeremy Youde, eds. New York: Routledge.

Department of Justice. 2011. White Paper, "Lawfulness of a Lethal Operation Directed Against a U.S. Citizen Who Is a Senior Operational Leader of Al-Qa'ida or An Associated Force." https://fas.org/irp/eprint/doj-lethal.pdf

John Dietrich and Caitlyn Witkowski. 2012. "Obama's Human Rights Policy: Déjà Vu with a Twist." *Human Rights Review* 13(1): 39–64.

Ken Dilanian. 2011. "CIA has Slashed its Terrorism Interrogation Role." *Los Angeles Times*, 10 April.

Adam Entous. 2010. "Drones Kill Low-Level Militants, Few Civilians: US." *Reuters*. www.reuters.com/article/us-pakistan-usa-drones-idUSTRE6424WI20100503

Food and Agricultural Organization. 2010. *The State of Food Insecurity in the World 2009*. Rome: FAO

David Forsythe. 2011a. "US Foreign Policy and Human Rights: Situating Obama." *Human Rights Quarterly* 33(3): 767–789.

David Forsythe. 2011b. *The Politics of Prisoner Abuse: The United States and Enemy Prisoners after 9/11*. New York: Cambridge University Press.

Douglas Gibler and Steven Miller. 2012. "Comparing the Foreign Aid Policies of Presidents Bush and Obama." *Social Science Quarterly* 93(5): 1202–1217.

Jack Goldsmith. 2007. *The Terror Presidency: Law and Judgment Inside the Bush Administration*. New York: W. W. Norton & Company

Vin Gupta, Alexander Tsai, Alexandre Mason-Sharma, Eric Goosby, Ashish Jha, and Vanessa Kerry. 2018. "Have Geopolitics Influenced Decisions on American Health Foreign Assistance Efforts during the Obama Presidency?" *Journal of Global Health*. doi: 10.7189/jogh.08.010417.

Lawrence Haas. 2012. *Sound the Trumpet: The United States and Human Rights Protection*. Lanham, MD: Rowman & Littlefield Publishers.

Lisa Hajjar. 2011. "Bagram, Obama's Other Gitmo." *Middle East Report* 260: 8–17.

Tobias Heinrich, Carla Martinez Machain, and Jared Oestman. 2017. "Does Counterterrorism Militarize Foreign Aid? Evidence from sub-Saharan Africa." *Journal of Peace Research* 54(4): 527–541.

Melissa Ho and Charles Hanrahan. 2011. *The Obama Administration's Feed the Future Initiative*. CRS Report R41612. Washington, DC: Congressional Research Service.

Eric Holder. 2009. Attorney General, Regarding a Preliminary Review into the Interrogation of Certain Detainees, 24 August. www.justice.gov/opa/speech/attorney-general-eric-holder-regarding-preliminary-review-interrogation-certain-detainees

Eric Holder. 2011. Statement of the Attorney General Regarding Investigation into the Interrogation of Certain Detainees, 30 June. www.justice.gov/opa/pr/statement-attorney-general-regarding-investigation-interrogation-certain-detainees

Eric Holder. 2012. "Remarks at Northwestern University School of Law." Chicago, IL. www.justice.gov/opa/speech/attorney-general-eric-holder-speaks-northwestern-university-school-law

Human Rights First. 2010. *The U.S. Army Field Manual on Interrogation: A Strong Document in Need of Careful Revision*. www.humanrightsfirst.org/wp-content/uploads/pdf/Army_Field_Manual.pdf

Human Rights First. 2011. *Detained and Denied in Afghanistan: How to Make U.S. Detention Comply with the Law.* www.humanrightsfirst.org/wp-content/uploads/pdf/Detained-Denied-in-Afghanistan.pdf

Human Rights First. 2017. "President Obama's Legacy on Human Rights." www.humanrightsfirst.org/sites/default/files/HRFBackgrounderObamaLegacy.pdf

Aziz Huq. 2017. "The President and the Detainees." *University of Pennsylvania Law Review* 165(3): 499–592.

Rebecca Ingber. 2013. "Interpretation Catalysts and Executive Branch Legal Decisionmaking." *Yale Journal of International Law* 38(2): 359–421.

Rebecca Ingber. 2018. "Bureaucratic Resistance and the National Security State." *Iowa Law Review* 104: 139–221.

Andy Irwin, Ed Krauland, Meredith Rathbone, Jack Hayes, Tom Barletta, and Peter Jeydel. 2014. "Foreign Military Sales: First Revision of the U.S. Conventional Arms Transfer Policy in Nearly Two Decades." www.steptoe.com/en/news-publications/foreign-military-sales-first-revision-of-the-us-conventional-arms-transfer-policy-in-nearly-two-decades.html

Richard Jackson. 2011. "Culture, Identity and Hegemony: Continuity and (the Lack of) Change in US Counterterrorism Policy from Bush to Obama." *International Politics* 48(2/3): 390–411.

Jameel Jaffar. 2016. *The Drone Memos.* New York: New Press.

Betcy Jose. 2017. "Not Completely the New Normal: How Human Rights Watch Tried to Suppress the Targeted Killing Norm." *Contemporary Security Policy* 38(2): 237–259.

Brad Knickerbocker. 2010. "WikiLeaks 101: Five Questions About Who Did What and When." *The Christian Science Monitor.* www.csmonitor.com/USA/2010/1201/WikiLeaks-101-Five-questions-about-who-did-what-and-when/Who-is-responsible-for-the-leaks

Harold Hongju Koh. 2010. "The Obama Administration and International Law." Annual Meeting of the American Society of International Law. Washington, DC. www.state.gov/s/l/releases/remarks/139119.htm

Anne Kornblut. 2008. "Obama Warns Economy 'Going to Get Worse,' Pushes Administration on Help for Homeowners." *Washington Post*, 8 December. www.washingtonpost.com/wp-dyn/content/article/2008/12/07/AR2008120702407.html

Larry Lewis and Sarah Holewinsk. 2013. "Changing of the Guard: Civilian Protection for an Evolving Military." *PRISM Security Studies Journal* 4(2): 56–65.

Piotr Lis. 2018. "The Impact of Armed Conflict and Terrorism on Foreign Aid: A Sector-level Analysis." *World Development* 110: 283–294.

Joseph Margulies and Hope Metcalf. 2011. "Terrorizing Academia." *Journal of Legal Education* 60(3): 433–471.

Jane Mayer. 2010. "The Trial." *The New Yorker* 15, February. https://www.newyorker.com/magazine/2010/02/15/the-trial-2

Trevor McCrisken. 2011. "Ten Years on: Obama's War on Terrorism in Rhetoric and Practice." *International Affairs* 87(4): 781–801.

MSN. 2013. "Justice Department Memo: It's Legal to use Drone Strikes against Americans." www.msnbc.com/msnbc/justice-department-memo-its-legal-use-dr

Robert Neustadt. 1980. *Presidential Power and the Modern Presidents: The Politics of Leadership.* Hoboken, NJ: Wiley and Sons.

New America. Online. America's Counterterrorism Wars: Tracking the United States' Drone Strikes and other Operations in Pakistan, Yemen, and Somalia. www.newamerica.org/in-depth/americas-counterterrorism-wars/

Mark Norris. 2013. "Bad 'Leaker' or Good 'Whistleblower'? A Test." *Case Western Reserve Law Review* 64(2): 693–710.

Barack Obama. 2008. Obama-Biden Transition Project: Office of the President-elect and Office of the Vice President-elect. www.Change.gov

Barack Obama. 2009a. President Barack Obama's Inaugural Address. 21 January. https://obamawhitehouse.archives.gov/blog/2009/01/21/president-barack-obamas-inaugural-address

Barack Obama. 2009b. Executive Order 13492- Review and Disposition of Individuals Detained at the Guantánamo Bay Naval Base and Closure of Detention Facilities. www.presidency.ucsb.edu/ws/?pid=85670

Barack Obama. 2009c. Executive Order 13493- Review of Detention Policy Options. www.presidency.ucsb.edu/ws/index.php?pid=85671

Barack Obama. 2009d. Remarks by the President on National Security. 21 May. www.nytimes.com/2009/05/21/us/politics/21obama.text.html

Barack Obama. 2009e. "Obama gives Intelligence Team Clear Lead on Torture." *New York Times*. www.nytimes.com/2009/01/09/world/americas/09iht-obama.4.19231282.html

Barack Obama. 2009f. Executive Order 13491- Ensuring Lawful Interrogations. www.presidency.ucsb.edu/ws?pid=85669

Barack Obama. 2011a. "Remarks by President Obama in Address to the United Nations General Assembly." 21 September. obamawhitehouse.archives.gov/the-press-office/2011/09/21/remarks-president-obama-address-united-nations-general-assembly

Barack Obama. 2011b. "Presidential Memorandum — International Initiatives to Advance the Human Rights of Lesbian, Gay, Bisexual, and Transgender Persons" www.hrionline.org/presidential-memorandum-international-initiatives-to-advance-the-human-rights-of-lesbian-gay-bisexual-and-transgender-persons/

Barack Obama. 2013. "Remarks by the President at the National Defense University." https://obamawhitehouse.archives.gov/the-press-office/2013/05/23/remarks-president-national-defense-university

Barack Obama. 2014a. Address Before a Joint Session of the Congress on the State of the Union. www.presidency.ucsb.edu/documents/address-before-joint-session-the-congress-the-state-the-union-21

Barack Obama. 2014b. Executive Order 13672 — Further Amendments to Executive Order 11478, Equal Employment Opportunity in the Federal Government, and Executive Order 11246, Equal Employment Opportunity. www.eeoc.gov/eeoc/history/50th/thelaw/11478_11246_amend.cfm

Barack Obama. 2014c. *Remarks by the President at Signing of Executive Order on LGBT Workplace Discrimination.* https://obamawhitehouse.archives.gov/the-press-office/2014/07/21/remarks-president-signing-executive-order-lgbt-workplace-discrimination

Open Society Foundations. 2010. *Confinement Conditions at a U.S. Screening Facility on Bagram Air Base.* Policy Brief #3. www.opensocietyfoundations.org/sites/default/files/confinement-conditions-20101014.pdf

Mary-Rose Papandrea. 2014. "Leaker Traitor Whistleblower Spy: National Security Leaks and the First Amendment." *Boston University Law Review* 94(2): 449–544.

Sandra Crouse Quinn and Supriya Kumar. 2014. "Health Inequalities and Infectious Disease Epidemics: A Challenge for Global Health Security." *Biosecurity and Bioterrorism: Biodefense Strategy, Practice, and Science* 12(5): 263–273.

Jose Rodriguez. 2012. *Hard Measures: How Aggressive CIA Actions after 9/11 Saved America Lives.* New York: Threshold Editions.

Jerel Rosati and James Scott. 2007. *The Politics of United States Foreign Policy.* 4th ed. Belmont, CA: Thomson Higher Education.

Kenneth Roth. 2010. "Empty Promises? Obama's Hesitant Embrace of Human Rights." *Foreign Affairs* 89(2): 10–16.

Kenneth Roth. 2017. "Barack Obama's Shaky Legacy on Human Rights." *Foreign Policy (blog).* https://foreignpolicy.com/2017/01/04/barack-obamas-shaky-legacy-on-human-rights/

Burcu Savun and Daniel Tirone. 2018. "Foreign Aid as a Counterterrorism Tool: More Liberty, Less Terror?" *Journal of Conflict Resolution* 62(8): 1607–1635.

Arthur Schlesinger. 2004. *The Imperial Presidency.* Boston, MA: Houghton Mifflin Co.

Martin Senn and Jodok Troy. 2017. "The Transformation of Targeted Killing and International Order." *Contemporary Security Policy* 38(2): 175–211.

Nina M. Serafino, June Beittel, Lauren Ploch Blanchard, and Liana Rosen. 2014. *"Leahy Law" Human Rights Provisions and Security Assistance: Issue Overview.* Washington, DC: Congressional Research Service.

Rajiv Shah. 2010. "Remarks by USAID Administrator Rajiv Shah on the Release of the 2011 World Hunger Report." *Bread for the World 2011.* www.usaid.gov/press/speeches/2010/sp101122.html

Stanford Law School and NYU School of Law. 2012. *Living Under Drones: Death, Injury and Trauma to Civilians from US Drone Practices in Pakistan.* https://law.stanford.edu/wp-content/uploads/sites/default/files/publication/313671/doc/slspublic/Stanford_NYU_LIVING_UNDER_DRONES.pdf.

Daniel Statman. 2012. "Can Just War Theory Justify Targeted Killing? Three Possible Models," in *Targeted Killings: Law and Morality in an Asymmetrical World.* Claire Finkelstein, Jens Ohlin, and Andrew Altman, eds. Oxford: Oxford University Press.

Paul Stephan. 2012. "The Limits of Change: International Human Rights Under the Obama Administration." *Fordham International Law Journal* 35(2): 488–509.

Rachel Stohl. 2014. "Promoting Restraint: Updated Rules for U.S. Arms Transfer Policy." *Arms Control Today* 44(2): 15–19.

Curt Tarnoff and Marian Lawson. 2016. *Foreign Aid: An Introduction to U.S. Programs and Policy.* Congressional Research Service, CRS Report to Congress R40213. Washington DC: Congressional Research Service.

Ward Thomas. 2000. "Norms and Security: The Case of International Assassination." *International Security* 25(1): 105–133.

Andrew Tutt. 2013. "*Boumediene*'s Wake." *Rutgers Law Review Commentaries* 65(1): 52–58.

USAID. 2017. *Feed the Future: Progress through 2017.* www.usaid.gov/sites/default/files/documents/1867/2017_Feed_the_Future_Progress_Snapshot_Final_-_508C_1.pdf

U.S. Department of State. 2009. *2009 Country Reports on Human Rights Practices.* Bureau of Democracy, Human Rights, and Labour. www.state.gov/j/drl/rls/hrrpt/2009/frontmatter/135936.htm

U.S. Department of State. 2013. Advancing the Human Rights of Lesbian, Gay, Bisexual and Transgendered Persons Worldwide: A State Department Priority. https://2009-2017.state.gov/r/pa/pl/2013/211478.htm

U.S. Senate. 2010. Senate Roll Call Vote #00196. On the Amendment S.Amdt.1133: Inouye Amdt. No. 1133; To prohibit funding to transfer, release, or incarcerate detainees detained at Guantánamo Bay, Cuba, to or within the United States. https://www.democrats.senate.gov/05/20/2009/senate-roll-call-vote-00196-21

White House. 2015. "The Global Health Security Agenda," Fact Sheet, 28 July, 2015, https://obamawhitehouse.archives.gov/the-press-office/2015/07/28/fact-sheet-global-health-security-agenda

Craig Whitlock. 2013. "Renditions Continue under Obama, Despite Due-process Concerns." *The Washington Post*, 1 January.

Robert Worth. 2009. "Freed by the U.S., Saudi Becomes a Qaeda Chief." *New York Times*, 22 January, A1.

Jordy Yager. 2011. "Bin Laden would be Held at Gitmo if Caught." *The Hill*. http://thehill.com/homenews/administration/144695-bin-laden-would-be-held-at-gitmo-if-he-were-caught

6 A Prevaricator Who Told the Truth
Donald Trump (2017–)

The 2016 election of Donald John Trump as President of the United States took place against a backdrop of growing inequality in the distribution of resources, a concentration of wealth, and a reduction in social mobility for the lower and middle classes in the United States. Trump came to the political scene claiming to be the voice of the forgotten American, the ordinary worker and taxpayer. In a campaign speech in Dimondale, Michigan, Trump pledged:

> It's going to be a victory for the people, a victory for the wage-earner, the factory worker. Remember this, a big, big victory for the factory worker. They haven't had those victories for a long time. A victory for every citizen and for all of the people whose voices have not been heard for many, many years. They're going to be heard again.
> (August 19, 2016)

Trump portrayed the working class as hard-working Americans who have been cheated by globalization. Globalization was the American project during the Clinton Administration and was now the cause of poor pay and lack of jobs for American workers. Manufacturing jobs, once the mainstay of well-paying blue-collar work, went overseas. With globalization, companies moved abroad for cheaper labor costs, providing no health or retirement benefits, and reduced safety and environmental regulations. The beneficiaries of globalization were the upper-class individuals who enjoyed growing economic profits. The reduction in production costs increased profits for the owners and stockholders while the American worker lost out. While the poor got poorer due to globalization, the rich got richer. Furthermore, American workers, both white and blue color, suffered downward mobility as a result of the 2008 recession. They were underwater on their home mortgages, many lost their pensions, and more lost their jobs. Working-class labor in the United States also believed that it was in an intense competition with illegal immigrants for the few jobs that remained in the country.

To "Make America Great Again" (Trump's slogan) its proponents believed would require a return to a time when the country was patriotic, prosperous, white, and Christian, and where women accepted their traditional gender roles. During the Obama Administration, the contributions of white Christian men were the "invisible and under-recognized 'backbone' of the American economy" (Lamont et al. 2017). Trump was able to tap into these fears and resentments, praised their virtues, and presented himself as an advocate of the working man (and sometimes woman).

Trump was vocal about his disdain of immigrants, refugees, Muslims, women, and Mexicans throughout his campaign. Thus, when he won the presidency, he assumed that he had a mandate to initiate the racist and sexist policies on which he had campaigned. Latino immigrants were scapegoated as dangerous rapists and murderers, drug-dealers, and job-stealers, who came to the United States to sponge off the U.S. welfare system. Muslim immigrants were all terrorists or terrorist sympathizers wishing to kill hard-working Americans and destroy American democracy and values.

What does this populist, nativist, and xenophobic turn in American politics mean for U.S. human rights policy? The Trump Administration's clearly stated focus for U.S. foreign policy was to promote U.S. economic and security interests. Human rights, democratic promotion, and moral principles would have no place in Trump's foreign or domestic policy.

A Billionaire as the Voice of the Everyman (and Perhaps Woman)

Populism is, according to Mudde (2007), characterized by three core attributes: antiestablishment belief, nativism, and authoritarianism. Populists are antiestablishment and critical of the corruption and self-serving immorality of political and economic elites. This includes elected politicians, but also big business, big banks, intellectuals, and the media. Populists claim that they represent the interests of ordinary working men and women, the forgotten people. Trump, a billionaire, declared himself to be the champion of the people against the power of the established elite. The concept of nativism means that ordinary people, the wise and decent citizens who own and built America, need to be defended from the intrusion of immigrants who threaten their lives and livelihoods. Illegal Mexican immigrants, unfair Chinese competition, and Muslim terrorists disguised as refugees are destroying the American way of life for real Americans. Immigrants and refugees are taking advantage of the healthcare and welfare system, a system that working Americans have been forced to pay for through taxes and other "contributions." In addition, foreigners are forcing changes in American culture because they refuse to assimilate.

The third characteristic is authoritarianism. Conventional political procedures, artifacts of the corrupt system that preceded the populist leader, are illegitimate. Power should be concentrated in the hands of a strong leader as the voice of the people motivated by their needs and aspirations. As the voice of the people and their true representatives, authoritarian leaders believe that their decisions ought not to be questioned or challenged. The established bureaucracy and the "fixed" political system would not restrain a decisive, strong, and commanding leader like Trump. And Trump was beguiled by human rights abusing autocrats. These autocratic "friends" wield the unchallenged political power he longs for. On the campaign trail, Trump praised Saddam Hussein by saying: "He killed terrorists. He did that so good. They didn't read them the rights —they didn't talk, they were a terrorist, it was over" (as reported by J. Johnson 2016a). He applauded Rodrigo Duterte, the President of the Philippines, for doing "an unbelievable job on the drug problem," even though Duterte's crackdown had killed a reported 12,000 people including journalists and innocent bystanders (Reuters 2017). Trump also believed the brutal military dictator and Egyptian President Abdel Fattah el-Sisi was "doing a fantastic job" (Conway 2017). In addition, he tweeted his congratulations to Chinese President Xi Jinping on "his great political victory" when appointed as the Communist Party's General Secretary for a second term. Trump declared that Turkey's President Erdoğan had become a friend and was getting very high marks, even though Turkey is still today under a state of emergency and the government is ruthlessly suppressing human rights advocates, journalists, and political opponents (McCaskill 2017). At a political rally in Wheeling, West Virginia, in September 2018, Trump announced that he loved Kim Jong-un, the dictator of North Korea, one of the world's most repressive states. Meanwhile, Trump's well-reported admiration for Vladimir Putin has been unrivaled.

Trump believes himself to be a strongman and displays acute authoritarian tendencies. For example, Trump repeated several times his desire to punish the media if they published negative stories that he did not approve (Gold 2016), to use federal regulators against his detractors (Savage 2016), to divest critics of their security clearances (Manchester 2018), to strip protesters of their citizenship (Savage 2016), and to jail his political opponents (Fallows 2016). The *New York Times* reported that Michael Chertoff, George W. Bush's Secretary of Homeland Security and coauthor of the Patriot Act, argued that Trump's behavior "smacks of what we read about tin-pot dictators in other parts of the world, where when they win an election their first move is to imprison opponents" (Savage 2016).

Müller (2017) includes an additional feature to populism. Populists are also anti-pluralists; they view the people as a single harmonized unit. The people do not have divergent interests, and only a populist leader can represent the whole of the people. Müller writes that

> populists are anti-pluralist. They claim that they and they alone represent the people. All other political competitors are essentially

illegitimate, and anyone who does not support them is not properly part of the people....The people are a moral, homogeneous entity whose will cannot err.

(2017)

Anti-pluralism allows neither acceptance nor vocalization of the interests, needs, or values of different groups. Thus, anti-pluralism can prompt undemocratic and illiberal policies.

The rise of populism, and Trump's success, was due to two trends: the economic downturn and the change in demographics. Economic insecurity from the loss of jobs due to immigration and globalization, and the loss of whole sectors of the economy due to deindustrialization and technological innovation, created grievances among workers. In addition, the collapse of the home mortgage bubble led to the 2008 recession whereby millions of Americans lost their homes, were unable to buy into the American dream of homeownership, or were underwater on their mortgages. Increased taxes, combined with stagnating wages, also meant that middle-class Americans could no longer pay for their kids' schooling, go on vacation, or pay their bills without relying on credit cards, bank loans, or dipping into their savings and retirement accounts.

Group-based deprivation, the belief that your group is suffering or receiving fewer benefits, compared to other groups, creates a sense of moral outrage and anger at the disadvantage of one's social group or community. This sense of deprivation led to growing frustration and dissatisfaction with the American political system. Valentino, Neuner et al. conclude that "Many whites now view themselves as an embattled and even disadvantaged group, and this has led to both strong in-group identity and a greater tolerance for expressions of hostility toward out-groups" (2018: 768). Work by Jost et al. (2012) found that community-based anger is one of the strongest predictors of political activism. It becomes an "us against them" populist movement, with the government, elite, and those receiving a perceived unfair or undeserving share of the benefits as the "them," and the white, working, and middle classes (mostly men) as the "us." This is not to say that there are not real economic grievances or that the government has been unresponsive to millions of Americans. Gilens (2014) found that the government did respond to the preferences of the affluent while "under most circumstances, the preferences of the vast majority of Americans appear to have essentially no impact on which policies the government does or doesn't adopt" (Gilens 2014: 1). Even "when large majorities of Americans favor policy changes—when 70 to 80 percent want change—they get it less than half the time" (Page and Gilens 2017: 71). The affluent classes are able to thwart the will of the majority and provide special benefits for themselves. This has led to anger, frustration, and resentment in American politics. American workers started to believe that traditional politicians defended the privileges of Wall Street and that, by contrast, a populist leader would protect the interests of Main Street.

The change in demographics threatened traditional American culture and American values, too. The United States was no longer white and Protestant and soon would become a "minority-majority" nation where the minority population outnumbers Caucasians. White Americans were experiencing declining status and influence as a group due to civil rights policies supporting diversity and social tolerance, and diminishing census numbers. Census data have shown that there are already more minority children, primarily Hispanic, under the age of five than white children (Wazwaz 2015). This trend resulted in a backlash against ethnic minorities, women, and other disparaged groups. Philpot (2018) found that racial issues, which he measured as support for preferential hiring and promotion for blacks, were a salient issue for white men. In reaction to the Obama presidency, white men withdrew their support for the Democratic Party and increased their support for the Republican Party.[1] White-male support of the Democratic Party, Philpot reported, dwindled to 31 percent in 2016.

Although much has been made of Trump's working-class supporters, the demographic that won the election for Trump was middle-class voters (Henley 2016). Trump won disproportionately in small towns and rural areas where residents tend to be older and less mobile though not necessarily poorer. Trump appealed to white voters, particularly men who were suffering economic hardship and felt a threat to their social and political status (Morgan 2018). The middle and perhaps upper middle class was afraid and angry that they were losing their place in American society, and they worried that they could lose their privileged status. Middle-class workers were living paycheck to paycheck, struggling to pay their bills, relying on credit to pay for the goods and services their middle-class status ought to afford them. Trump won 49 percent of voters who earned more than $50,000 a year (compared to 47 percent who voted for Clinton). Furthermore, Trump energized the working-class voter to come out in record numbers to vote, and he won 67 percent of votes from white voters without a college degree. In fact, Trump's insurgent outsider campaign generated enthusiasm among chronic nonvoters.

Governmental Policies toward Socially Constructed Groups

Similar to the hierarchy erected by the concept of populism, where the ordinary people are situated below the elite and above the marginal class, social construction theory also conceives of hierarchical categorization of groups ranging from the powerful and deserving to the powerless and undeserving. In their early work on policy design based on the social construction of recipient target groups, Schneider and Ingram (1993) developed four idealized types: the advantaged, the contenders, the dependents, and the deviants.[2] The advantaged groups were perceived to be those who are deserving and politically powerful. Groups in this category are the military, doctors, small businessmen as job creators, and, of course, the American worker. Contenders are politically powerful but are less deserving, such as the rich, big banks, big pharma, and lawyers. Dependents are deserving but powerless. This group includes children, veterans, or the disabled. And deviant groups are the undeserving and powerless, notably criminals, drug addicts, illegal aliens, and terrorists. A group's placement into a given category is based on "social constructions [that] are stereotypes about particular groups of people that have been created by politics, culture, socialization, history, the media, literature, religion, and like" (Schneider and Ingram 1993: 335). Being placed in one or the other category will affect the distribution of rights and entitlements, but also of burdens and punishments.

Policymakers develop and implement public policy built on these stereotyped classifications. As Schneider et al. note, "the allocation of benefits and burdens to target groups in public policy depends on the extent of their political power and their positive or negative social construction on the deserving or undeserving axis" (2014: 110). By labeling some groups as deserving and powerful (the advantaged group), policies toward these target groups garner strong public support. Their concerns and demands are viewed as legitimate. Deserving and powerless groups (the dependents group) are treated sympathetically, but policies do not adequately respond to their needs or interests. Powerful but undeserving groups (the contenders) garner government benefits covertly since they are unworthy of public endorsement and are found to be morally suspect. For example, the corporate tax cut from 35 percent to 21 percent in Trump's tax cut plan of 2017 was hidden by the Trump Administration's touting of the individual tax cut, which will expire, unlike the corporate tax cut. And finally, policies aimed at undeserving deviant groups, such as illegal immigrants or terrorists, revolve around policing, imprisonment, and deportation. Deviant groups are easily scapegoated and blamed for the social problems suffered by the deserving groups and they must be sanctioned.

Schneider and Ingram (1993) do recognize that social constructions can be subject to dispute and, over time, these stereotypes do change and evolve. LGBTQ individuals were historically viewed as deviants, but the social constructed stereotype has shifted somewhat for them. As a result, the LGBTQ target group has gained some government rights and protections in the United States. Because sexual orientation is believed to be an immutable characteristic, it is "not their fault" that they are gay, and, therefore, they can be "forgiven" and not penalized. LGBTQ individuals are consequently worthy of protection (Solanke 2017). Kreitzer and Watts Smith (2018) report that illegal immigrants were in the deviant group, ensuring that policymakers would enact policies to punish these groups. But upon closer examination, they found that, for the illegal immigrant target group, there was a lack of consensus as to whether this group was deserving or not. Kreitzer and Watts Smith (2018) speculate that there may be a partisan divide, with Democrats and liberals viewing illegal immigrants as deserving since they are in the United States to make a better life for themselves and their families and seek to flee poverty and violence. Republicans and conservatives, on the other hand, are more likely to regard this group as criminals entering the United States to take advantage of the system and to trade in illegal drugs. Hillary Clinton supporters tended to view undocumented aliens as deserving (placing them in the dependent category) while Trump supporters believed that illegal immigrants were undeserving (placing them clearly in the deviant group).

The Deviants

Kreitzer and Watts Smith suggest that "policy entrepreneurs can capitalize by scapegoating negatively constructed groups" (2018: 774). Policymakers expect approval for policies allocating costs and punishments to undeserving groups (Schneider and Ingram 2018). Voters appreciate a get-tough attitude directed toward deviant target groups. Trump's policy statements and initiatives exemplify this statement. Trump's deserving groups, the advantaged target groups and the dependent target groups, were being unfairly taxed and deprived of justified benefits because of the invasion of illegal immigrants, the "nasty feminist women" who advocate for women's rights, the social inclusion of the LGBTQ community, and furtive ambitions of Muslim émigrés. Trump reinforced the negative social construction of illegal immigrants as violent criminals, LGBTQ as violators of social morals, women seeking equality as a threat to the American family, and Muslim refugees as sleeper terrorists. Valentino, Neuner et al. (2018) found that Trump's explicit racist and sexist statements won him more support than they cost him. This is because deviant groups "are widely disliked or even 'hated': political leaders have much to gain by punishing them, and almost nothing to lose, since these groups have very low participation rates and in some cases are even barred from voting" (Schneider and Ingram 2017: 324–25).

Scapegoating Muslim Refugees and Mexican Immigrants

Tough immigration enforcement was a central plank of Trump's presidential campaign. Prevaricate Trump often exaggerated or overstated the threat of illegal immigration or Muslims undermining traditional American values, thus appealing to the fear, frustration, and anger of his supporters. Trump initiated a variety of policies intended to restrict or deny the immigration of foreign nationals into the United States. But the courts blocked many of his intended policies.

Trump's immigration enforcement program began within days of his inauguration. Executive Order 13767 "Border Security and Immigration

Enforcement Improvements" (2017b) declared that illegal aliens were a "significant threat to national security and public safety." To secure the southern border, Trump ordered the construction of a border wall, increased detention of illegal aliens at or near the border, expanded removals and deportations, and provided greater resources to border agents by increasing the number of personnel at the Border Patrol Agency and Immigration and Customs Enforcement (ICE) by 5,000 and 10,000, respectively. Yet, as of this writing, the wall is still not built, nor has the additional personnel been hired. Thus, Trump ordered the deployment of the national guard to the U.S.-Mexico border to assist U.S. Customs and Border Protection units in order to crackdown on illegal immigration.[3] In addition, Trump stepped up immigration workplace raids by ICE.

Trump initiated a zero-tolerance approach to illegal immigration that resulted in the separation of families in detention centers. Children were removed from their parents or other adult relatives. While the adults were held in jail awaiting their hearings, the children were sent to shelters in the care of the Department of Health and Human Services. The Trump Administration's zero-tolerance policy labeled the adults as criminals. They had, after all, entered the United States illegally. However, housing children in jail with their parents was inappropriate. There was no better option, according to the Trump Administration, than family separation. Furthermore, family separation would serve as a "tough deterrent" to illegal immigrants if they understood that their children would be removed. In an NPR interview, John Kelly, White House Chief of Staff, said that the "name of the game is deterrence…they elected to come illegally into the United States and this is a technique [family separation] that no one hopes will be used extensively or for very long" (Burnett 2018). In June 2018, Attorney General Jeff Sessions was more emphatic on the notion that family separation deters illegal immigration. In an interview with conservative talk show personality Hugh Hewitt, Sessions stated:

> We believe every person that enters the country illegally like that should be prosecuted. And you can't be giving immunity to people who bring children with them recklessly and improperly and illegally.… If people don't want to be separated from their children, they should not bring them with them.
>
> (Hewitt 2018)

However, under a firestorm of controversy, the policy of family separation was rescinded, leaving the gargantuan task of family reunification. A federal court judge in San Diego ordered all separated children to reunite with their parents within 30 days. With Executive Order 13841 "Affording Congress an Opportunity to Address Family Separation" (2018b), the Department of Homeland Security was to maintain custody of parents with their children, as appropriate. The executive order also instructed the Justice Department to expand the time limits on detaining alien children as part of the Flores Agreement. Under the Flores Agreement, the government can only hold children for 20 days, at which point it must release the child to the parents or other relatives. However, the courts have denied the JOD's request to modify the Flores Agreement.

In June 2017, Kelly, the Secretary of the Department of Homeland Security, announced that the Deferred Action for Parents of Americans and Lawful Permanent Residents was officially rescinded. This Obama-era program was intended to benefit illegal immigrants who came to the United States and had American children. The program would have provided a path to citizenship for approximately four million illegal immigrants. Since the Supreme Court blocked this program in June 2016, it was never formally implemented.

President Trump terminated the Deferred Action for Childhood Arrivals (DACA) program in September 2017. Five years earlier, on June 15, 2012, Obama's Secretary of Homeland Security, Janet Napolitano, had announced the DACA program that shielded young undocumented immigrants brought to the United States as children from deportation. DACA allowed illegal immigrants who were brought to the United States before the age of 16, who lived in the country since 2007, and were less than 31 years of age to apply for a renewable, two-year permit to legally live, work, or study in the United States. DACA recipients receive various benefits, such as employment authorization, and a limited number of federal benefits such as the Earned Income Tax Credit and disaster relief assistance. DACA was instituted by executive authority under Obama rather than through a legislative act of Congress. DACA rescission was challenged by several states claiming that Trump's action violated the equal protection clause of the Constitution by explicitly targeting Mexican-born immigrants. The federal courts ordered the U.S. Citizenship and Immigration Services to resume accepting DACA applications. Still, the issue is still working its way through the federal courts as of the writing of this book.

Trump also wanted to remove Temporary Protection Status (TPS) for hundreds of thousands of immigrants from Sudan, Haiti, El Salvador, Honduras, and Nicaragua. Under TPS, foreign nationals from designated countries who do not qualify as refugees or asylum seekers, but are unable to return to their homes due to conflict or natural disasters, can legally stay in the United States. These immigrants are to return home once the emergency in their countries of origin has ended. TPS, however, has allowed immigrants to live and work legally in the United States for decades. A removal of TPS would pave the way for deportation. On October 3, 2018, a federal judge issued a preliminary injunction preventing the Trump Administrations from deporting TPS holders, citing a violation of the Equal Protection Clause and acknowledging that thousands of children holding U.S. citizenship, born to TPS parents, would be harmed.

The Trump Administration also announced that, in FY2019, the United States would reduce the number of refugees allowed to settle in the United States to 30,000, down from 45,000 in FY2018 (the lowest ceiling since 1980). Secretary of State Mike Pompeo blamed the decrease on a lack of resources and an immense backlog:

> This year's refugee ceiling reflects the substantial increase in the number of individuals seeking asylum in our country, leading to a massive backlog of outstanding asylum cases and greater public expense.
> (2018)

In addition, refugees and asylum seekers would undergo a thorough screening and vetting process in order to "prioritiz[e] the safety and well-being of the American people," adding to the expense and backlog (Pompeo 2018). Border and national security is under the purview of the Executive. But Congress, not the President, sets the criteria for admission to the United States. Congress, however, has delegated some aspects of immigration authority to the Executive branch. For example, under the Immigration and Nationality Act (1952, amended 1965) Congress has granted all Presidents the right to deny "entry of any aliens or of any class of aliens" whose admission would be "detrimental to the interests of the United States" (8 U.S.C. § 1182(f)). In addition, the State Department's overseas consular officers are the ones who determine whether an individual fits within congressionally imposed criteria when they apply for visa.

In order to counter what was seen as a growing threat of terrorists entering the United States, Trump also issued Executive Order 13780 "Protecting the Nation from Foreign Terrorist Entry into the United States" on January 27, 2017 (Trump 2017c). The order suspended the issuance of visas and other immigration benefits to nationals of countries of particular concern, namely from the seven Muslim-majority countries of Iran, Iraq, Libya, Somalia, Sudan, Syria, and Yemen, for 90 days. Signing the Executive Order Trump pledged to "keep radical Islamic terrorists out of the United States of America" (Merica 2017). Opponents of the ban claimed that it violated equal protection by discriminating based on religion. With growing opposition and lawsuits, Trump issued a revised version of the travel ban in March 2017 (Executive Order 13780) that removed Iraq and the indefinite ban on Syrian refugees from the list. In September 2017, a third version of the ban was issued to withstand court review. The third travel ban modified the list of countries, excluding Iraq and Sudan, and added two non-Muslim-majority countries, North Korea and Venezuela. Trump's Muslim ban and inflammatory rhetoric emboldened hate-based groups in the United States. CNN reports that there were on average nine attacks, acts of vandalism, or arson on mosques each month in 2017 in the United States. In comparison, in 2016, there were a total of 46.

As an indication of the contested nature of the social construction of immigrants as deviants, many local communities provided safe haven to immigrants and undocumented workers. Trump then attempted to deny federal funding to "sanctuary cities," cities that failed to comply with federal immigration authorities and policies. The Ninth Circuit Court of Appeals found that Trump had exceeded his authority and the order was deemed unconstitutional.

The building of a contiguous wall, a physical barrier to illegal immigration, along the southern border of the United States proved to be more difficult than Trump imagined. There are several reasons for this. First, were the costs. According to the Department of Homeland Security, the wall has been estimated to cost over $22 billion, and Mexico has not chosen to pay for it. Second, the wall may not be effective due to topographical restrictions and changing immigration dynamics. Due to the Rio Grande and mountainous terrain, there are sections of the border that clearly cannot be walled. Plus, there are the limitations of the wall itself. A wall 30 feet high can be scaled and a foundation six feet deep can be tunneled under (Felbab-Brown 2017). Also, research indicates that most people in the country illegally are people who have simply overstayed their visas after having entered legally in the first place (Gonella 2017). Third, the building of the wall would require seizure of privately owned property. A good number of seized properties would be from the red state of Texas where private property is a sacrosanct right.

Still, the Trump Administration did not soften its stance on immigration. In a speech to the U.N. General Assembly, Trump stated:

> Illegal immigration funds criminal networks, ruthless gangs, and the flow of deadly drugs. Illegal immigration exploits vulnerable populations, hurts hardworking citizens, and has produced a vicious cycle of crime, violence, and poverty. Only by upholding national borders, destroying criminal gangs, can we break this cycle and establish a real foundation for prosperity.
>
> (2018a)

Trump, citing concern over U.S. sovereignty, refused to support the Global Compact for Safe, Orderly and Regular Migrations (the United States withdrew from its deliberation and drafting last year). The Global Compact on Migration is a nonbinding collective international framework whose purpose is to strengthen international cooperation on migration. The Global Compact on Migrations affirms the human rights of refugees and migrants. The compact specifically upholds the concept of state sovereignty, but also sustains states' obligations under international law.

In 2017, immigration reform was introduced in Congress with Trump's full support. The Reforming American Immigration for Strong

Employment (RAISE) Act, sponsored by Senators Tom Cotton (R-AR) and David Perdue (R-GA), sought to reduce the level of legal immigration by 50 percent and to cap refugee admissions to 50,000 per year. The RAISE Act would also greatly reduce the number of family reunification visas, limiting these visas to spouses and minor children of U.S. citizens and lawful permanent residents. The majority of visas would be based on merit, that is to say, to persons with advanced degrees, who have high-paying jobs, or have the money to invest in the U.S. economy. The RAISE Act would reduce legal immigration and shift allowances away from family-based visas toward individuals with high levels of education, job skills, and English proficiency.

The RAISE Act would appeal to Trump's anti-immigration supporters. Zong et al., of the Migration Policy Institute, report that "29 percent of all immigrant adults lacked a high school diploma or General Educational Development (GED) certificate" (2018). Thus, Trump's lower- and working-class constituents were in direct competition for low and unskilled employment and believed that immigrants were taking their jobs and receiving welfare benefits. The RAISE Act also called for the elimination of the visa diversity lottery that makes available an additional 50,000 visas to countries with low numbers of immigrant populations.[4] Because Congress has been unable to protect citizens from an influx of illegal immigrants, many U.S. citizens became staunchly anti-immigrant, confusing illegal immigration with legal immigration, and thus viewing all foreigners as illegal.

The Nasty Women: Dismantling Women's Reproductive Rights

Within days of his inauguration, Trump reenacted and expanded the Mexico City Policy and defunded the U.N. Population Fund. Trump's reinstatement of the Mexico City gag rule, now known as the Protecting Life in Global Health Assistance, applies to all agencies that receive U.S. health assistance, not just to those health organizations whose principal mission is family planning. According to Shannon Kowalski, Director of Advocacy and Policy at the International Women's Health Coalition (IWHC), the result of the Trump policy would cost women's and girls' lives by denying them access to safe abortions and other essential health services (IWHC 2017). Furthermore, the IWHC reports that previous implementations of the gag rule increased unintended pregnancies, abortions, and maternal deaths in sub-Saharan Africa. The World Health Organization (2018) reports that up to 13.2 percent of all maternal deaths are due to unsafe abortions. The report further documents that around seven million women are admitted to hospitals every year to complications from unsafe abortions at the annual cost of $553 million. The Protecting Life in Global Health Assistance program awards approximately $8.8 billion in health-related funds through the DOS, USAID, and the DOD.

In order to receive funding, the NGO must agree to neither promote nor perform abortions. Even mentioning abortion would violate the terms of funding. The State Department asserted that "the President has made very clear: U.S. taxpayer money should not be used to support foreign organizations that perform or actively promote abortion as a method of family planning in other nations" (U.S. Department of State 2017). If a health professional were to answer a patient's request for information on abortion, she could risk the health clinic's funding. Funding would be removed from the entire health clinic, not just the sector of the clinic dedicated to women's reproductive health. This would also have profound implications for NGOs and state health services in their treatment and prevention of such diseases as the Zika virus, AIDS, and Ebola (diseases that pose a particular threat to the pregnant woman and fetus). Access to reproductive health care has also been identified as an important determinant for reducing maternal mortality and infant mortality rates.

To add insult to injury, the United States under Trump rejected a Canadian proposal to the U.N. Human Rights Council that sought to protect women in conflict zones. Recognizing that women are at a higher risk of sexual assault and rape in war zones, the Canadian resolution called for comprehensive sexual and healthcare services, including access to safe abortions. What was the reason the United States rejected a proposal to shield women from the violent consequences of conflict? The Trump Administration did "not recognize abortion as a method of family planning, nor do we support abortion in our reproductive health assistance" whether or not the pregnancy is the result of rape (Sampathkumar 2017). In addition, the Trump budgets for FY2018 and FY2019 called for drastic decreases in funding to international healthcare organizations, such as Right to Care, a South African NGO dedicated to HIV prevention and treatment. Yet, Ian Sanne of Right to Care insisted that his biggest concern was Trump's plan to cut funding by nearly 20 percent to the U.S. National Institutes of Health (NIH). The NIH is the leading HIV-tuberculosis research organization, and the cut in funding could lead to a TB epidemic (Powell 2017).

Although women's rights both domestically and internationally have been institutionalized in a variety of legal and policy documents, there remains an undercurrent of patriarchal and misogynistic beliefs in the United States. Many faith-based organizations object to the core principles of women's rights and have successfully block and rolled back protections. In an effort to turn back women's reproductive rights globally, the Trump Administration appointed two conservative organizations, the Center for Family and Human Rights, and the Heritage Foundation, to the U.S. delegation to the Commission on the Status of Women's 2017 annual meeting. Among U.S. government officials for the 2018 meeting, Bethany Kozma (USAID) and Valerie Huber (Department of Health and Human Services) attended. Both women are anti-LGBTQ, anti-contraceptives, and anti-abortion advocates who believe in natural family planning only. Rather than advocate for comprehensive sex education, the U.S. delegation, claiming that the United States was a pro-life nation, attempted to negotiate for abstinence-oriented education and teaching women sexual refusal skills (Anapol 2018). This position ignores the fact that when women lack status and power, they have little or no ability to refuse their partner's sexual demands.

The Trump Administration also attempted to restrict women's rights domestically. Women's rights and empowerment are typically a threat to traditional social norms. The threat posed by women's advancement and progress was amplified in the 2016 presidential election since the Democratic candidate was a woman and Trump "carried a reputation for being insensitive and even hostile toward women, making headlines on several occasions with anti-feminist, chauvinist, or sexist statements" (Valentino, Wayne et al. 2018: 215).

The Affordable Care Act guaranteed coverage for FDA-approved contraceptives without out-of-pocket costs. This allowed millions of women with limited financial resources access to birth control. However, in October 2017, the Trump Administration issued an interim final rule that created a broad exemption allowing any employer, health insurance provider, or university to claim a religious or moral objection that would allow them to deny coverage for contraception. In December 2017, two federal district courts granted injunctions. Louise Melling, deputy legal director at the American Civil Liberties Union, believes that

> What's at stake with these rules is women's equality in the sense of access to contraception ... What's also at stake here is... a question about religious objections and whether religious objections can entitle you not to comply with anti-discrimination measures.
> (quoted in Frieden 2018)

Contraceptives include issues of sexuality beyond fertility and child bearing. Contraceptives allow women decision-making control over their body and sexuality, threatening the patriarchal family and Christian beliefs. The Trump Administration studied and revised the exception clause (the final rule on exemptions is not out yet but will be soon).

Roger Severino, who directs the Office for Civil Rights in the U.S. Department of Health and Human Services, created the Conscience and Religious Freedom Division (CRFD) to "vigorously and effectively enforce existing laws protecting the rights of conscience and religious freedom" for healthcare workers (HHS 2018). CRFD protects medical and healthcare workers who refuse to perform "any lawful health service or research activity...on the grounds that doing so would be contrary to his or her religious beliefs or moral convictions, or because of his or her religious beliefs or moral convictions" (as quoted in Raifman 2018).

Religious freedom, for Severino, was the first freedom. Thus, employers could be allowed to refuse to cover birth control in their health insurance plans, and doctors or nurses could refuse to participate in medical procedures and care. Women gaining rights over their bodies and reproductive health could be viewed as a threat to traditional American values (religious freedom) and the masculine hierarchy whereby the man is the head of the family.

The social construction of women has evolved significantly within the past several decades. Pierce et al. (2014) describe how middle-class women were viewed as a dependent group in the 1960s and 1970s. But with their increased entrance into the workforce and institutions of higher education by the 1990s, women were classified as an advantaged group. However, women's success has come at a comparative cost to men. Men were no longer the sole breadwinners and perhaps not even the primary breadwinners thus threatening traditional family dynamics. Schneider et al. (2014) report that, by 2007, strong, independent, feminist women moved into the quadrant of contenders, that is, powerful but undeserving. However, Stabile (2016) suggests that women who reject or wish to delay motherhood or to engage in sexual activity without the fear of an unwanted pregnancy, thereby, failing to embrace their traditional gender roles, have experienced a negative social construction, moving toward the deviant category. Government policy toward deviant women is to impede access to contraceptives and abortions. Pierce et al. (2014) report that poor women, criminal women, and women of color have always been placed in the deviant category and seen as undeserving of government assistance and responsible for their own plight.

LGBTQ Community

LGBTQ advocates have feared that lesbian, gay, bisexual, transgendered, and queer people could be refused health care altogether under the Trump Administration. A leaked draft of Trump's executive order "Establishing a Government-Wide Initiative to Respect Religious Freedom" sought to protect the right of healthcare professionals to refuse to treat LGBTQ patients for religious reasons. Furthermore, the August 25th Presidential Memorandum for the Secretary of Defense and the Secretary of Homeland Security (2017d), "Military Service by Transgender Individuals," prohibited openly transgender individuals from joining the U.S. military and authorized DOD to discharge individuals who were transgender. To disallow transgendered individuals from serving their country via the military, to authorize their discharge, and to prohibit expenditure of military resources for sex-reassignment health care violated these individuals' equal protection rights.

Valcore believes that LGBTQ have now moved from the deviant category to the dependent category as they are recognized as "a minority group in need of enhanced support from the government because of the existence and potential for acts of violence and harassment, which is indicative of dependent status" (2018: 1625). As a dependent social construction (sympathetic but powerless), they receive symbolic and inadequate policy support. Policymakers have little incentive to provide significant benefits. However, Valcore acknowledges that the move of LGBTQ groups in the socially constructed categorization (deviant or dependent) is still highly contested. Schneider and Ingram warn that "Periods of beneficial policy, however, may be short-lived as the political capital gained from being 'tough' rather than 'soft' on an issue is enormous" (2017: 325). Socially constructed categories are fluid, susceptible to public sentiments regarding a public policy, but also tend to change slowly over time.

LGBTQ individuals fleeing from Trump's travel ban countries were at particular risk since their countries of origin imposed the death penalty for homosexual activity. These individuals fell into three deviant categories: homosexual/transgender (foreign LGBTQ may not yet move to the dependent category), immigrants, and those from Muslim-majority countries.

Terrorists: Continuity with the Policies of Torture and Assassination

Punishment and retaliation have come to dominate public policy toward the deviance of terrorism. When the deviant group is perceived to be a threat to the morals and safety of society, it becomes politically beneficial to implement punitive policies toward that group. Anticipating the fear and anger of his constituents, Trump announced that it is his belief that torture absolutely works and he pledged to "fight fire with fire" when dealing with terrorists (Ackerman 2017). As a candidate, Trump openly promised that his administration would practice assassinations and abuse human rights. Voters rewarded him for promising to take a hard stand against negatively constructed groups since, as Nicholson-Crotty and Meier have stated, "there is often significant electoral benefit in pandering to public fears" (2005: 228).

While the George W. Bush Administration first hid the use of torture, then as an act of prevaricate, it redefined and renamed what torture encompassed, and the Obama Administration later apologized for the use of torture and officially rescinded the Bush-era approval of tit, the Trump Administration escalated the shameless, insolent talk about torture. Going beyond the policies of the George W. Bush Administration, Trump pledged to reinstitute enhanced interrogation techniques. But he also wished to expand the law and go beyond mere waterboarding by utilizing tougher and harsher methods (Ackerman 2017). Upon taking office, Trump passed around a draft executive order that would roll back restrictions on the interrogation and detention of detainees. The late

Senator John McCain (R-AZ) spoke out against a proposed draft executive order, "Detention and Interrogation of Enemy Combatants," that would revive the use of torture by stating that "The President can sign whatever executive orders he likes. But the law is the law. We are not bringing back torture in the United States of America" (Carney 2017). Still, thus far, there has not been any evidence of torture by U.S. officials as a result of an undisclosed Trump executive order.

If the United States were to institute torture as a policy, it would confront strong international pressure, opposition from federal law, and antagonism from members of Congress. James Mattis, Secretary of Defense, convinced Trump that torture does not work. Mattis was of the opinion that gaining the confidence of a suspect is more effective and provides better intelligence. Yet, many of Trump's appointees approved of the use of torture. Trump persuaded the Senate to confirm Gina Haspel as CIA director in 2018. Haspel oversaw the CIA's Rendition, Detention and Interrogation program that tortured detainees at the CIA black site in Thailand. Haspel also participated in covering up and destroying torture evidence under the direction of Jose Rodriquez, head of the CIA Counterterrorism Center under the George W. Bush Administration (Blanton 2018). In addition, Mike Pompeo, a former Director of the CIA and Trump's new Secretary of State, has been on record in supporting the use of torture and praising its use by the CIA (Pitter 2018). Pompeo also said that he would attempt to have the National Defense Authorization Act (2015) revised if it proved to constrain interrogators. Yet, any revisions would have to be approved by the Secretary of Defense, and Mattis has made clear his position on the use of torture. Despite his belief that torture works, Trump also indicated that he would accede to the judgment of Mattis and Pompeo. In an interview with David Muir on *ABC World News Tonight*, Trump said, "I will say this, I will rely on Pompeo and Mattis and my group. And if they don't wanna do [torture], that's fine. If they do wanna do, then I will work for that end" (2017a). Trump publically claimed to have changed his mind on the use of torture after meeting with Mattis.

Trump also stated that a terrorist's family could be targeted. Trump declared: "The other thing with the terrorists is you have to take out their families, when you get these terrorists, you have to take out their families" (LoBianco 2015). Intentionally targeting the innocent family members of a terrorist is a grave breach of the Fourth Geneva Conventions, the War Crimes Act (1996), and the Uniform Code of Military Justice because family members are civilians not combatants.[5] Former CIA Director and Air Force General Michael Hayden opined that the military would be barred from following an illegal order and therefore would be required to refuse to obey a direct order from the commander in chief (Holley 2016).

Trump promised to continue the practice of preventive detention used by his predecessors. Trump tweeted that there would be no further releases of detainees. Attorney General Jeff Sessions called Guantánamo a "very fine place" to hold and interrogate terror suspects. The prison was spacious and could be used to hold future enemy combatants and domestic terrorists (K. Johnson 2017). Guantánamo would stay open, and "we're gonna load it up with some bad dudes, believe me, we're gonna load it up" (Trump, as quoted in Corera 2017). Pompeo also supported Trump's intention to keep Guantánamo open and populated.

Moreover, Trump increased targeted assassination of Islamic State of Iraq and Syria, (ISIS) operatives. Savage and Schmitt (2017) report that the Trump Administration relaxed two rules of drone engagement thereby rolling back the admittedly weak limits set by Obama.

> First, the targets of kill missions by the military and the C.I.A., now generally limited to high-level militants deemed to pose a "continuing and imminent threat" to Americans, would be expanded to include foot-soldier jihadists with no special skills or leadership roles. And second, proposed drone attacks and raids would no longer undergo high-level vetting.
>
> (Savage and Schmitt 2017)

The targeting of rank-and-file insurgents would likely increase the number of civilian casualties, either by mistaken identification or by their physical proximity to the suspected insurgents. Additionally, the ability to strike without a high-level terrorist posing an active threat to the United States and its citizens would allow a geographical expansion of CIA drone activities. Trump granted the CIA and the military secret new strike authority to conduct covert drone attacks. The drone strikes could now be carried out without first getting approval of the Pentagon or the White House (Shinkman 2017). However, the near certainty standard may be downgraded as the CIA is given complete discretion to operate on its own strikes.

The rules of engagement for airstrikes against ISIS were also relaxed, resulting in greater civilian deaths. According to Borger (2017), 60 percent of the officially acknowledged civilian deaths from Operation Inherent Resolve (which began in August 2014) against ISIS occurred during the Trump Administration. Due to Trump's "strategy to more proactively target extremist groups that threaten the stability and security of the Afghan people" (as quoted in Losey 2017), airstrikes reached their highest level in seven years. Many of Trump's senior staff members had military backgrounds and played critical roles in developing and executing the war on terror strategy. They had a vested interest in seeing their policies continue.

The Pew Research Center found that the American public was divided over whether it is acceptable or not to use torture to combat terrorism. Forty-eight percent believed that there could be some theoretical circumstances where it might be permissible to torture, while 49 percent said that it was never acceptable. Men, white respondents, and Republicans (Trump's core supporters) were the most likely to favor the use of torture against the deviant policy group of terrorists (Tyson 2017). Political leaders often gain political capital from punishing the deviant when an anxious public believes that the deviant is undeserving of better treatment and poses a threat to their lives and values.

Foreign Aid as a Discarded Tool of Foreign Policy

Moral considerations have held a revered, although not always principal, place in U.S. foreign aid allocations. Security and economic concerns have always been the priority in aid allocations, with human rights and humanitarian interests regulated to a secondary yet important position. The Trump foreign aid budget is an important case because it illustrates what could happen if the United States, the largest aid donor globally, were to turn its focus inward. An "America First" strategy could have long-term consequences for human rights, poverty alleviation, and economic development, even after Trump is out of office. The contradictions between the current aid request under Trump and the U.S. historic, albeit often inconsistent and disputed, position on human rights promotion can have global repercussions. Although it is only half way through Trump's term as of the writing of this book, we can begin to determine how significant the change in U.S. foreign aid policy would be, as the President's intentions are clear.

Traditionally, presidents have asked for large foreign aid budgets and Congress cuts the amount due to its overriding concern with the budget and budget deficit. But Trump himself drastically cut foreign aid budget and Congress, for the most part, has maintained funding to FY2017 levels. The budget is an important signal of the Trump Administration's priorities. As Parker notes, "the central reflection of a society's values lies in the overall pattern of its allocation of resources ... and a shift in allocations in favour of human priority concerns" (1994: 9). The FY2019 budget, like the FY2018 budget request, has proposed large cuts to the DOS and USAID, with increased or stable funding for the military and homeland security programs.

The reduction of the foreign aid budget is among the campaign pledges Trump promised to enact. Reducing foreign aid funding is consistent with Trump's America First message and an expedient way to appeal to Trump's political base by focusing on domestic needs. Trump's budget blueprint "puts America first by keeping more of America's hard-earned tax dollars here at home" in order to fund domestic priorities (Office of Management and Budget 2017: 1). Mulvaney, White House Office of Management Budget director, stated that "The overriding message is fairly straightforward: less money spent overseas means more money spent here" (as reported in Shepardson 2017). This sentiment has resonated well with Trump supporters. Foreign aid was blamed for high taxes, a reduction in American living standards, the crumbling of American infrastructure, and a skyrocketing deficit because other developed countries simply are not doing their share to help when it comes to foreign aid. Although the United States allocates only about 1 percent of its budget to foreign aid, polls show that Americans believe that foreign aid accounts for 25 percent of the budget (Ferrarello 2017).

Trump, under the guise of America First, has wanted to reduce America's long-standing commitment to humanitarianism, democracy, poverty reduction, women's health, and human rights. Trump did not believe that foreign aid could serve America's long-term interests. For FY2018, the Trump Administration attempted to cut the International Affairs Budget to $40.5 billion (of which $29.5 billion is base and $12.0 billion is OCO), down approximately 32 percent from FY2017. Fortunately, Congress did not go along with Trump's drastic budget cuts for foreign assistance. Senator Lindsey Graham (R-SC), Chairman of the Senate's Subcommittee on the DOS, Foreign Operations, and Related Programs, commented that Trump's cuts would eliminate the U.S. soft power, or the ability to encourage and motivate foreign governments. Graham declared: "this budget is not going to go anywhere" (Torbati 2017). Likewise, for FY2019, the Trump request for the International Affairs Budget was $42.2 billion (of which $42.2 billion is base and 0 is OCO), down about 25 percent ($13.7 billion) from the enacted FY2018 budget. Later, in 2018, the Trump Administration proposed to rescind (that is to say, to take back funds appropriated by Congress but not yet spent) billions of dollars from the foreign aid budget. Again, Congress pushed back, and the Trump Administration backed off. Congress, again, proposed a restoration of much of the funding to the International Affairs Budget for FY2019.

Foreign aid designated OCO allows the Congress to appropriate greater amounts of aid without violating the Budget Control Act (BCA) of 2011, which establishes caps on discretionary funding. Any funds designated as OCO do not count against the budget limit set by the act. Originally, the OCO or "emergency funding" was used for war-related funding. But since the Obama years, OCO has been used to fund regular operations in violations of the spirit and intent of the BCA. In this way, the Congress and the President can spend additional money while still complying with statutory spending limits intended to cap government spending and reduce the deficit. Furthermore, they can claim to the American people that they are spending taxpayer money responsibly. OCO accounted for 37 percent of the State and USAID budget in 2017. The Trump Administration proposed to eliminate the use of OCO for DOS and U.S. Agency for International Development budgets.

Trump's FY2019 budget request asked for a reduction of nearly $2 billion or 23 percent in global health funding from the enacted FY2018 budget. Both the Senate and House appropriations bills have proposed global aid budgeting levels to FY2018 or higher. The United States is the largest funder and implementer of global health programs worldwide. The major programs are PEPFAR, Tuberculosis, the President's Malaria Initiative, Neglected Tropical Diseases, Family Planning and Reproductive Health, Maternal and Child Health, Feed the Future, and Global Health Security. Trump also requested a reduction of $1.29 billion in humanitarian assistance compared to FY2018 (that is $1.48 billion from FY2017). International Disaster Aid (IDA) is reduced by nearly 17 percent. Trump's FY2019 budget request also eliminated food aid (P.L. 480 Title II). The elimination was disingenuously justified because IDA "retains sufficient funding for emergency food assistance" even at IDA's significantly reduced funding levels (OMB 2018: 76). Both the House and Senate appropriations bills would increase the amount of humanitarian assistance at or near FY2017 levels. Trump also sought to reduce contributions to the U.N. by $703 million including a complete withdrawal from the U.N. Educational and Cultural Organization. In both FY2018 and FY2019, Trump's funding for multilateral assistance eliminated funds for International Organizations and Programs (IOP). IOP encompass voluntary contributions to U.N.-affiliated organizations such as the United Nations International Children's Emergency Fund (UNICEF), the United Nations High Commissioner for Human Rights (UNHCHR), the United Nations Development Programme (UNDP), U.N. Trust Fund to End Violence Against Women, and the United Nations Population Fund (UNPF). The Administration pledged that support for an unidentified, unspecified, undisclosed, limited number of U.N.-affiliated organizations, determined to be important to U.S. strategic objectives, would still be funded by the Economic Support and Development Fund (ESDF). Congress, once again, provided funding to IOP, reasoning that granting IOP funding would serve basic humanitarian purposes: for example, to eradicate poverty and hunger, to save the lives of children, and to improve the health of the poor.

In both FY2018 and FY2019 budget proposals, the Trump Administration also called for the elimination of the Development Assistance Fund and Economic Support Fund in order to create a new ESDF. The Administration claimed that the combination of ESF and DA would streamline assistance and allow the DOS and USAID greater flexibility to respond to "emerging challenges and opportunities within one account" (OMB 2018: 69). This would greatly reduce foreign aid expenditures. The Office of Management and Budget maintained that the new ESDF would be directed toward partner countries of greatest strategic importance in order to assure the effectiveness of taxpayer money. Congress has rejected the Trump Administration's proposal to consolidate the ESF and

DA funding programs because it would obstruct Congressional oversight of DA and ESF spending.

Trump has elevated the transactional nature of foreign aid to quid pro quo arrangement, vowing to provide aid only to America's friends. In a speech to the U.N. General Assembly Trump stated:

> The United States is the world's largest giver in the world, by far, of foreign aid. But few give anything to us. That is why we are taking a hard look at US foreign assistance... whether the countries who receive our dollars and our protection also have our interests at heart... Moving forward, we are only going to give foreign aid to those who respect us and, frankly, are our friends.
> (September 25, 2018)

Voting with the United States in the U.N. is one measure of friendship, that is, following lockstep with Trump's foreign policy agenda. Development would no longer be a pillar in U.S. foreign policy, along with defense and diplomacy, but rather a bargaining chip to get other countries to make policy concessions. Given the fact that U.S. military and economic interests are global, oftentimes autocrats are in a position to do as Trump wants in return for foreign aid. Trump has been vociferously clear that U.S. foreign aid would be used to advantage negotiations for U.S. security and commercial interests.

In sum, historically, the President is more supportive of foreign aid than Congress. Congress usually appropriates less, sometimes far less, foreign aid than the President requests. However, Trump proposed massive reductions in foreign aid for FY2018 and FY2019. Congress pushed back against the excessive cuts in foreign aid and the State Department budget by providing more funds than Trump requested.

Military Aid and Arms Sales Making America Great Again

The Trump Administration has lifted human rights conditions on arms sales that were imposed by the Obama Administration due to human rights violations. For example, the Trump Administration announced a multibillion-dollar arms deal with Bahrain, overlooking Bahrain's brutal repression of opposition leaders and its crackdown on the Shiite majority. Cole Bockenfeld, Deputy Director for Policy at the Project on Middle East Democracy, reports that Bahrain's Sunni monarchy is in a "full-scale crackdown" of the majority-Shiite population (Rogin 2017). Nonetheless, the State Department approved the sale of Meter Fast Patrol Boats (estimated cost of $60.25 million), F-16V aircraft with support ($2.785 billion), TOW missiles with equipment and support ($27 million), and an upgrade of F-16 Block 40 aircraft to F-16V configuration ($1.082 billion).[6] The Trump Administration lifted the human rights conditions that once blocked military sales to Bahrain. With the human rights restrictions removed, the U.S. administration was able to sell 19 F-16 fighter jets, worth $2.8 billion, and an upgrading package of older F-16s worth an additional $4 billion (Capaccio 2017). The arms deal was announced over the objections of several members in Congress, but with the full support of the military. Army General Joseph Votel, commander of U.S. forces in the Middle East, objected to human rights conditions placed on arms sales to allies stating:

> While we have historically enjoyed a strong mil-to-mil relationship with our Bahraini counterparts, the slow progress on key FMS cases, specifically additional F-16 aircraft and upgrades to Bahrain's existing F-16 fleet, due to concerns of potential human rights abuses in the country, continues to strain our relationship.
> (as reported in Capaccio 2017)

Human rights groups worry that the lifting of human rights conditions on the sale of military weapons and equipment has signaled to repressive governments that there is no need to reform or improve (Sanger and Schmitt 2017).

Likewise, the Trump Administration announced the sale of military aircraft to Nigeria despite Nigeria's history of human rights abuses and bombing of civilian targets, including refugee camps. Amnesty International's recent report stated that the Nigerian military continues "to commit serious human rights violations including extrajudicial executions and enforced disappearances. The police and military continued to commit torture and other ill-treatment" (2016/2017 online). Furthermore, the Nigerian military still routinely arrests civilians based on random profiling rather than on evidence, and it frequently employs torture as an investigatory tool. Conditions in Nigerian military prisons are cruel. Two hundred forty detainees died due to disease and starvation. Nevertheless, selling twelve (12) A-29 Super Tucano aircraft to Nigeria worth $593 million, in the opinion of the Defense Security Cooperation Agency, "supported Nigerian military operations against terrorist organizations Boko Haram and ISIS West Africa, and Nigerian efforts to counter illicit trafficking in Nigeria and the Gulf of Guinea" (DSCA 2017). Boko Haram has been a serious problem in Nigeria, and the United States has had security concerns in the country. But it ought to be noted that Nigeria is currently (2018) one of the countries on the verge of a widespread famine.

The Trump Administration also declared its intention to sell the Saudi Arabian government more than $460 billion in defense articles over the next ten years. At issue is the sale of $500 million of precision-guided munitions and other offensive weapons. Pursuant to the Arms Export Control Act of 1976, U.S. Senators Rand Paul (R-KY), Chris Murphy (D-CT), and Al Franken (D-MN) introduced a joint resolution of disapproval of the proposed export, thereby forcing a Congressional vote on the arms sale (Paul 2017). Senator Paul stated that

> given Saudi Arabia's past support of terror, poor human rights record, and questionable tactics in its war in Yemen, Congress must carefully consider and thoroughly debate if selling them billions of dollars of arms is in our best national security interest at this time.
> (Reuters 2017)

Previously, in December 2016, the Obama Administration had suspended the arms deal due to Saudi Arabia's repeated attacks against civilian targets (including hospitals) in its war in Yemen. Dafna Rand, Deputy Assistant Secretary of State for Democracy, Human Rights, and Labor under the Obama Administration, testified in a Senate Foreign Relations Committee hearing that Saudi Arabia had selected civilian targets and failed to adhere to a no-strike list (as reported in Abramson 2017). The three-year conflict, with the United States providing material aid to the Saudi-led coalition's war, resulted in a humanitarian crisis with the destruction of basic social services, devastation of the economy, destruction of health services, and ravage of the agricultural sector in Yemen. Millions of civilians, including the majority of Yemeni children and pregnant women, have faced acute malnourishment and starvation. U.N. Secretary-General António Guterres, in an April 2017 appeal for humanitarian aid to Yemen, stated: "On average, a child under the age of five dies of preventable causes in Yemen every ten minutes" (2017). Senator Chris Murphy (D-CT) affirmed:

> The United States has its fingerprints all over a famine inside Yemen that is killing a child under 5, every 10 minutes through causes that are preventable.... Part of the responsibility lies in the failure of the United States to tell the Saudis to get serious about stopping targeting civilian and humanitarian assets inside that country.
> (as quoted in Sprusansky 2017: 54)

In 2017, the Trump Administration also approved the direct commercial sale of lethal weapons to Ukraine as it was battling pro-Russian separatists in its eastern provinces. The weapons, worth $41.5 million, including sniper systems, ammunition, and accessories, were described as defensive in nature (Correll 2017). Trump also approved sales of Javelin anti-tank missiles.

The Security Assistance Monitor (2018) reports that, in his first year in office, Trump notified Congress of 157 commercial arms sales to 43 states, worth over $84 billion. Many of the countries the United States sold weapons to posed little or no risk to the human rights of their citizens (Canada, Japan, Sweden, or New Zealand, for example). But the United

States also sold billions of dollars' worth of weapons to countries that have regularly used violence against their own citizens or were involved in intrastate conflicts with sectarian/ethnic groups or posed a threat to their neighbors. Among Trump's buyers have been the conflict-riddled, human rights abusing countries of Bahrain, Honduras, India, Iraq, Saudi Arabia, and Turkey.

Trump even reversed a George W. Bush Administration policy to phase out cluster bombs by 2019.[7] Currently, the United States maintains a stockpile of 1.5 million cluster weapons and 90 million bomblets housed in South Korea (Peck 2018). A cluster bomb releases small bomblets that indiscriminately destroy a wide range of targets at one time. Amnesty International (2010) described the destruction caused, stating that a cluster bomb

> is designed to carry a payload of 166 cluster submunitions (bomblets) which each explode into over 200 sharp steel fragments that can cause injuries up to 150m away. An incendiary material inside the bomblet also spreads fragments of burning zirconium designed to set fire to nearby flammable objects.

Peck (2018) reports that many of the bomblets (up to 30 percent) do not explode as intended but remain live, thus posing a threat to anyone who unwarily comes upon it. Human Rights Watch recounts that cluster bombs "typically open in the air, dispersing multiple bomblets or submunitions over a wide area. Many submutions fail to explode on initial impact, leaving unexploded duds that can act like landmines for years to come" (HRW 2017). Farmers, children, and livestock are common post-conflict victims.

Trump has touted international commercial arms sales as a source of jobs in the United States. However, William Hartung of the Security Assistance Monitor argues that jobs created by arms sales are often hindered by offset and coproduction agreements (2018). As part of the sale, U.S. manufactures agree to invest in the purchaser's economy to offset the costs of the deal. This frequently involves producing parts of the weapon or weapon system in the recipient's country, thereby augmenting the recipient's manufacturing capacity and employing their citizens, not American citizens. Commercial arms sales, consequently, "will likely create jobs in foreign countries rather than in the United States" (Hartung 2018: 11). Worse, with the increase in the buyer's manufacturing capacity, and their lower labor costs, Trump's arms sales could slash American jobs in the future because U.S. companies would be unable to compete.

Congressional Push Back to Trump's Agenda

In an era of extreme partisan Congressional politics, it is unlikely that the Republicans would be a check on Trump's overreach and hyperbole.

As one would expect, Republicans in Congress have largely backed Trump's agenda. Although Trump enjoyed his highest approval rating of a mere 45 percent on January 29, 2017 (term average to date is only 39 percent), among self-identified Republicans, Trump has had a fairly stable 80–85 percent approval rating, and 70 percent among conservatives throughout his term in office (Gallup 2018). Neustadt (1980) identified "public prestige" as a source of presidential influence and support in Congress. Public prestige assists the president in pushing his agenda through Congress because Congressional members are attentive to the president's public approval. Rivers and Rose go as far as to state that "presidential influence in Congress rises and falls with the president's public prestige" (1985: 195). Legislators support a popular president's agenda in hopes of pleasing his, and their, constituency. Although Trump may have held prestige among his base, his lack of prestige among the general public has allowed both Democrats and Republicans some leeway to pursue their own agendas. Apparently, Trump's coattails have not been strong enough to coerce Congressional support for his foreign aid budget and other controversial policies.

With regard to the two determinants of Presidential success outlined by Cohen et al. (2013), personal skills of leadership and political context, Trump has had a difficult time in successfully implementing his political agenda. Even though the President's party controlled both chambers of Congress up until the midterm elections of 2018, Trump has had great difficulty in passing legislation. Trump could not get healthcare reform, spending on infrastructure, foreign aid reduction, and immigration reform, notably the massive wall protecting the U.S. southern border, through Congress. Edwards (2018) believes that successful presidents understand that they persuade, facilitate, and guide legislation. They do not direct and command Congress to pass legislation. Congress is more willing to negotiate with the President to further his agenda if they believe he has a mandate from the people. Trump claimed to have such a mandate, but it is widely known that he won with only 46 percent of the popular vote and nearly three million fewer votes than Hillary Clinton (Edwards 2018). In fact, many Trump voters voted against Clinton rather than voted for Trump. The Republican Party lost several Congressional seats but still retained control of Congress in 2016 (until the 2018 midterm elections where the Republicans lost the House of Representatives). Because the Republicans did not have large enough majorities to assure passage of the presidential agenda, they had to rely on at least minimal support from the Democrats. However, as Edwards notes, "The degree of polarization will affect the potential for the president to reach across the aisle and obtain support from the opposition party" (2018: 460). Ideological polarization in Congress has been extremely high. Furthermore, Trump's hyperbolic rhetoric and derogatory or insulting remarks toward revered institutions, like the military, the intelligence, and the justice department, fractured party cohesion.

Although Republicans were the majority in both houses of Congress (until the midterms), they have not been blind supporters of Trump's resolve to reduce or eliminate foreign aid. Eichensehr (2018) suggests that due to Trump's perceived incompetence and inattention to diplomacy, Congress may have had to conduct in a more prominent and forceful fashion U.S. foreign relations. Diplomacy and U.S. alliances have not been a priority for the Trump Administration. As evidence, Trump cut the staffing and budget of the DOS and, at the NATO summit, he declined to endorse the mutual defense pledge, complaining instead that other members chronically underpaid into the military alliance.

However, there have also been instances of bipartisan cooperation. For example, in 2017, Republicans and Democrats jointly and overwhelmingly backed a package of sanctions against Russia for meddling in the 2016 elections against the wishes of Trump (Schor 2017). Included in the bill, "Russia Sanctions Review Act of 2017," were stringent congressional oversight provisions that the White House resisted. In addition, there was strong bipartisan support against Trump's attempt to eviscerate the foreign affairs budget for FY2018 and FY2019. Foreign aid was often thought to be a divisive foreign policy issue between Republicans and Democrats in Congress. Nevertheless, there was strong bipartisan opposition to Trump's efforts to drastically reduce foreign aid. Congress did cut the foreign aid budget, but not by the draconian levels requested by Trump.

In the realm of foreign aid, the president must negotiate with Congress. Congress has the ability to both pass legislation and appropriate funds that directly influence foreign aid policy. Binder (2018) suggests that the inability of the Republican Party to pass the President's agenda has been due to the split in the Republic Party between the "hard-core conservatives, often representing southern states, hold decidedly more far-right views and are less willing to compromise than their more centrist, pragmatic colleagues" (2018: 83). It is particularly noteworthy that both the House and the Senate proposed to reduce international security assistance from FY2017, but not by as much as proposed by Trump's "skinny budget" of FY2018 and his "efficient budget" of FY2019. Both chambers of Congress have appropriated more for security assistance than what Trump asked for. Congress fears that Trump's budget did not do enough to protect the national security interests related to the threats posed by terrorism, weak or failed states, and transnational criminal organizations. Congress also opposed Trump's hope to transform foreign aid from grants to interest accumulating loans. The transition from grants to loans could not only threaten jobs but also cause a loss of U.S. influence if China or Russia provided the arms.

Bureaucratic Resistance to Trump's Agenda

The bureaucracy has a strong tendency toward maintaining the status quo, has a proclivity for inertia, and is renowned for its resistance to change. Instituted policies, standard operating procedures, and embedded routines are difficult to reform or amend. Human rights have been a feature in U.S. foreign policy since the Nixon Administration with legislation binding and restricting presidential prerogative, under normal circumstances.[8] Human rights are also an accepted and admired American value, at least in theory if not always in practice. Individuals, attracted by the human rights, democracy, and development missions of the DOS and the USAID, have chosen to work in these departments and support their missions. Thus, there is no surprise that mid- and lower-level bureaucratic and embassy employees protect and advance U.S. human rights policy. The turbulence and chaos that have characterized the Trump Administration have allowed lower-level State and USAID employees' substantial leeway in implementing human rights, development, and democratization policies (The Economist 2017). Cooper et al. suggest that "bureaucratic jockeying at lower levels sometimes plays a not inconsequential role in shaping decisions, even those that are ultimately resolved at much higher levels" (2018: 522). Admittedly, mid- and low-level bureaucrats have greater influence on issues that do not attract the attention of the highest level elites.

Ingber suggests that there are two opposing opinions of the U.S. executive bureaucracy. The first "views the entrenched bureaucracy as a benevolent, apolitical constraining force that might otherwise be an imperial autocrat...reining in the President from abuses of power" (2018). Senior officials in Trump's Administration have been working to serve the greater good by restraining Trump's "worst inclinations" and thwarting his misguided, adversarial, and shortsighted agenda (Anonymous 2018). Anonymous further argues that senior officials are not attempting to take down the president but are interested in protecting their agencies and the country from his "half-baked, ill-informed and occasionally reckless decisions." Anonymous has assured us that this is not a deep state, of which Trump has continually complained, but rather a steady state. To protect democracy in the face of imperial executives, the bureaucracy must act as an "internal separation of powers" when Congress fails to balance (Katyal 2006). Bureaucratic resistance can take the form of officials, administrators, and civil servants simply doing their jobs, that is, fulfilling the duties of their position (Ingber 2018). Resistance is satisfying the legislative requirements that incorporate human rights into U.S. foreign policy despite Presidential wishes. The professionalism, along with a bit of inertia, helps to ensure that U.S. human rights policy has remained relatively stable regardless of a change in leadership.

In contrast, the second opinion of the entrenched executive bureaucracy "views the bureaucracy as a self-interested, power-hungry cabal of conspiratorial operators, a 'deep state,' acting in darkness to wield the vast military and surveillance powers of the state at the expense of the accountable, elected government" (Ingber 2018). The entrenched bureaucracy, particularly the national security bureaucracy, is feared to be a "deep state," secretive, independent, and unaccountable to the American public, Congress, or even the President (Ambinder and Grady 2013, Lofgren 2016).[9] In this view the bureaucracy is also restraining presidential powers, but as a shadow government undermining presidential initiatives to further its own nefarious agenda. Trump would have us believe that the deep state is undermining his agenda to eliminate consumer protections, increase trade tariffs, and reduce federal regulations, and thwarting his efforts to Make America Great Again.

What Trump has feared as the "deep state" is what Michaels (2017) simply calls the "state." The state is the "large, complex hive of people and procedures that constitute the U.S. federal government" (Michaels 2017). Trump has deliberately crippled the hive by removing its leadership. Trump was slow to fill cabinet and political appointee positions. Ten months after his inauguration, of the 704 key executive branch positions requiring Senate approval, Trump only had 381 confirmed and 143 still had not been nominated (Washington Post 2017). Haas (2018 reports that 46 of the 47 federal prosecutors were fired along with all U.S. ambassadors. But Trump claimed he would not hire new officials until he had the opportunity to evaluate their loyalty. In addition, approximately 16,000 permanent bureaucratic civil servants were let go. Haas suspects that Trump's reason was to cripple the deep state by eliminating personnel.

Trump has left many political appointees and civil service positions in the State Department and USAID unfilled. This, in the opinion of Prendergast (2018), has sent the message that diplomacy, democracy, and development were not high on the President's agenda. Concerned that the position of Assistant Secretary for Democracy, Human Rights, and Labor remained vacant, Senators Marco Rubio (R-FL) and Bob Menendez (D-NJ) presided over a bipartisan group of 15 Senators urging Trump to nominate a qualified individual (Rubio 2018). It was not until June 20, 2018, a year and a half into his presidency, that Trump nominated Robert Destro to be Assistant Secretary of State for DRL. As of this writing, he has yet to be confirmed by the Senate. Without leadership, DRL will have a difficult time sustaining its work in protecting and promoting human rights in U.S. foreign policy. The implementation of U.S. human rights policy has clearly not been a priority for the Trump administration.

Use of Loyalty Oaths and the Presidential Pardon

The military and intelligence personnel swear an oath to uphold the U.S. Constitution. However, Trump has demanded loyalty oaths, and pledges of allegiance, to him rather than to the party, the country, or the U.S. Constitution. At an open campaign rally in Vermont (January 8, 2016), Trump's staff denied entrance to anyone who refused to take a loyalty oath to Trump. Later, on a March 2016 campaign stop in Orlando, Florida, Trump requested the crowd to take the following loyalty oath: "I do solemnly swear that I—no matter how I feel, no matter what the conditions, if there's hurricanes or whatever — will vote, on or before the 12th for Donald J. Trump for president" (as quoted in J. Johnson 2016b). When an individual refused to offer a pledge of loyalty to Trump (for example, former Federal Bureau of Investigation director James Comey),[10] he fired them. Hypocritically, when the Republican Party attempted to require a loyalty oath before a citizen was allowed to cast a vote during the 2015 Virginia Republican primary election, candidate Trump took to Twitter to condemn the proposal. Pledges of loyalty to the Republican Party would disenfranchise Trump supporters, typically less educated, lower income, older men, many of whom have avoided voting in the past.

Trump has had another tactic for assuring loyalty to his brand. FBI special counsel Robert Mueller's Russia probe has led to the arrest and plea deals of several members of Trump's Administration. There is concern among Trump critics that he could use post-conviction and pre-emptive pardons to exonerate his aides, allies, family, perhaps even himself, in order to cover up past and present crimes and misdemeanors.[11] "The presidential pardon power," opines S. Johnson, "is a significant grant of authority that could be used in a self-interested manner by an executive to shield criminal or unethical activities from public scrutiny" (2018: 290). And this concern is not founded as the *Washington Post* reported that Trump has asked his lawyers about the limits of his pardoning powers (Leonnig et al. 2017). And Rudy Giuliani, former New York mayor and currently an attorney to the President, when commenting on the Mueller's Russia investigation decision to talk to Manafort,[12] Flynn,[13] and Cohen,[14] stated: "When the whole thing is over, things might get cleaned up with some presidential pardons." In the opinion of Rivkin and Casey, two attorneys who served in the White House Counsel's office and the Department of Justice, not only could he, but he ought to issue a "blanket presidential pardon to anyone involved in supposed collusion with Russia or Russians during the 2016 presidential campaign" (2017). And that blanket pardon would cover the president himself. Rivkin and Casey would give the president a grant of full, unlimited, and complete immunity for virtually any crime he wishes to engage in, with the exception of impeachable offenses that would have to be investigated by Congress. On June 4, 2018, Trump tweeted that he has an "absolute right to PARDON myself."

Conclusion

Mounk and Stefan Foa (2018) believe that the appeal of democracy is less about its ideological precepts and more about its ability to provide economic growth and prosperity to its citizens. The economic prosperity of

Western liberal democracies, the United States the first among them, has allowed the United States to project its interests and values (for example, human rights, democracy, and good governance) abroad, but also to buy domestic stability. Stability was possible in an era of relative equality and rapidly growing incomes. The United States is no longer economically dominant globally and cannot provide its citizens with the material resources necessary to acquire the American Dream. Mounk and Stefan Foa (2018) report that less than one-third of young people under the age of 35 believe that it is absolutely important to live in a democracy. Democracy can no longer persuade voters of its economic and political advantages. Authoritarian economic models are providing viable alternatives for economic prosperity while promising to reduce the perceived rapid rise of crime and terrorism in the country. Democracy has not prevented and perhaps has exacerbated crime and terrorism.

Eichengreen (2018) proclaims that the United States has been ripe for a populist insurgence for a while. The economic recovery of the 2010s restored Wall Street while Main Street experienced slow growth. Inequality was rising; the middle classes suffered downward social mobility; and globalization created a loss of manufacturing jobs. Thus, "the success of Donald Trump and his fellow populists … is not a temporary or geographic aberration" (Stefan Foa and Mounk 2017: 8). Populism was the logical political outcome when the needs and desires of the socially constructed deserving and powerful groups were neglected.

These problems are real and immediate but, in the words of Kenneth Roth, Executive Director of Human Rights Watch, "populists tend to respond less by proposing genuine solutions than by scapegoating vulnerable minorities and disfavored segments of society" (2018). Populist leaders represent the "real people," but this excludes undeserving minority ethnic and religious groups. Populism is in opposition to pluralism, a defining feature of democracy, whereby different groups holding different interests and values are allowed to be heard and their needs satisfied.

Trump's tweets and statements of support for autocrats have made it clear that, in foreign policy, he has been less concerned with human rights and democracy promotion than with shoring up his version of American economic interests. The Trump's efforts to downgrade diplomacy and human rights by reducing State Department personnel and slashing the international affairs budget have come at the expense of America's leadership and furtherance of its national interest, while his desire to eliminate foreign aid has been at the expense of the lives of millions of poor people around the world.

Resistance to Trump's regressive populism has come from his own party, Congress, and the courts. In the United States, the executive is held in check by the power and prerogatives of Congress and the Judiciary. The Federal Courts have played an important role in reversing or blocking many of Trump's undemocratic and illegitimate policies. However, with two Trump nominees sitting on the Supreme Court, the ability of the court to balance the executive may be in question. Stefan Foa and Mounk (2017) suggest that a key method of control for an authoritarian is censoring of the press. Trump has believed the press is attacking him personally by spreading information that is critical of his governance. Censoring of the press can take the extreme overt form of closing office and purging personnel, but it can also be to silence the press by referring to it as "fake news," the "opposition party," or calling the media the "enemy of the American people," as Trump has done on numerous occasions. Yet, Cooley optimistically concludes that "Under Trump, the balance of power between the branches of government has been maintained, news outlets that are critical of the government have survived, and non-governmental organizations have kept the right to peacefully express dissenting opinions" (2018: 36).

All in all, Trump, widely viewed as a prevaricator, has been true to his anti-pluralist, racist, and misogynistic campaign and presidential rhetoric. He is a prevaricator who told the truth. Where does the future of U.S. human rights policy go from here? The final chapter of this book will offer a scholarly prognostication.

Notes

1 White males have identified with the Republican Party and voted for a Republican presidential candidate in greater numbers since the 1990s. However, the Obama years intensified this trend (Philpot 2018).
2 By 2018, Schneider and Ingram refined their categories to include subgroups. For example, the deviant category was broken down into "borderline deviant" made up of deadbeat dads, low-income poor, the homeless, and welfare recipients; "negative construction deviants" made up of prisoners, sex offenders, and terrorists; and "divided construction deviants" include refugees and illegal immigrants.
3 Trump is not the first president to use the National Guard to protect the borders. Both George W. Bush (in 2006) and Obama (2010) mobilized the National Guard to the border.
4 The program was discredited by the terrorist actions of Sayfullo Habibullaevic Saipov. Saipov used a truck to plow into pedestrians and bicyclists in New York City, killing eight people and injuring twelve more in 2017. Saipov entered the United States from Uzbekistan in 2010 under the Diversity Visa Lottery Program.
5 Incidental deaths of family members are not illegal if the attack was directed on lawful target and proportional to the military advantage anticipated.
6 Figures taken from the Defense Security Cooperation Agency website.
7 Cluster bombs have been declared a violation of the laws of war. The International Criminal Tribunal for the former Yugoslavia (ICTY) indicted Milan Martić, President of the Republika Srpska Krajina (the Serb Republic in Croatia), for violations of the laws and customs of war for using cluster bombs. The ICTY found that cluster bombs are "anti-personnel weapon designed only to kill people" (ICTY, Martic Indictment, ¶ 7). NATO also used

A Prevaricator Who Told the Truth 177

cluster bombs but there was no indictment since it is argued that NATO was targeting military instillations. Western countries also provided the funding for these tribunals. The United States last used cluster bombs in Yemen in 2009 under President Obama. However, Saudi Arabia has used cluster bombs provided by the United States in Yemen up until 2015.

8 Human rights legislation, specifically Sections 116 and 502B of the FAA, and the Leahy Laws, contain loopholes that allow foreign aid to be provided to human rights abusing recipient states under exceptional circumstances (see Chapter 1).

9 It should be noted that the concept of the deep state goes beyond the recognition that the bureaucracy has values and interests it wishes to protect and advance, as explained by the bureaucratic politics model. It is well recognized that bureaucrats work with "great devotion and integrity to preserve and protect the interests" of the American people, but that they also maintain an interest in promoting their agencies and careers (Cooper et al. 2018: 524). However, the deep state conspiracy claims that the bureaucracy is an undemocratic, megalomaniac, shadow government bent on undermining the president.

10 Comey was overseeing the investigation into Russian interference in the 2016 presidential election. Trump attempted to derail the FBI investigation into National Security Adviser Michael Flynn's undisclosed communications with Russia.

11 There has been controversy over the modern use of the presidential pardon: Ford pardoned Richard Nixon in 1974; George H. W. Bush pardoned several of the Iran Contra offenders; Clinton pardoned his own brother, Roger; George W. Bush pardoned I. Lewis "Scooter" Libby (Chief of Staff for Vice President Richard Cheney); and Obama pardoned Oscar Lopez Rivera, a Puerto Rican terrorist. However, no other president has sought council on pardoning themselves.

12 Paul Manafort was Trump's campaign chairman and a principal in a federal investigation into Russian interference with the 2016 presidential elections. On August 21, 2018, he was convicted of tax and bank fraud. Three weeks later, he pleaded guilty to conspiracy and agreed to cooperate with the Mueller investigation. By the end of 2018 it was determined he lie to the Muller investigators and his deal may be revoked.

13 Michael Flynn, a retired Army Lieutenant General and National Security Advisor to Trump, pleaded guilty to lying to the FBI about his relationship with Russian government officials. He also agreed to cooperate with the Mueller investigation.

14 Michael Cohen was Trump's personal attorney until August 21, 2018 when he pleaded guilty to charges of tax evasion, bank fraud, and campaign finance violations. His plea deal did not include an agreement to cooperate with the Mueller investigation.

References

Jeff Abramson. 2017. "Arms Sales to Saudi Arabia and Bahrain Should Be Rejected." *Arms Control Association, Issue Briefs* 9(3). www.armscontrol.org/issue-briefs/2017-05/arms-sales-saudi-arabia-bahrain-should-rejected

Spencer Ackerman. 2017. "Trump's Impending Executive Order Heralds 'Dangerous' Return to Torture, Official Warns." *The Guardian*, 25 January.

Amnesty International. 2010. *Yemen: Images of Missile and Cluster Munitions Point to US Role in Fatal Attack*. www.amnesty.org/en/press-releases/2010/06/yemen-images-missile-and-cluster-munitions-point-us-role-fatal-attack-2010/

Amnesty International. 2016/2017. *Nigeria 2016/2017.* www.amnesty.org/en/countries/africa/nigeria/report-nigeria/

Marc Ambinder and D. Grady. 2013. *Deep State: Inside the Government Secrecy Industry.* Hoboken, NJ: Wiley and Sons.

Avery Anapol. 2018. "Trump Official Claimed US is a 'Pro-life Nation' in UN Meeting: Report." *The Hill*, 17 April.

Anonymous. 2018. "I Am Part of the Resistance Inside the Trump Administration." Op-ed, *New York Times*, 5 September.

Sarah Binder. 2018. "How to Waste a Congressional Majority Trump and the Republican Congress." *Foreign Affairs* 97(1): 78–86.

Tom Blanton. 2018. "Gina Haspel CIA Torture Cables Declassified." *National Security Archive.* https://nsarchive.gwu.edu/briefing-book/foia-intelligence-torture-archive/2018-08-10/gina-haspel-cia-torture-cables-declassified

Julian Borger. 2017. "Civilian Deaths from US led Strikes on ISIS Surge Under Trump Administration." *The Guardian*, 6 June.

John Burnett. 2018. "Transcript: White House Chief of Staff John Kelly's Interview with NPR." *NPR*, 11 May.

Anthony Capaccio. 2017. "Trump Drops Human Rights Demand in Bid to Sell Bahrain F-16 Jets." *Bloomberg*, 29 March.

Jordain Carney. 2017. "McCain to Trump: 'We're Not Bringing Back Torture.'" *The Hill*, 25 January.

Jeffrey Cohen, Jon Bond, and Richard Fleisher. 2013. "Placing Presidential-Congressional Relations in Context: A Comparison of Barack Obama and His Predecessors." *Polity* 45(1): 105–126.

Madeline Conway. 2017. "Trump: 'We are very much behind' Egypt's el-Sisi." *Politico*. 3 May.

Jason Cooley. 2018. "American Exceptionalism During the Populist Wave." *Fletcher Forum of World Affairs* 42(1): 27–38.

David Cooper, Nikolas Gvosdev, and Jessica Blankshain. 2018. "Deconstructing the 'Deep State': Subordinate Bureaucratic Politics in U.S. National Security." *Orbis* 62(4): 518–540.

Gordon Corera. 2017. "Donald Trump says Guantanamo Bay Releases Must End." *BBC News*, 3 January.

Diana Stancy Correll. 2017. "US Approves Sale of Lethal Defensive Weapons to Ukraine." *Washington Examiner*, 20 December.

Defense Security Cooperation Agency. 2017. *News Release: Defense Security Government of Nigeria – A-29 Super Tucano Aircraft, Weapons, and Associated Support.* www.dsca.mil/major-arms-sales/government-nigeria-29-super-tucano-aircraft-weapons-and-associated-support

The Economist. 2017. "Donald Trump's Administration is Promoting Democracy and Human Rights. Fortunately He Has Yet to Notice." *The Economist*, 6 December.

George Edwards. 2018. "Closer" or Context? Explaining Donald Trump's Relations with Congress." *Presidential Studies Quarterly* 48(3): 456–479.

Barry Eichengreen. 2018. *The Populist Temptation: Economic Grievance and Political Reaction in the Modern Era.* Oxford: Oxford University Press.

Kristen Eichensehr. 2018. "Courts, Congress, and the Conduct of Foreign Relations." *The University of Chicago Law Review* 85(3): 609–675.

James Fallows. 2016. "Trump Time Capsule #136: 'She'd be in Jail.'" *The Atlantic*. www.theatlantic.com/notes/2016/10/trump-time-capsule-136-shed-be-in-jail/503507/

Vanda Felbab-Brown. 2017. "The Wall: The Real Costs of a Barrier between the United States and Mexico." *The Brookings Institute*. www.brookings.edu/essay/the-wall-the-real-costs-of-a-barrier-between-the-united-states-and-mexico/

Molli Ferrarello. 2017. "What 'America First' Means for US Foreign Aid." *The Brookings Institute*. www.brookings.edu/blog/brookings-now/2017/07/27/what-america-first-means-for-us-foreign-aid/

Joyce Frieden. 2018. "Final Rule Expected Soon on Birth Control Coverage Exemption." *MedPage Today*, 18 October.

Gallup. 2018. "Trump Job Approval (Weekly)." https://news.gallup.com/poll/203207/trump-job-approval-weekly.aspx

Martin Gilens. 2014. *Affluence and Influence: Economic Inequality and Political Power in America*. Princeton, NJ: Princeton University Press.

Hadas Gold. 2016. "Donald Trump: We're Going to 'Open Up' Libel Laws." *Politico*, 26 February.

Catalina Gonella. 2017. "Visa Overstays Outnumber Illegal Border Crossings, Trend Expected to Continue." *NBC News*, 7 March.

António Guterres. 2017. "Secretary-General's Opening Remarks to Yemen Pledging Conference." www.un.org/sg/en/content/sg/statement/2017-04-25/secretary-generals-opening-remarks-yemen-pledging-conference

Michael Haas. 2018. *Why Democracies Flounder and Fail: Remedying Mass Society Politics*. New York: Palgrave.

William Hartung. 2018. *Trends in Major U.S. Arms Sales in 2017: A Comparison of the Obama and Trump Administrations*. Security Assistance Monitor. https://securityassistance.org/sites/default/files/US%20Arms%20Sales%202017%20Report.pdf

Health and Human Services. 2018. *HHS Announces New Conscience and Religious Freedom Division*, 18 January.

Jon Henley. 2016. "White and Wealthy Voters Gave Victory to Donald Trump, Exit Polls Show." *The Guardian*, 9 November.

Hugh Hewitt. "US Attorney General Jeff Sessions on Children Separated from Parents at Border, F-1 Visas for PRC Students, and Masterpiece Cakeshop Decision," 5 June. www.hughhewitt.com/attorney-general-jeff-sessions-on-the-immigration-policies-concerning-children-apprehended-at-he-border-and-f-1-visas/

Peter Holley. 2016. "Former CIA Director: Military May Refuse to Follow Trump's Orders if He Becomes President." *Washington Post*, 28 February.

Human Rights Watch. 2017. *US Embraces Cluster Munitions: Reverses Course on Internationally Banned, Reviled Weapons*. www.hrw.org/news/2017/12/01/us-embraces-cluster-munitions

Rebecca Ingber. 2018. "Bureaucratic Resistance and the National Security State." *Iowa Law Review* 104: 139–221.

The International Criminal Tribunal for the former Yugoslavia (ICTY). Prosecutor of the Tribunal against Milan Martić, ICTY case no. IT-96-11-R61; Rule 61 Evidentiary Review (27 February, 1996) at 5. www.un.org/icty/transe11/960227IT.txt

International Women's Health Coalition (IWHC). 2017. "Trump Expanded Global Gag Rule Will Cost Women's Lives." 16 May. https://iwhc.org/press-releases/trump-expanded-global-gag-rule-will-cost-womens-lives/

Jenna Johnson. 2016a. "Donald Trump praises Saddam Hussein for killing terrorists 'so good.'" *Washington Post*, 5 July.

Jenna Johnson. 2016b. "Donald Trump's supporters swear their allegiance in Orlando." *Washington Post*, 5 March.

Kevin Johnson. 2017. "Sessions Calls Guantanamo Bay Prison Camp 'A Very Fine Place.'" *USA Today*, 9 March.

Scott Johnson. 2018. "President Donald J. Trump and the Potential Abuse of the Pardon Power." *Faulkner Law Review* 9(2): 289–328.

John Jost, Vagelis Chaikalis-Petritsis, Dominic Abrams, Jim Sidanius, Jojanneke van der Toorn, and Christopher Bratt. 2012. "Why Men (and Women) Do and Don't Rebel: Effects of System Justification on Willingness to Protest." *Personality and Social Psychology Bulletin* 38(2): 197–208.

Neal Katyal. 2006. "Internal Separation of Powers: Checking Today's Most Dangerous Branch from Within." *Yale Law Journal* 115(9): 2314–2349.

Rebecca Kreitzer and Candis Watts Smith. 2018. "Reproducible and Replicable: An Empirical Assessment of the Social Construction of Politically Relevant Target Groups." *P.S. Political Science and Politics* 51(4): 768–774.

Michele Lamont, Bo Yun Park, and Elena Ayala-Hurtado. 2017. "Trump's Electoral Speeches and His Appeal to the American White Working Class." *The British Journal of Sociology* 68(S1): S153–S180.

Carol Leonnig, Ashley Parker, Rosalind Helderman, and Tom Hamburger. 2017. "Trump Team Seeks to Control, Block Mueller's Russia Investigation." *Washington Post*, 21 July.

Tom LoBianco. 2015. "Donald Trump on Terrorists: 'Take Out their Families.'" *CNN*, 3 December.

Mike Lofgren. 2016. *The Deep State: The Fall of the Constitution and the Rise of a Shadow Government*. New York: Penguin Random House.

Stephen Losey. "Afghanistan Airstrikes Hit Highest Point in Years." *Military Times*, 9 October.

Julia Manchester. 2018. "Ex-CIA Chief on Trump Stripping Critics of their Security Clearances: 'You just can't let that stand.'" *The Hill*, 24 August.

Jon Michaels. 2017. "Trump and the 'Deep State.'" *Foreign Affairs* September/October.

Nolan McCaskill. 2017. "Trump says Turkish President gets 'Very High Marks.'" *Politico*, 21 September.

Dan Merica. 2017. "Trump Signs Executive Order to Keep Out 'Radical Islamic Terrorists.'" *CNN Politics*, 30 January.

Stephen Morgan. 2018. "Status Threat, Material Interests, and the 2016 Presidential Vote." *Socius: Sociological Research for a Dynamic World* 4: 1–17.

Yascha Mounk and Roberto Stefan Foa. 2018. "The End of the Democratic Century: Autocracy's Global Ascendance." *Foreign Affairs* (May/June). www.foreignaffairs.com/articles/2018-04-16/end-democratic-century

Cas Mudde. 2007. *Populist Radical Right Parties in Europe*. New York: Cambridge University Press.

Jan-Werner Müller. 2017. *What Is Populism?* Philadelphia: University of Pennsylvania Press.

Robert Neustadt. 1980. *Presidential Power: The Politics of Leadership from FDR to Carter.* Hoboken, NJ: Wiley and Sons.

Sean Nicholson-Crotty and Kenneth Meier. 2005. "From Perception to Public Policy: Translating Social Constructions into Policy Design," in *Deserving and Entitled: Social Construction of Public Policy.* Anne Schneider and Helen Ingram, eds. Albany, NY: SUNY Press.

Office of Management and Budget (OMB). 2017. *America First: A Budget Blueprint to Make America Great Again.* Washington, DC: OMB.

Office of Management and Budget (OMB). 2018. *Efficient, Effective, Accountable: An American Budget, Major Savings and Reforms, FY2019.* Washington, DC: OMB.

Benjamin Page and Martin Gilens. 2017. *Democracy in America? What Has Gone Wrong and What We Can Do About It.* Chicago, IL: University of Chicago Press.

David Parker. 1994. "Resources and Child Rights: An Economic Perspective." *Innocenti Occasional Papers,* Child Rights Series, No, 6, International Child Development Centre, Florence: UNICEF.

Rand Paul. 2017. "Sens. Paul, Murphy, and Franken Demand Senate Vote on Proposed Weapons Sale to Saudi Arabia." www.paul.senate.gov/news/press/sens-paul-murphy-and-franken-demand-senate-vote-on-proposed-weapons-sale-to-saudi-arabia

Michael Peck. 2018. "Cluster Bombs Are Back—and America and Russia Can't Get Enough." *The National Interest,* 21 April.

Tasha Philpot. 2018. "Race, Gender, and the 2016 Presidential Election." *P.S. Political Science and Politics* 51(4): 755–761.

Jonathan Pierce, Saba Siddiki, Michael Jones, Kristin Schumacher, Andrew Pattison, and Holly Peterson. 2014. "Social Construction and Policy Design: A Review of Past Applications." *Policy Studies Journal* 42(1): 1–29.

Laura Pitter. 2018. "'I Won't Torture' Is Not Enough: Question Pompeo on US Rendition Policy." *Human Rights Watch.* www.hrw.org/news/2018/04/11/i-wont-torture-not-enough-question-pompeo-us-rendition-policy

Michael Pompeo. 2018. Remarks to the Media, 17 September. www.state.gov/secretary/remarks/2018/09/285960.htm

Anita Powell. 2017. "Aid Officials Concerned at Proposed US Aid Cuts." *Africa News Service.* www.voanews.com/a/africa-aid-officials-concerned-at-proposed-us-aid-cuts/3773854.html

Liza Prendergast. 2018. "Confronting a Global Democracy Recession: The Role of United States International Democracy Support Programs," in *Democracy's Discontent and Civic Learning.* Charles White, ed. Charlotte, NC: Information Age Publishing, Inc.

Julia Raifman. 2018. "Sanctioned Stigma in Health Care Settings and Harm to LGBT Youth." *JAMA Pediatrics* 172(8): 713–714.

Douglas Rivers and Nancy Rose. 1985. "Passing the President's Program: Public Opinion and Presidential Influence in Congress." *American Journal of Political Science* 29(2): 183–196.

David Rivkin Jr. and Lee Casey. 2017. "Begging Your Pardon, Mr. President." *The Wall Street Journal,* 29 October.

Josh Rogin. 2017. "The Trump Team's Deal with Bahrain Could Ignore Its Human Rights Abuses." *The Washington Post*. www.washingtonpost.com/opinions/global-opinions/the-trump-teams-deal-with-bahrain-could-ignore-its-human-rights-abuses/2017/02/19/f5e4737c-f543-11e6-b9c9-e83fce42fb61_story.html?utm_term=.1f3ecbc985bb

Kenneth Roth. 2018. *The Pushback Against the Populist Challenge*. Human Rights Watch. www.hrw.org/world-report/2018/pushback-against-the-populist-challenge

Reuters. 2017. "Philippines' Duterte Says to Deal with Trump in 'Most Righteous Way.'" *Reuters*, 29 October. www.reuters.com/article/us-philippines-usa/philippines-duterte-says-to-deal-with-trump-in-most-righteous-way-idUSKBN1CY0OR

Marco Rubio. 2018. "Press Release: Rubio, Mendez Lead Bipartisan Letter urging President Trump to Nominate a Qualified Candidate to Lead the Bureau of Democracy, Human Rights, and Labor," 5 June. www.rubio.senate.gov/public/index.cfm/2018/6/rubio-menendez-lead-bipartisan-letter-urging-president-trump-to-nominate-a-qualified-candidate-to-lead-the-bureau-of-democracy-human-rights-and-labor

Mythili Sampathkumar. 2017. "US Rejects UN Resolution on Violence Against Women Due to Abortion Clause." *Independent*, 22 June.

David Sanger and Eric Schmitt. 2017. "Rex Tillerson to Lift Human Rights Conditions on Arms Sale to Bahrain," *New York Times*, 29 March.

Charlie Savage. 2016. "Threat to Jail Clinton Smacks of 'Tin-Pot Dictators,' Experts Say." *New York Times*, 10 October.

Charlie Savage and Eric Schmitt. 2017. "Trump Poised to Drop Some Limits on Drone Strikes and Commando Raids." *New York Times*, 21 September.

Anne Schneider and Helen Ingram. 1993. "Social Construction of Target Populations: Implications for Politics and Policy." *American Political Science Review* 87(2): 334–347.

Anne Schneider, Helen Ingram, and Peter deLeon. 2014. "Democratic Policy Design: Social Construction of Targeted Populations," in *Theories of the Policy Process*, 3rd ed. Paul Sabatier and Christopher Weible, eds. Boulder, CO: Westview Press.

Anne Schneider and Helen Ingram. 2017. "Framing the Target in Policy Formulation: The Importance of Social Constructions," in *Handbook of Policy Formulation*. Michael Howlett and Ishani Mukherjee, eds. Cheltenham: Edward Elgar.

Anne Schneider and Helen Ingram. 2018. "Social Constructions, Anticipatory Feedback Strategies, and Deceptive Public Policy." *Policy Studies Journal*. doi: 10.1111/psj.12281

Elana Schor. 2017. "Congress Sends Russia Sanctions to Trump Desk, Daring a Veto." *Politico*, 27 July.

Security Assistance Monitor. 2018. "Total U.S. Arms Sales Notifications under the Trump Administration," *Security Assistance Monitor*, 8 March.

David Shepardson. 2017. "Trump Administration to Propose 'Dramatic Reductions' in Foreign Aid." *Reuters*, 4 March.

Paul Shinkman. 2017. "Report: Trump Gives CIA Authority for Drone Strikes." *U.S. News and World Report*, 14 March.

Iyiola Solanke. 2017. *Discrimination as Stigma: A Theory of Anti-discrimination Law.* Oxford: Hart Publishing.

Dale Sprusansky. 2017. "Sen. Chris Murphy Decries Militarization of U.S. Foreign Policy." *Washington Report on Middle East Affairs* 36(4): 53–54.

Bonnie Stabile. 2016. "Reproductive Policy and the Social Construction of Motherhood." *Politics and the Life Sciences* 35(2): 18–29.

Roberto Stefan Foa and Yascha Mounk. 2017. "The Signs of Deconsolidation." *Journal of Democracy* 28(1): 5–15.

Yeganeh Torbati. 2017. "Republicans Push Back against Trump Plan to Cut Foreign Aid." *Reuters*, 23 May.

Donald Trump. 2016. Remarks at the Summit Sports and Ice Complex in Dimondale, Michigan, 19 August. www.presidency.ucsb.edu/documents/remarks-the-summit-sports-and-ice-complex-dimondale-michigan

Donald Trump. 2017a. Interview by David Muir with President Donald Trump, Transcript: ABC *World News Tonight*, 25 January.

Donald Trump. 2017b. Executive Order 13767 "Border Security and Immigration Enforcement Improvements," 25 January. www.whitehouse.gov/presidential-actions/executive-order-border-security-immigration-enforcement-improvements/

Donald Trump. 2017c. Executive Order 13780 "Protecting the Nation from Foreign Terrorist Entry into the United States," 27 January. www.whitehouse.gov/presidential-actions/executive-order-protecting-nation-foreign-terrorist-entry-united-states-2/

Donald Trump. 2017d. Presidential Memorandum for the Secretary of Defense and the Secretary of Homeland Security: "Military Service by Transgender Individuals," 25 August. www.whitehouse.gov/presidential-actions/presidential-memorandum-secretary-defense-secretary-homeland-security/

Donald Trump. 2018a. "Remarks by President Trump to the 73rd Session of the United Nations General Assembly," 25 September. https://ee.usembassy.gov/remarks-president-unga2018/

Donald Trump. 2018b. Executive Order 13841 "Affording Congress an Opportunity to Address Family Separation," 20 June. www.whitehouse.gov/presidential-actions/affording-congress-opportunity-address-family-separation/

Alec Tyson. 2017. "Americans Divided in Views of Use of Torture in U.S. Anti-Terror Efforts." The Pew Research Center. www.pewresearch.org/fact-tank/2017/01/26/americans-divided-in-views-of-use-of-torture-in-u-s-anti-terror-efforts/

U.S. Department of State. 2017. "Background Briefing: Senior Administration Officials on Protecting Life in Global Health Assistance." www.state.gov/r/pa/prs/ps/2017/05/270879.htm

Jace Valcore. 2018. "Sexual Orientation in State Hate Crime Laws: Exploring Social Construction and Criminal Law." *Journal of Homosexuality* 65(12): 1607–1630.

Nicholas Valentino, Fabian Neuner, and L. Matthew Vandenbroek. 2018. "The Changing Norms of Racial Political Rhetoric and the End of Racial Priming." *Journal of Politics* 80(3): 757–771.

Nicholas Valentino, Carly Wayne, and Marzia Oceno. 2018. "Mobilizing Sexism: The Interaction of Emotion and Gender Attitudes in the 2016 US Presidential Election." *Public Opinion Quarterly* 82(S1): 213–235.

Washington Post. 2017. "Tracking How Many Key Positions Trump Has Filled So Far." *Washington Post*. www.washingtonpost.com/graphics/politics/trump-administration-appointee-tracker/database/?utm_term=.cc9592e209e2

Noor Wazwaz. 2015. "It's Official: The U.S. Is Becoming a Minority-Majority Nation." *U.S. News and World Report*, 6 July.

World Health Organization. 2018. *Preventing Unsafe Abortions*. World Health Organization. www.who.int/news-room/fact-sheets/detail/preventing-unsafe-abortion

Jie Zong, Jeanne Batalova, and Jeffrey Hallock. 2018. "Frequently Requested Statistics on Immigrants and Immigration in the United States." *Migration Policy Institute*. www.migrationpolicy.org/article/frequently-requested-statistics-immigrants-and-immigration-united-states#Demographic

7 The Future of U.S. Human Rights Policy

The United States has always had a disputed, complex, and complicated relationship with human rights. The United States is among the oldest and best functioning democracies in the world and it embraces human rights as a founding principle. Nonetheless, U.S. foreign policy, even human rights policy, has wavered between two important objectives: one, to protect the state from external threats and to defend the national interest; and two, to defend and project American values, such as democracy and human rights. The United States assumed a leadership role in human rights norm setting following WWII. Eleanor Roosevelt chaired the U.N. Human Rights Commission and was the driving force in creating the Universal Declaration of Human Rights.[1] The power and prosperity of the United States has positioned it as a dominant norm entrepreneur.[2] After WWII, the acceptance and inclusion of human rights norms into U.S. foreign policy and foreign aid allocations led to a norm cascade, where other states adopted human rights. Human rights became a global phenomenon due to the leadership of the United States. It was not until the 1970s, however, when Donald Fraser began his hearings that human rights secured a foothold in U.S. foreign policy. Although U.S. foreign policy has provided a normative framework for human rights, there has been enormous variation in terms of practice between and within administrations over the past five decades.

The United States did incorporate human rights into its foreign policy, as evidenced by its sizeable foreign aid commitments linking human rights to aid allocations, its financial support of U.N. human rights bodies, its annual reporting of human rights conditions globally, and its deployment of troops to prevent humanitarian crises. Still, the U.S. failure to ratify human rights treaties or to adhere to those it ratified has also left the United States in the company of rogue states, out of step with democratic partners, and sometimes facing accusations of duplicity. As the Cold War and post-Cold War eras have unfolded, the United States found itself increasingly open to accusations of hypocrisy and double standards. The United States has used and shaped human rights policy and foreign aid allocations to advance its interests and security. As a result, the United States has an inconsistent and contradictory record on human rights promotion, not to mention adherence, but given the human rights records of the two emerging (or reemerging) global powers, China and Russia, the United States is still seen as the world's best hope for a compassionate and charitable foreign aid policy aimed at securing human rights and poverty alleviation. For example, Obama affirmed, in an interview with the *Atlantic*:

> for all our warts, the United States has clearly been a force for good in the world. If you compare us to previous superpowers, we act less on the basis of naked self-interest, and have been interested in establishing norms that benefit everyone. If it is possible to do good at a bearable cost, to save lives, we will do it.
>
> (Goldberg 2016)

U.S. human rights policy and legislation are still important despite the challenges over time in achieving presidential compliance or a lack of evidence in improving human rights conditions globally.

Complying with Human Rights Norms

In 2013, Risse, Ropp, and Sikkink published the influential book *The Persistent Power of Human Rights: From Commitment to Compliance*, a book that investigates the conditions and mechanisms that lead a state from the acceptance of the validity of human rights norms to sustained practices conforming to those norms. Risse and Sikkink (2013) warned that advocates for human rights ought to maintain realistic expectations about the possibility and speed of governmental compliance with international norms of human rights. States that are unwilling or lack the material capacity for change are hard cases, but "this does not mean change cannot and should not be promoted" (2013: 294). Because norm internationalization does not always mean persistence in norm compliance, hard time-consuming work and patience are required.

Risse et al. (2013) also identified four mechanisms for moving human rights commitment to compliance: coercion, incentives, persuasion, and capacity-building. Coercion is the use of force by external actors to compel a state to adhere to human rights standards. The United States did employ coercion in order to protect the lives of foreign citizens, for example, in Somalia or Bosnia in the 1990s. However, there are two significant limitations to the use of coercion. The first is that compliance is often only maintained while force is being applied. When troops are withdrawn, there is no guarantee that the state will continue to comply. Second is the high cost of using force. Beyond the financial costs, there are human costs. In trying to forcefully maintain control and secure human rights norms, human lives are lost and human rights are violated. Foreign troops under the aegis of the United States, NATO, or the U.N.

have been implicated in aggressive acts and sexual violence against civilians. In the case of the U.S. backsliding into human rights violations, coercion as a mechanism to enforce compliance with human rights norms is simply impracticable. The United States is the most militarily powerful state in the world.

Second, Risse et al. (2013) discussed capacity-building as a mechanism for moving a state from commitment to compliance with human rights standards. Even when the country has internalized and committed to human rights norms, if the target country does not have the capacity to change its political and economic institutions, human rights standards simply cannot be met. Capacity-building involves the creation or strengthening of state institutions to promote democracy, protect the rule of law, and fight corruption. This can also involve supporting the target country's local NGOs and human rights activists. The United States has a strong civil society, a court system, and a belief in democracy. Although the election of Trump initiated a populist turn in the United States, thus far the courts and political opposition in the United States have blocked anti-pluralist and authoritarian policies.

Persuasion is the third mechanism identified by Risse et al. Persuasion requires inducing, coaxing, and convincing the state to voluntarily comply with human rights norms and to allow democratic participation. NGOs, IGOs, and governmental advocacy campaigns of naming and shaming are intended to be forms of leverage against recalcitrant governments so as to encourage their compliance with legal and moral human rights standards. Persuasion is the strength of the U.S. DOS. The State Department can persuade using either quiet or public diplomacy to convince the target state that it is in its best interest to conform to human rights norms. Quiet diplomacy involves private discussion with the target state, while public diplomacy involves naming and shaming through open criticism and perhaps public condemnation. Among the most important U.S. public diplomacy instruments are the Congressionally mandated *Country Reports on Human Rights Practices*. The *Country Reports* are made public, widely distributed to the press and other media outlets, and provided to various academic researchers in order to pressure a government to implement changes. No state wants to be stigmatized as a human rights violator, and states will often go to great lengths to deny or repudiate that stigma. The hope is that states will modify their egregious human rights behavior. Thus, persuasion can be an effective tool in the United States return to human rights compliance. The United States has always been sensitive to maintaining its reputation and standing as the first democracy and champion of human rights. The United States would like to avoid the reputational costs associated with failing to meet its human rights obligations.

The final mechanism mentioned by Risse et al., incentives (such as sanctions or rewards), is more likely to generate compliance than the other mechanisms. Incentives are used to alter the rational cost-benefit calculation in order to modify the targeted state's behavior. Countries that are dependent on trade and aid flows are most susceptible to incentive promises and threats. Thus, U.S. human rights policy assumes its most tangible form with the granting or restricting of economic and military foreign assistance.

Over the years, foreign aid has become an indispensable tool of U.S. foreign policy. Since the Marshall Plan, the first and most successful U.S. foreign aid program, the objectives and motivations for aid allocation have experienced several shifts. The rationale for foreign aid in the Cold War era was the need to contain communism, support allies, and utilize as a soft power tool to draw developing countries into the U.S. sphere of influence. In order to achieve its foreign policy goals, the United States placed various conditionalities, stipulations, and provisions on aid eligibility. In the 1970s, the promotion of democracy and human rights became a requirement for aid receipt. Congress linked U.S. economic as well as military assistance to respect for human rights in the recipient state. With the collapse of the Soviet Union and the need to contain communism eliminated, the motivation for granting foreign aid shifted to strengthening U.S. dominance in a globalizing world economy. With the end of the Cold War, human rights advocates believed that human rights would be elevated and unified in U.S. foreign policy. But, this was not to be.

The funding of foreign aid has always been a contentious project. Yet, counterintuitively, the self-interested, pragmatic, and perhaps mercenary allocation of U.S. foreign assistance may actually guarantee its survival. Foreign aid is an effective tool in support of U.S. foreign policy. It can be used either to contain threats to U.S. security or to tackle the root causes of foreign threats. Foreign aid can be used to promote strategic interests, to secure the right to build and maintain foreign bases, to strengthen alliances, or to keep pro-American regimes in power. Foreign aid is also used to maintain friendly relations with foreign governments, and it is given as a reward for backing the U.S. interests. The United States provides foreign assistance to help develop foreign economies and to reduce the tensions generated by extreme inequalities by raising the living standard of the poor. Foreign aid, by providing hope for a better future to downtrodden populations, can reduce the call of terrorist or insurgent ideologies too. Poverty and repression are often causes of social instability and civil unrest, which in turn can produce flows of refugees and acts of terrorism, thus potentially making the United States less secure. In addition, foreign aid allocations have been shown to have significant favorable effects on the U.S. economy by providing employment for American workers, opening foreign markets, and subsidizing domestic firms.

The Populist Turn

With the U.S. turn to populism more recently, there is no longer a global hegemonic power to effectively foster human rights. The concept of human rights is increasingly vociferously and abrasively contested by states, religions and religious organizations, and patriarchies of all hues. Yet, Alston reminds us that the human rights regime "emerged out of the ashes of the deepest authoritarian dysfunction" of post WWII (2017: 3). What is new, according to Alston, is the fact that in the post-9/11 era, citizens are now convinced that they have to trade their civil liberties and freedoms for safety and security.

Rodríguez-Garavito and Gomez (2018) believe that the main threat to human rights is the result of the anti-pluralism of populist regimes that slowly chip away at civil liberties, free and independent media, protections of religious and ethnic minorities, and judicial and legislative checks on executive power. The tension between minority and majority rights-holders is settled by the populist regime's protection of majority rights. In fact, Helfer warns, rights become "a zero-sum conflict in which a 'win' for minority rights is often portrayed, however implausibly, as a 'loss' for majority rights," thus justifying restrictions on the rights of minority groups (2018: 7).

The increasing lack of relevance of human rights in the United States for the American population can be explained by two phenomena. First, human rights, for the U.S. politician, policymaker, bureaucrat, and public, have primarily meant civil and political rights. Economic and social rights were always seen as socialist principles incompatible with American values and neoliberal agendas. Moyn (2018a) argues that the blame for the turn toward populism can be, in no small part, placed on human rights advocates because they ignored the distributive justice grievances of newly mobilized lower and middle classes in the United States. In order to campaign against their chosen human rights violations and to gain the resources to do so, human rights advocates cozied up with powerful wealthy donors, both governments and upper-class benefactors. Thus, the U.S. human rights regime neglected the growing distributive inequality and downward mobility of lower- and middle-class Americans. Although there are violations of civil and political rights in the United States, for the most part, this set of rights is protected through constitutional provisions. When human rights advocates sought to improve human rights in the United States, they did so by trying to improve the status of historically inferior and excluded groups, such as women or LGBTQ individuals (Moyn 2018b).

The second reason the international human rights regime was believed to have little relevance for the protection of U.S. citizens was that American human rights advocates worked tirelessly to get the United States to sign and ratify international treaties but actually placed little effort in having these treaties apply domestically. Human rights were seen as something for foreigners. From the beginning, starting with the Fraser Committee hearings, U.S. human rights policy was focused externally, that is, toward encouraging or coercing foreign governments to fulfill their human rights obligations toward their own citizens. Given the inequality inherent to the American economy and the downward mobility of the American middle class, Alston warns that human rights advocates need to work against the perception "that human rights groups really are just working for 'asylum seekers', 'felons', 'terrorists', and the like" (2017: 6). Fearful and resentful voters are unlikely to support the rights of the most disadvantaged in society.

Apocalyptic Predictions: Sikkink vs. Hopgood

Erosion of American power and the enhanced power of authoritarian states, such as China and Russia, as well as increasing and often violent contestation of fundamentalist movements, have brought what some have referred to as the endtimes of human rights (Hopgood 2014). Hopgood believes that human rights will decline as the power and dominance of Western countries, specifically the United States, recede (2013). Without the force of the U.S. cultural globalization, its military might, and its economic power, human rights will wither. Hopgood also blames the failed human rights project on American hypocrisy. While the United States engaged in neocolonialism and human rights violations (Nixon in Vietnam, Reagan in El Salvador, W. Bush in relation to the global war on terror, for example), it denounced violations by foreign governments and threatened the withdrawal of foreign aid.

The universality, inalienability, indivisibility, interdependence, and interrelatedness of human rights are being challenged by both nationalism and the recent resurgence of religious "neoconservatism, evangelism, and Islamism" (Hopgood 2013: 156). Human rights, particularly women's and sexual minorities' rights, have been under attack from rising nationalist and religious forces around the world, as illustrated by the conflict between "Shari'a law and women's rights, Catholicism and abortion, evangelism and homosexuality, national identity and freedom of expression, public morality and individual choice" (Hopgood 2014: 18).

This apocalypitic prediction that human rights have reached the endtimes is overstated. "Powerful countries," Sikkink claims,

> have never been a constant, or even a primary, source of support for the international protections of human rights .... because the history of the human rights movement is much more diverse than Hopgood presents, its future is likely to be more promising.
> (Sikkink 2017: 30)

Sikkink is optimistic that the human rights regime will survive the rise of populism because human rights are not simply a Western invention, but rather originated in many diverse cultures. In fact, Sikkink believes that human rights' "momentum and progress depended on the actions of smaller countries, with support from emerging NGOs and civil society" (2017: 231).

Thus, there is still hope that human rights will continue to influence U.S. foreign policy. Donnelly and Whelen (2018) expect human rights diplomacy to remain a feature of U.S. foreign policy since the American public and Congressional members still adhere, at least in theory, to the moral values and principles of human rights. Donnelly and Whelen write that "there are many in Congress, supported by a sophisticated human rights lobby, who will insist on raising human rights issues even where the administration may prefer not to" (2018: 128). Without a doubt, the United States has played a pivotal role in the global diffusion of human rights norms. There are still many advocates for human rights within and outside of the U.S. executive bureaucracy and Congress. Human rights norms are still institutionalized in U.S. law and policy. And, thus far, the courts have blocked the most egregious illiberal policies of the Trump Administration. Trump's political opponents, Congress, and human rights advocates, although increasingly sidelined, have not yet been cowed into silence.

Prevaricating Policy

The fact that a prevaricator reveals a willingness to distort the truth and practice policy deception is merely an unavoidable reality of politics. Presidential prevarications are designed to deceive Congress and the American public. Foreign governments, as targets of the policy, experience the policy directly. For example, Nixon's secret bombing in Cambodia and Laos was hidden from the American electorate but the governments of North Vietnam, Cambodia, and Laos were well aware of the bombings. Likewise, George W. Bush's secret CIA black sites and use of extraordinary renditions were known by the many governments involved in the transport, housing, and torturous interrogation of the noncombatant terrorist suspects.

Prevarications are also used to sell Congress and the American public on a favored presidential policy. In the United States, the people elect a president to govern them and to be responsive to their policy choices. A president who makes grand speeches to promise a certain policy but instead implements another "strikes at the very essence of democratic government" (Bok 1978: 182). Pfiffner (1999) warns that policy deception is the worst type of prevarication because it violates the basic premise of democracy.

As this book has shown, presidents have prevaricated time and time again in their commitment to and implementation of human rights in foreign policy. Presidents use the noble language of human rights to pontificate and to compel small, vulnerable, and dependent countries to adhere to international norms of human rights. However, presidents do not criticize or censure allies or strategically important nations on their human rights performance. Nor do presidents seek to deny these countries economic and security assistance, as required by law. In order to evade the law, presidents have to dance around and evade the truth. Simply put, U.S. human rights policy is a policy of prevarication.

The Nixon Administration fought wars, killing thousands of innocent civilians in Laos, Vietnam, and Cambodia, to secure human rights and democratic forms of government in these nations. Kissinger argued that there was no objective way to distinguish between good and bad countries since human rights abuses were widespread and hidden. Indeed, Kissinger claimed, the United States could not adequately define what a human rights violation was. Under Kissinger, the State Department attempted to evade the Congressional mandate to collect and publish accurate and factual information on human rights in U.S.-allied states. The *Country Reports* were fragmentary and rudimentary then, praising allies and disparaging enemies, no matter the human rights conditions.

The Carter Administration pledged to implement a foreign policy based on moral considerations. Yet, Carter's words of support for human rights failed to be realized due to double standards. The Carter Administration imposed human rights conditions in Latin America while ignoring equally vile human rights practices in countries where the United States maintained strong military, economic, or strategic interests. In addition, as a result of the Soviet Union's increasingly aggressive international behavior, Carter, the "human rights president," focus on human rights fell under the weight of power politics. The issue of human rights could not sustain continued salience in the face of power politics, and therefore it failed to unify American foreign policy.

The Reagan Administration claimed that communism was the worst violation of human rights. The Reagan Administration prevaricated by using the terms "communism" and "human rights violations" interchangeably. Defending its support of rightwing ruthless dictatorships, Reagan claimed that the United States was actually supporting human rights by providing military and economic assistance to friendly, yet repressive, governments. Nevertheless, the Reagan Administration soon learned that human rights could prove advantageous in the ideological struggle against the Soviet Union.

The passing of the Cold War led to dramatically changed world conditions. The dissolution of the Soviet Union and the collapse of communism initiated important questions concerning the nature and future of the advancement of U.S. human rights policy. There was great hope that perhaps now human rights and democracy could now be successfully pursued globally. This hope was short lived though. Without superpower competition safeguarding the power of Third World dictators, many would fall prey to civil wars, ethnic conflicts, and genocide. George H.W. Bush mismanaged the opportunity to redirect America's foreign policy toward human rights concerns due to his renowned lack of vision and his desire to remain convivial with foreign nations, regardless of their human rights record. Bush, Sr.'s new world order rhetorically drew heavily from the Wilsonian tradition, but in practice the new world order frequently ignored human rights altogether. The new world order looked much the same as the old world order where human rights were easily bargained away when it proved politically expedient or convenient to do so.

For the most part the United States wanted to withdraw from international engagements simply wishing to enjoy the peace dividend that came with the end of the Cold War. Clinton's rhetoric raised expectations that human rights would have a central place in his administration's guiding principles. However, Clinton's narrow focus on the economy, often to the detriment of human rights, quickly crushed those rising expectations. When the human rights abuses could no longer be ignored, the United States under Clinton reluctantly and halfheartedly became involved. Human rights would be relegated to a secondary position behind the commercial interests of corporate America. Clinton's foreign policy was one that stressed trade expansion and the opening of foreign markets at the expense of human rights.

The terrorist attacks of September 11, 2001 initiated a regression in the U.S. commitment to human rights protections, both domestically and internationally. George W. Bush's own prevarication over human rights violations during his tenure in office has been widely recognized. George W. Bush prevaricated on the decision to go to war with Iraq that would result in the deaths of and human rights violations against innocent Iraqis. Bush also issued a series of executive orders, introduced several pieces of legislation, and issued exemptions that annulled human rights guarantees. Bush's practices of torture, extraordinary renditions, widespread public surveillance of American citizens, and overall restriction of civil liberties were accepted by a fearful public, a surrendering Congress, an obedient bureaucracy, and a hesitant judiciary. George W. Bush used U.S. foreign aid to further the security interests of the United States by significantly increasing U.S. military aid and contributing funding to an even greater number of states, many of which were known to be egregiously undemocratic and repressive. Economic aid was deployed in an attempt to win the hearts and minds of Muslim populations, hoping that they would not be tempted by radical ideologies of terror.

After the human rights violations associated with the Bush Administration, the majority of Americans welcomed the change seemingly offered by the Obama Administration. The human rights community celebrated the new President in anticipation of a renewed commitment to human rights. Obama shut down secret CIA detention facilities and stopped enhanced interrogation techniques of suspected terrorists and their sympathizers. However, Obama also continued many of the W. Bush-era counterterrorism policies, including the use of administrative detention by holding suspected terrorists and their supporters indefinitely without charges, extraordinary rendition, and the use of military commissions.

Furthermore, Obama increased the reliance on drone attacks in the ongoing war on terror, and he continued the highly controversial surveillance programs by the NSA. The Obama Administration did attempt to improve a number of human rights issues, specifically LGBTQ rights. In the realm of foreign aid, Obama increased both economic and military aid beyond the amounts of the W. Bush Administration.

Prior to September 11, presidents hid their use of human rights violations in pursuit of U.S. security interests. The Bush and Obama Administrations, on the other hand, practiced "plausible legality" with regard to human rights violations (Sanders 2018). They reinterpreted human rights documents, redefined human rights standards, and reconstructed the law to accommodate their use of torture, indefinite detention, and/or assassination.

Trump, who prevaricates on most matters, is clear and truthful regarding the place of human rights in U.S. domestic and foreign policy. Trump was hostile to legal norms and judicial review that could restrict his behavior, and he openly claimed to fully embrace the use of human rights violations to secure economic, political, and security goals. Trump argued that the U.S. failure to successfully counter the terrorist threat was the result of political correctness and a refusal to acknowledge the threat posed by radical Islamic extremists. Trump also wanted to reduce the U.S. long-standing pledge to humanitarianism, poverty reduction, democracy, women's health, and human rights. Trump's repeated attempts to cut the funding for the International Affairs Budget could have disastrous effects on the prospects of health, education, and even life in several developing countries.

Nevertheless, optimists believe that since Trump's rhetoric and posturing have foreshadowed a return to the use of torture, a reversal in women's and LGBTQ rights, and an increase in exclusionary policies, human rights advocates now "are highly motivated to fight back" (Sanders 2018: 164). Trump's policies have inspired passionate debates and incited considerable pushback from human rights advocates, promoters of women's equality, and supporters of social justice. The moral defiance from human rights advocates could push executive behavior toward compliance with domestic and international legal norms. Thus, rather than making the endtimes of human rights, the Trump Administration could unwittingly usher in a deep commitment to democracy, human rights, and equality. After all, the recent rise of populism is not the first setback experienced by U.S. human rights policy. The prospect of human rights acceptance and enforcement has been cyclical, oscillating from the hard times to the not-so-hard times. As Forsythe concludes, "the struggle to implement international human rights can rightly be seen as enduring hard times. But there have never been easy times" (2017: 250). What there has been and what will likely continue to be though is presidential prevarication.

Notes

1 To say that the United States was an early champion of international human rights does not imply that human rights standards were a Western project that was imposed on other countries. Sikkink (2017) details how active and enthusiastic the global south was in shaping human rights law and institutions.
2 Norms are "shared expectations about appropriate behavior held by a community of actors [for example, states]" but "unlike ideas which may be held privately, norms are shared and social; they are not just subjective but intersubjective" (Finnemore 1996: 22–23).

References

Philip Alston. 2017. "The Populist Challenge to Human Rights." *Journal of Human Rights Practice* 9(1): 1–15.
Sissela Bok. 1978. *Lying: Moral Choice in Public and Private Life*. New York: Vintage
Jack Donnelly and Daniel Whelan. 2018. *International Human Rights*. 5th ed. New York: Westview Press.
Martha Finnemore. 1996. *National Interests in International Society*. Ithaca, NY: Cornell University Press.
David Forsythe. 2017. "Hard Times for Human Rights." *Journal of Human Rights* 16(2): 242–253.
Jeffrey Goldberg. 2016. "The Obama Doctrine: The U.S. President Talks through His Hardest Decisions about America's Role in the World." *The Atlantic*, April. www.theatlantic.com/magazine/archive/2016/04/the-obama-doctrine/471525/
Laurence Helfer. 2018. "Populism and International Human Rights Institutions: A Survival Guide." iCourts Working Paper Series, No. 133. Duke Law School Public Law and Legal Theory Series No. 2018-150.
Stephen Hopgood. 2013. *The Endtimes of Human Rights*. Ithaca, NY: Cornell University Press.
Stephen Hopgood. 2014. "The Endtimes of Human Rights," in *Debating The Endtimes of Human Rights: Activism and Institutions in a Neo-Westphalian World*. Doutje Lettinga and Lars van Troost, eds. Amsterdam: Amnesty International Netherlands.
Samuel Moyn. 2018a. "How the Human Rights Movement Failed." *New York Times*, 23 April.
Samual Moyn. 2018b. *Not Enough: Human Rights in an Unequal World*. Cambridge, MA: Harvard University Press.
James Pfiffner. 1999. "The Contemporary Presidency: Presidential Lies." *Presidential Studies Quarterly* 29(4): 903–917.
Thomas Risse, Stephen Ropp, and Kathryn Sikkink. 2013. *The Persistent Power of Human Rights: From Commitment to Compliance*. Cambridge: Cambridge University Press.
Thomas Risse and Kathryn Sikkink. 2013. "Conclusions," in *The Persistent Power of Human Rights: From Commitment to Compliance*. Thomas Risse, Stephen Ropp, and Kathryn Sikkink, eds. Cambridge: Cambridge University Press.
César Rodríguez-Garavito and Krizna Gomez. 2018. "Responding to the Populist Challenge: A New Playbook for the Human Rights Field," in *Rising*

to the Populist Challenge: A New Playbook for Human Rights Actors*. César Rodríguez-Garavito and Krizna Gomez, eds. Bogotá: Dejusticia.

Rebecca Sanders. 2018. "Norm Spoiling: Undermining the International Women's Rights Agenda." *International Affairs* 94(2): 271–291.

Kathryn Sikkink. 2017. *Evidence for Hope: Making Human Rights Work in the 21st Century*. Princeton, NJ: Princeton University Press.

Index

Note: page numbers followed by "n" denote endnotes.

Abrams, Elliot 46, 48, 49
Abu Ghraib 76, 78
Albright, Madeleine 62, 66
Al-Qaeda 70, 82, 85, 86, 89, 113, 121, 123, 124
America First 163, 164
anti-pluralism 147–8, 176
Army Field Manual on Intelligence Interrogation 87, 122, 129, 135
Ashcroft, John 96

Bagram Airbase 114, 119, 121–2, 137
Bin Laden, Osama 85, 114
Boko Haram 167
Budget Control Act 119, 164
bureaucratic politics 5–9, 10, 38, 41, 43, 65, 94, 98–100, 135–6, 171–3
Bureau of Democracy, Human Rights, and Labor (DRL) 17–18, 62, 68, 70, 110, 131, 168, 173
Bureau of Human Rights and Humanitarian Affairs 11, 16–17, 27, 35, 37, 39, 43, 46, 48, 56
Bush, George H.W. 54, 57–61, 65, 71, 72, 192, 193; administration 54–61
Bush, George W. 76, 77, 78, 81, 83, 85, 87, 88, 109, 110, 112, 115, 125, 133, 136, 191, 193; administration 76–102, 110, 128, 129, 160, 161, 169, 194
Bush, Laura 85, 86
Bybee Memorandum 79–81, 102n5

Carter administration 21, 34, 40–5, 61, 62, 192
Carter, James (Jimmy) 29, 48, 66
Cheney, Richard (Dick) 77, 128, 129
Christopher, Warren 62, 66

Church Committee 41, 42, 44
Clinton administration 54, 55, 61–71, 145
Clinton, Hillary 110, 149, 151, 170
Clinton, William (Bill) 62–5, 67, 69, 71, 81, 118, 133, 193
coalition of the willing 84–5
Conscience and Religious Freedom Division (CRFD) 158–9
Contract with America 67, 73n5
Convention against Torture and Other Cruel, Inhuman or Degrading Treatment or Punishment (CAT) 68, 79, 129
Convention on the Elimination of All Forms of Discrimination Against Women (CEDAW) 66–7, 128
Country Reports on Human Rights Practices 11, 15, 17–18, 37, 54, 65, 69, 70, 130, 187, 192

deep state 172, 173, 177n9
Deferred Action for Childhood Arrivals (DACA) 153
Derian, Patricia 41, 43, 51n7
development assistance or aid (DA) 8, 47, 84, 88, 89, 93, 94, 116
drones 115, 122–7, 137
Draft Executive Order "Protecting the Nation from Foreign Terrorist Entry into the United States" 154

economic aid 20, 22–3, 27, 47, 60, 87–90, 94, 193
Economic Support Funds (ESF) 22–3, 47, 69, 90, 116, 165, 166
Executive Order 13492 "Review and Disposition of Individuals Detained

at the Guantánamo Bay Naval Base and Closure of Detention Facilities" 112
Executive Order 13493 "Review of Detention Policy Options" 112
Executive Order 13567 "Periodic Review of Individuals Detained at Guantánamo Bay Naval Station Pursuant to the Authorization for Use of Military Force" 113
Executive Order 13767 "Border Security and Immigration Enforcement Improvements" 151
Executive Order 13841 "Affording Congress an Opportunity to Address Family Separation" 152
executive orders (EO) 36, 124, 133, 160, 161; *see also specific executive order*

Feed the Future (FtF) 116, 117, 165
Ford administration 19, 28, 35–40, 77
Ford, Gerald 36, 39, 40, 124, 177n11
foreign aid: battlefield 2–9; disregarded 163–6; tool in the global war on terror 87–95; tool of counterterrorism 115–19; types 21–5
Foreign Assistance Act 3, 36, 69, 87, 91, 94
Foreign Military Financing (FMF) 39, 42, 117
foreign military sales 23, 94
Fraser Committee 3, 11, 13–16, 26, 189
Fraser, Donald 13, 14–16, 20, 27, 28, 35, 37, 185

Global Health Security Agenda (GHSA) 116, 165
Gonzales, Alberto 99
Graham, Lindsey 112, 164
Guantánamo Bay, Cuba 66, 79, 100, 112–15, 121, 126, 133, 134, 136, 162
Gulf War 56, 58, 72

Harkin Amendment (Section 116) 20, 36, 45, 48, 177n8
Harkin, Tom 14, 35, 65
Haspel, Gina 161
Helms, Jesse 40, 67, 68, 88
Helsinki Accords 40
Holder, Eric 125, 127, 129
Hughes-Ryan Amendment 20, 39
Human Rights in the World Community: A Call for U.S. Leadership 15, 18, 38

Humphrey Cranston Amendment (Section 502B) 15, 16, 19, 20, 36, 45, 48, 64, 69, 70, 91
Hussein, Saddam 57–9, 82, 83, 147

Inter-Agency Group on Human Rights and Foreign Assistance (aka the Christopher Committee) 41, 44, 62
International Financial Institutions Act (Section 701) 21, 24, 43, 48
International Military Education and Training (IMET) 23, 24, 94
Iraq Relief and Reconstruction Fund 91, 102n13
Iraq's Coalition Provisional Authority 83, 91
Iraq War 82, 95, 128
Islamic State of Iraq and Syria (ISIS) 162, 167

Jackson-Vanik Amendment 20, 34

Kirkpatrick, Jeanne 45, 46
Kissinger, Henry 7, 13, 14, 16, 17, 25–8, 35–40, 192
Koh, Harold Hongju 62, 110, 123

Lake, Anthony 62, 63, 66
Leahy laws 64, 69, 70, 73n6, 94, 134, 135
LGBQT 130–2, 150, 151, 157, 159–60, 189, 194
Lister, George 29n8, 34, 48, 49
loyalty oaths 173–4

Make America Great Again 145, 166, 173
Military Commissions Act (MCA) 113
Millennium Challenge Corporation 88, 89, 117
multilateral aid 22, 24–5, 47, 165

National Defense Authorization Act 133–5
Nelson-Bingham Amendment 20
New World Order 50, 54, 58, 59, 71, 72, 193
Nixon administration 17, 19, 20, 25–9, 34–6, 50n3, 56, 59, 191
Noriega, Manual 60–1

Operation Freedom's Sentinel 127
Overseas Contingency Operations (OCO) 110–12, 118, 119, 137, 164
Ottawa Treaty 71

Index 199

Patriot Act 95, 96, 111, 147
Populism 146–9, 175, 188–90, 194
Powell, Colin 82, 83, 94, 112, 128
President's Emergency Plan for AIDS Relief (PEPFAR) 88–9
principal-agent model 6–8

Reagan administration 44–9, 57, 58, 98, 192
Reagan, Ronald 29, 36, 40, 55, 60, 61, 190
Reforming American Immigration for Strong Employment (RAISE) 156
Religious Freedom Act 68–9
rendition 77–9, 81, 90, 92, 97, 101, 112, 114–15, 127, 135, 161, 191, 193
Rodriguez, Jose 127
Rumsfeld, Donald 77, 78, 80–3, 94, 128
Rwanda 65, 70

Salzberg, John 114
security assistance (military assistance) 8, 16, 19, 21, 23–4, 37, 40, 42, 47, 57, 58, 60, 64, 69, 70, 91–3, 116, 171, 188, 192

Sessions, Jeff 152, 162
Shattuck, John 62, 64
Smoot-Hawley Tariff Act 59
socially constructed groups: advantaged 149–51, 159; contenders 149, 150, 159; dependents 149, 150; deviants 149–60, 176n2
Special Defense Acquisitions Fund (SDAF) 49, 51n9

Taliban 66, 79, 85–7, 98, 120
Temporary Protection Status (TPS) 153
Tor Jail 122
torture memos 79–81
two-president thesis 2

whistleblowers 119–21, 136
Wilson, Jr., James 16, 38
Wolfowitz, Paul 59, 83, 128
women's rights 7, 66, 67, 85–7, 151, 156–9, 190, 194

Yoo memorandum 79–81, 102n5

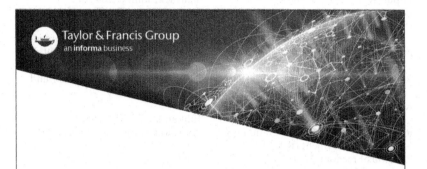